This Old House Kitchens
A Guide to Design and Renovation

This Old House Kitchens
A Guide to Design and Renovation

Steve Thomas and Philip Langdon

Little, Brown and Company
Boston   Toronto   London

First Edition

Library of Congress Cataloging-in-Publication Data

Thomas, Steve.
    This old house kitchens : a guide to design and renovation / Steve
Thomas and Philip Langdon. — 1st ed.
        p.   cm.
    Includes index.
    ISBN 0-316-84106-4
    1. Kitchens — Remodeling.   2. Kitchens — Design and construc-
tion.
    I. Langdon, Philip. II. Title.
TH4816.3.K58T48   1992
643'.3 — dc20   91-20413

10 9 8 7 6 5 4 3 2 1

RRD-OH

Published simultaneously in Canada by Little, Brown & Company
(Canada) Limited

Printed in the United States of America

In Memory of
Marilyn Ruben

A kitchen can be many things — social, practical, warm, busy — but above all, it's your domain. Dream big to get the most enjoyment out of it.

Introduction

Steve Thomas

Introduction

At the end of the working day, my wife and son and I often stroll across town to visit our longtime friends Peter and Françoise. We let ourselves in by the back door, announce our arrival, and help ourselves to a glass of *vin rouge* from the uncorked bottle on the round kitchen table. Our son finds his special box of toys, long ago outgrown by our friends' two sons, dumps them on the floor, and begins to play. A soup or *pot-au-feu* bubbles on the stove, French bread warms in the oven, a platter of fruits and cheeses stands on a side counter, and freshly washed lettuce glistens on the draining board. Whether we are expected or not, Françoise will invite us to eat, for she possesses that remarkable capacity to improvise an extension to just about any meal to accommodate guests.

And so we spend the evening. Our hosts' sons eat with us then go up to their rooms to do their homework, or across to the parking lot to skateboard. Peter takes a few phone calls in an adjoining room, and our son raids the lower cupboard for the cookies Françoise stashes there just for him.

Françoise's kitchen is by no means fancy, yet it exudes all the warmth and well being one dreams of in a kitchen. I suppose it's really no mystery, for her family ran the bistro in their small village of Saint-Julien and she and her four sisters grew up at the center table. Now, as it was in her childhood in France, Françoise's kitchen is the heart and soul of her household.

●

My own house is an 1836 Colonial Revival on Boston's North Shore, which my wife and I have renovated in several stages, the most recent being the conversion of the attic to office space in the summer of 1989. In fact, I was in the thick of the project when WGBH publicist Daphne Noyes called me concerning *The Last Navigator*, a film I had done for Public Television's "Adventure" series. When she learned I was pounding nails, she suggested I apply for the host position of "This Old House," which Bob Vila had recently left. I thought it over, applied, was screen-tested, and much to my astonishment ended up with the job. It was just ten days from the time I learned the job was open to the day I became host.

In any case, our house has four bedrooms, three and a half

baths, formal living and dining rooms with lovely period details, and, now, an office suite in the attic. Yet with all these rooms, we, along with guests and friends, end up spending most of our time in the kitchen. Everyone seems most comfortable there. Upon completion of the initial 1986 renovation we threw a housewarming party. At one point in the evening, I looked around and noted (with some chagrin) that virtually all of our twenty-five guests were arrayed around the island in the kitchen.

●

The entire team at "This Old House" wanted to put this book together because, in more than a decade of doing renovations for television, it was the kitchen that posed the most challenging design and construction problems and offered the greatest satisfaction when these problems were solved. These days renovating a kitchen is more challenging than it ever was because families are placing new demands on this room. Just take my own case, which seems fairly typical. My wife and I both work, we have a family, we correspond with friends both on the phone and in writing, we like to listen to music, we entertain frequently, and we love to cook. My wife, Evy, specializes in desserts and baked goods. I experiment with the cuisines of Thailand, India, and Indonesia, while also pursuing the ultimate bouillabaisse.

Since Julia Child, James Beard, and Pierre Franey introduced the cuisines of the world to the American cook, many of us want to satisfy our curiosity about these recipes in our own kitchens. And when we turn out a new dish and invite our friends to be the first victims, we likely eat right there where we cooked it, in the kitchen.

When our kitchens are not gourmet workshops, they facilitate the production of everything from Thanksgiving feasts for the extended family to baby bottles, workday breakfasts, school lunches, and midnight snacks. To accomplish these tasks speedily, we want our kitchens to contain a variety of appliances our grandparents and even parents never had: microwave ovens, ice-makers, boiling- and chilled-water dispensers, food processors, garbage compactors, water-filtration systems, and restaurant-style mixers and stoves. In addition, we generally want our kitchens equipped with a telephone, stereo and television, a place to store and consult our cookbooks, and perhaps a small office with a typewriter or computer where we can pay bills and conduct family correspondence. Of course, the room must be well heated, air conditioned, ventilated, and illuminated by both natural and artificial means.

This plethora of equipment and mechanical systems makes today's kitchens a far cry from those of a generation ago, which were utilitarian spaces used primarily to prepare sturdy American meals.

Concord barn kitchen for "This Old House"

If in your new or remodeled kitchen you can get all these elements to work harmoniously together in a space that is also aesthetically pleasing, you will have a room that will satisfy you for many years.

●

"This Old House" began working on kitchens in 1979, when, as our very first undertaking, we renovated a rundown late-Victorian house in the Dorchester section of Boston. For that project, in which we re-habbed an entire house in just thirteen weeks, we used moderately priced, widely available kitchen products, such as stock cabinets and plastic laminate countertops.

Weatherbee kitchen for "This Old House"

Sante Fe kitchen for "This Old House"

For our next project, the Bigelow House, we converted an abandoned mansion and barn into condominiums. In these kitchens we used higher-grade components such as custom-made cabinetry and solid-surfaced countertops. We gave each kitchen a unique character by doing the cabinets in different species of wood, but designed them all with an openness that would encourage informal socializing.

At the Weatherbee Farm, we built a brand-new kitchen in the "ell," or wing addition, of a mid-nineteenth-century farmhouse. We installed radiant heating in the floor (thus overcoming the intractable problem of finding space for radiators or baseboard heating elements), and we asked a custom-cabinet shop in Maine to fabricate

Norm Abram, master carpenter for "This Old House"

simple, Shaker-style wood cabinets. Just off the kitchen we built a red-wood deck accessed by sliding glass doors so one could easily dine indoors or outdoors.

In renovating a two-family Greek Revival home, we designed a combination kitchen, solarium, and small office. It had a skylight for daytime illumination and track lighting for night. We laid tile floors in the solarium area and hardwood in the rest, and also experimented with tiled countertops edged in wood.

In still another project, an adobe house in the historic center of Santa Fe, New Mexico, we treated ourselves to a bit of "Santa Fe style." "This Old House" master carpenter Norm Abram built the kitchen cabinets right on the site. We used hydronic radiant heat under the flagstone floor, and we went to Juárez, Mexico, for pink marble countertops. As in the Weatherbee Farm, the kitchen opened to the yard, but in this case through a *portal,* or covered porch, to protect the diners from the hot Santa Fe sun.

In more than ten years of doing "This Old House" shows all over the United States, we've worked on the whole range of kitchens, from small ones in which space and budget were tight, to grand "dream" kitchens. In each project, we've tried to learn new things about materials, products, installation and building procedures, lay-outs, and aesthetic considerations. In working with a succession of homeowners, each with his or her own agendas and goals, we've learned to have a flexible attitude toward this most important room of the house.

The challenge we've faced at "This Old House" has been to find the solution that fits the house, the budget, and the homeowners' way of living. There is no one "best" counter material, no "best" flooring, no one "best" kind of cabinetry or appliances. The diverse ways in which we all use our kitchens, and the amount of space and money we can allocate to them, make it impossible to cast a set of rules for creating the ultimate kitchen. What's *best* is the kitchen that *works* for you. In remodeling an old kitchen or designing a new one, you have an opportunity to accommodate — and yes, celebrate — your family's ways of doing things. If you are one of the many people who have spent your life in a house someone else designed, we think you'll find that creating a kitchen that fits the way you use the room will be an exhilarating, if sometimes frustrating, experience.

●

We hope this book represents the collective wisdom of the "This Old House" team. Master carpenter Norm Abram has been with "This Old House" from its beginning, infusing his experience and great common sense into everything we've done. Jock Gifford, along with Chris

Dallmus and the staff at Design Associates of Cambridge and Nantucket, Massachusetts, have designed many of our kitchens, as well as conceived and executed the drawings you see in this book. Richard Trethewey, our plumbing and heating expert, keeps us informed about the state-of-the-art in plumbing, heating, ventilation, and kitchen appliances. Dick Metchear brings to the program his knowledge as a third-generation lighting specialist and Glenn Berger his expertise as a cabinetmaker and kitchen designer. Creator and director of "This Old House," Russ Morash is no stranger to kitchens either. He brought Julia Child to television and produced and directed her cooking shows for thirty years. Russ still films Chef Marian in "The Victory Garden" cooking sequences.

Richard Tretheway, plumbing and heating specialist for "This Old House"

My co-writer Phil Langdon is also an architectural writer for *The Atlantic Monthly.* He interviewed all the "This Old House" experts as well as other experts dealing with every aspect of kitchen design and renovation. He revisited many of the kitchens we renovated to see how our work stood the test of time. Our homeowners showed no reluctance in telling him about what worked great and what they would do differently.

Russ Morash, producer of "This Old House," in his kitchen

One of the great freedoms we've enjoyed in the course of "This Old House" renovations has been the opportunity to try innovative products, materials, and ways of doing things. In the pages that follow, we present a realistic appraisal of our experiences, successful and otherwise.

We designed the book to guide you in an organized way through the entire process of renovating your kitchen. (Those of you building from scratch will find it equally useful simply by skipping the irrelevant sections.) We start with design and planning, including how to identify your needs and tastes in kitchen design, then we move on to explain how to draft contracts and agreements that can help assure a productive relationship with your tradesmen. From there we take the renovation process step by step, from the removal of obsolete kitchen components to framing, plumbing, electrical, heating, ventilating, lighting, flooring, appliances, cabinets, counters, and the final painting and papering. We've organized the book in the sequence a typical kitchen renovation follows, so you can learn what you need to know in the order you need to know it. We recommend looking through the whole book before getting started on your project, as information in later chapters on subjects like lighting and appliances may help you make critical design and budget decisions now.

●

Great good luck from all of us at "This Old House"!

This Old House
Kitchens

Planning

This farmhouse kitchen was given a new look by adding a laminate counter, painting the cabinets and floor, and by opening up the ceiling and painting the exposed beams. The addition of a butcher block–topped table improves the convenience of the layout, without the expense of creating a built-in island. A simple color scheme enhances the richness of the owner's collection of pottery, baskets, and pots. Notice the simple lighting above the sink and the spotlights added to the beams to dramatize the room at night.

Jillian's Snack Bar was one of those wonderful New England finds: a little shack out on a pier in a quaint and historic harbor. Al, both owner and cook, served the best and cheapest lobster and fried clams on Boston's North Shore. He'd named the place after his favorite customer. Jillian was about seventy-five years old, yet she came almost every night to eat lobster and sip the martinis she brought with her in a mayonnaise jar at her table under the stars.

My wife and I loved the place. Far off the beaten path, it had all the character you could ask for and was known only to a small cadre of regulars. But one evening, after we'd dined there twelve nights in a row, we looked at each other and declared we could never stare another lobster in the claws again. We were renovating our kitchen, and had just hit the dining-out wall.

•

Don't delude yourselves, as I have several times: Renovating the kitchen is a monumental pain in the neck. Nothing disrupts the smooth flow of life more than having the kitchen out of commission. Renovation is messy, expensive, and complicated. It involves nearly every building trade, from carpenters, plumbers, cabinetmakers, and plasterers, to HVAC (heating, ventilating, and air conditioning) specialists, floor men, and painters. For most families, it's difficult to deal with the chaos for more than a few days. Sure the refrigerator can be moved to the living room, the cooking done on a camp stove, and the dishes washed in the bathtub, but this kind of camping out pales after a week or so and leaves everybody irritable. Nor is it cheap or much fun to escape the chaos by eating out — the luxury of restaurant meals wears off fast. I have renovated four kitchens and planned several others. Before each one, I have inured myself to the chaos to come with pure self-delusion: "Oh," I tell myself and my wife, "it will only take a week or so."

As host of "This Old House," I've participated in a number of kitchen rehabs. My experience there confirms what I learned on my own. Our first word of advice is: Step back from the warm images of the future kitchen now swirling through your head and be coldly realistic about what you want your renovation to achieve.

The first question to ask yourself is how long you plan to stay in your house. Answer realistically, because it is the first major fork in your decision strategy.

If your answer is three years or less, then we recommend you do the minimum in the kitchen. While a kitchen in poor condition is often the biggest negative to a potential buyer of your home, *Remodeling* magazine has found, you can only expect to recover 80 to 90 percent of the cost of a full renovation. Therefore, we think it best to defer that dream kitchen until you're settled somewhere else, and concentrate here on doing the most with the least. New paint, wallpaper, lighting, a new or refinished floor, and some new appliances can make a dramatic difference in the way the room looks at a fraction of the cost of a total rehab.

My wife and I were faced with just this problem in one of our houses, an 1846 Greek Revival with a kitchen from the 1940s. The floor was covered in rotting black and white linoleum tiles, the white walls were stained yellow, the wooden cabinets were greasy, badly in need of paint, and trimmed with ugly hardware, and the rock maple counters were slathered in such an accumulation of grease and filth that you wouldn't want to put your toolbox down on them, let alone your cheese sandwich. The dishwasher was ancient, as was the stove, and the room was lit by a single glass globe in the center. My wife thought I was out of my mind for wanting to buy the house, and yet the basic layout was quite nice. If you could see past the filth and the rusting appliances, it *could* be a delightful kitchen.

We stripped the linoleum to find a fir floor, which was lovely when refinished; we removed the hardware from the cabinets, sanded and repainted them, and upgraded their look with white wire pulls. I scraped the grease from the counters with a paint scraper, then sanded and urethaned them. We painted the whole room white, removed a bank of cabinets to open the kitchen onto a breakfast nook, replaced the stove and dishwasher (tasks easily accomplished by a handy homeowner), and installed track lighting above the counters. Total cost was under $2,000. We did everything ourselves except the floor refinishing and the electrical hookup for the stove. Two years later we sold the house to the first couple who walked in. They said they had fallen in love with the kitchen.

Predesign

At "This Old House," we think a full-blown kitchen remodel should serve you well for the next ten to fifteen years. You may change counters and appliances and refinish the floor, but the basic design, like the one in our Greek Revival, should last. Over that time it will pay for itself in function, beauty, and enjoyment, and in all probability enhance the resale value of your house. For a kitchen to fulfill these expectations it must be thoroughly thought-out and well designed. And so, the first and most critical stage in the kitchen remodeling process is design.

Jock Gifford feels that the design phase of a successful kitchen remodel will take *at least* as long as the construction phase. This adds to the cost, but paying a design professional what he or she is worth to help you develop and build the right design for your house and family is far cheaper than building the wrong kitchen. Paper and pencils are cheap; cabinets, plaster, and plumbing are dear.

If design is critical, "predesign" is just as critical. There are two exercises I do before I even contact an architect or designer. Chances are, if you've been thinking about your kitchen for some time you have already done both, perhaps without realizing it.

One is simply to critique your existing kitchen. This exercise involves trying to articulate what *you* think is "right" and "wrong" with the room. I like to go into my kitchen when the house is quiet and really look around. I try to identify what bothers me about the room as it exists, and what, if anything, I could do to change it. Mentally, I alter the room's colors, flooring materials, and lighting scheme; I move cabinets, change traffic patterns, install or remove windows, skylights, and doors. Often, I have found, what bothers me is not one major flaw, but many small things that cumulatively ruin the feeling or the function of the room.

I added a garbage disposal to my island sink to make the prep area more useful. Now lettuce and vegetables coming out of the fridge can be washed and chopped right on the island. Such an arrangement gives work areas for two cooks, as well as keeping people from barging into the work area to get at the main sink.

For some people, the dream kitchen is the ultimate in "cool" design. This one is an elegant exploration of the possibilities of natural and manmade materials: a continuous stainless-steel counter, sink, backsplash, and paneling, combined with marble island top, ash cabinets, and stained oak floors. Placement of the kitchen equipment is carefully thought out, even down to the entertainment center in the cabinets. Speakers for the sound system are located behind the grilles above the cabinets and refrigerator.

Since the kitchen is first a workshop, I look at how the room *works*. Sometimes identification of what's wrong is elusive. A case in point is our current kitchen, which we thoroughly renovated. Last year it occurred to me that even though the kitchen was fairly large, it was functioning like a small kitchen. I spent a few evenings contemplating this until it hit me that the area next to the prep sink on the island was being used as a staging area rather than a preparation area. We were removing lettuce and vegetables from the refrigerator, placing them in the prep area, then taking them over to the main sink for washing and cutting. One solution was to add a garbage disposal to the prep sink, so that cuttings could be easily swept into it. This minor change has given us a second work area, making it much easier for two cooks to work at the same time.

You might wonder why you should bother with this exercise if you're already sure you will renovate the kitchen. The answer is that you can only know if your new design *will* work if you can articulate why your current design *doesn't*.

The next part of predesign is dreaming. Again, you've probably done a good deal of this already, which is partly why you're reading this book. Once I've determined the kitchen is too dilapidated or outmoded to save, I jump to the other extreme and try to visualize what I would do if I could do *anything*, cost no object. Move the kitchen to the living room, extend it into a greenhouse addition in the backyard, take over the whole first floor — *anything*. The purpose of this exercise is to articulate what you most love. Dream big; it's only costing you a little time and maybe some paper on which to sketch your ideas. You can scale back later when you must.

Dreaming is critical to the design phase because it helps to break up any preconceived limitations you may have placed on your project. You may find that you *can* have your dream kitchen, but phased in over several years. You should spend your first money knocking down walls, putting on an addition, rearranging doors and windows — whatever it takes to organize the space for a sound design that will last. You can always upgrade the cabinets, counters, floors, or fixtures later, as budget permits. We have seen too many people rush into a kitchen rehab telling themselves they must do it quickly and cheaply. As they get into it, they inevitably introduce a series of minor upgrades to cabinets, appliances, and so on, and in the end they have spent much more than they planned, yet have built a compromised design.

People tend to think that major restructuring of space — moving partitions, bearing walls, windows, doors, even whole chimneys — is prohibitively expensive. It may be more or less expensive

depending on your house's structural characteristics. But the lion's share of the cost in a kitchen renovation is the finishing: cabinets, floors, lighting, appliances, and the labor to install them. You may well find (as I often have) that you can rearrange your space in a major way and still maintain your budget by, say, installing cabinets of plastic laminate instead of custom walnut. Later, when you're feeling flush, you can replace the laminate doors with wooden ones, while keeping the cabinet carcasses.

To feed your dreams, page through design magazines and kitchen books and visit (or, better, cook in) other kitchens. Talk to people about what they did right, and more important what they would do differently in their kitchen renovations. Browse through kitchen stores to get an idea of what kinds of cabinetry, faucets, appliances,

For others a kitchen is a living room, replete with fireplace, comfortable chairs, and ample windows onto a lush garden. This kind of kitchen emphasizes a social, convivial environment. One senses the smell of baking bread, the tinkle of wineglasses, and the sound of family laughter. An unfitted collection of workspaces and appliances makes the kitchen feel friendly and casual.

and special features are available and to start to build an inventory of layout ideas. In all the kitchens you look at, whether in person or in print, critique each one as you did your own to articulate what you like and dislike.

Think about the features and appliances you want in your kitchen, and also how they will relate to each other in the ultimate layout. Also start thinking about style and decor. The materials, surfaces, colors, and style of appliances will be much different for, say, a French country kitchen than for a sleek, postmodern one.

The whole point of this predesign phase is to get ideas suspended in your mind so that you can make the most efficient use of your architect or designer in the next phase, design.

Using a Design Professional

At "This Old House," we would not consider doing a renovation without an architect or design professional whose work we know and admire. We've trusted their advice in nearly all our projects and have been glad we did. We like the fact that architects work directly for their client, either for a flat fee or at an hourly rate, and earn no commissions by selling particular products. This gives architects the freedom to recommend whatever they think best suits the project's needs.

Personally, I would not undertake *any* renovation without consulting an architect or designer. I've done so in the past and regretted it. Even if know what I want I always run my plans past an architect to get his or her input. Each time I've done so the architect has improved the design to the extent that I considered that fee some of the best money I spent.

Architects have a comprehensive approach to building. They are generalists trained in all phases of design and construction: structural engineering, framing, cabinets, counters, appliances, floors, and finishes. Architects are also trained in project management and have experience in bidding and contracting, scheduling, budgeting, and managing relations with subcontractors.

Our homeowners have been surprised at the depth and breadth of the questions our architects have asked them in the early phases of design. These questions are critical, for the architect is doing, in perhaps a more structured and thorough way, what we strive for in the "critique" and "dreaming" phases of predesign.

"I consider it my job to help people realize their dreams; to assist them in designing their lifestyle," says Jock Gifford. Your architect must understand not just how you live, but how you want to live, before he or she can start to design your kitchen. We'd avoid anyone who instantly tells you how to lay out or furnish your kitchen, whether it's a contractor, cabinetmaker, kitchen designer, or architect.

If we've convinced you to use an architect, the next logical question is: "Where do I find one?" Not every architectural firm is available to handle kitchen projects. Large firms tend to be geared toward large commercial projects, leaving residential kitchens to smaller firms with lower overhead. Yet, not every small firm can do a good job. Finding the right architect is a bit like finding the right barber or psychiatrist. The one that's right for you is the one that's right for you. Peruse books and periodicals for designs that catch your eye. Architects who are just beginning to win recognition are not necessarily more expensive than those who are little known.

Perhaps the best method of finding an architect is by word of mouth. Ask friends and business associates for recommendations. Homeowners who have just taken on a kitchen remodel are usually more than happy to discuss their projects with you. You can get lots of free advice, some of it valuable. Talk to the architects they recommend, look at their work, and make your own judgments.

It is important that you feel the personal chemistry is good with your prospective architect. It's equally, if not more, important that he or she has personal experience cooking in his or her own kitchens. No matter how the architect comes to your attention, be sure to talk to other clients and visit other jobs. This will give you a lot of insight into his or her style and capabilities.

Having spent all this time beating the drum for architects, I must confess that my wife and I have never used one for our kitchens. Instead, we have enjoyed the talents of a designer, the late Marilyn Ruben. She was self-taught, and after twenty years in the business she had risen to the top of her profession, routinely doing multimillion-dollar projects in Manhattan, Beverly Hills, Chicago, Dallas, and Santa Fe. Her designs were simple, spare, and elegant, yet infused with the great good sense born of many years of caring for a large and active family while pursuing her career. Be prepared to recognize talent in a design whether or not the drawings bear the stamp of the American Institute of Architects.

Accordingly, you may find sympathetic advice at a kitchen design store. These are firms that design kitchens, and either custom-manufacture their own cabinets, order them from other manufacturers, or both. They will do the design for a fee, sometimes deductible from the cost of the cabinets. In dealing repeatedly with kitchens, the designers at these stores may have become adept at solving common problems. They can help select counter materials and major appliances. Often these firms will install the kitchen as well. "This Old

An architect's list of programming questions like this one is essential to help get you thinking in terms of the interaction of form, function, and space — the language of architecture.

D E S I G N   A S S O C I A T E S

58 Main Street
Nantucket
Massachusetts
02554
508-228-4342
FAX 508-228-3428

432 Columbia Street
Cambridge
Massachusetts
02141
617-661-9082
FAX 617-661-2550

July 18, 1991

Mr. & Mrs. Hartford
161 Park Hill Avenue
Yonkers, New York 10705

Dear Pam & Jack:

It was a pleasure speaking to you on the phone last week, discussing your thoughts about renovating your kitchen.

Now is your chance to fantasize about your perfect kitchen. I've put together a list of programming questions I'd like you both to read and think about. They are designed to help you expand your thinking about your kitchen, and to provide a mechanism through which your dreams can be verbalized. This gives us a way of providing the best possible planning and design service. Try to formulate a "wish list" based on these questions.

ORIENTATION
> Would you prefer a view from your kitchen?
> Would you prefer a sunny exposure or more light?
> Do you need direct access to outside and inside play areas?
> Do you use an outdoor dining area? How often?
> Do you garden? Grow vegetables or herbs?
> Is the route to the car cumbersome for groceries and garbage?

SPACE USE & PLANNING
> Who uses the kitchen regularly?
> Do you get in each other's way?
> Do you entertain? How often? How many people?
> Is your everyday lifestyle different from your entertaining style?
> What other activities would you ideally like to have better space for:
>> sewing; laundry; homework; paying bills; reading mail; planning meals and shopping; phone center; clothes closet; sports equipment; bulk food storage; recycling; gift wrapping
> How often do you shop?
> What are the features of your current kitchen that you like?
> What frustrates you about your current kitchen?
> How long do you plan to stay in this house?
> Do you have a budget for renovation?

STYLE
> What are your favorite kitchen "looks"? (clip magazines to show us!)
> Is the kitchen a public show place or private retreat?
> What features of the rest of your house are you particularly proud?
> (architecture, colors, details, furnishings, decorations, etc.)
> How would you describe your approach to housekeeping? (honestly, not ideally!)

As you can see, these questions will get you thinking and talking about big and little things, not all necessarily related to the kitchen. The more we know about you, the better we can help you get what you want, and what you need. Please call me with any questions, and let's get together soon to talk through your wish list.

Sincerely,

Christopher L. Dallmus, AIA

Planning for Special Needs

The terms *barrier-free design* and *universal design* have mercifully replaced the dread rubric "handicapped accessible." They are used to describe an architectural approach that utilizes standard appliances, materials, and construction techniques in designs flexible enough to be enjoyed by people of all ages and physical abilities — from children to folks on crutches or confined to a wheelchair, to people with poor eyesight.

At first glance there is nothing remarkable about the two kitchens pictured here. One is sleek and rather futuristic looking; the other, with its glowing cherry cabinets, is reserved and distinguished. Indeed, that is one of the goals of universal design; to create kitchens (and living spaces in general) that are appealing and functional for everyone.

A circular dining area doubles as a workspace for children and wheelchair bound; the television is a large format for the benefit of those with poor eyesight and pivots for viewing anywhere in the room; a dropped ceiling over the table increases effectiveness of the downlights for task lighting; the radiused corners and edges of the solid surfacing counters make for a generally safer setting; wide aisles and a smooth floor surface make it easy to navigate the room.

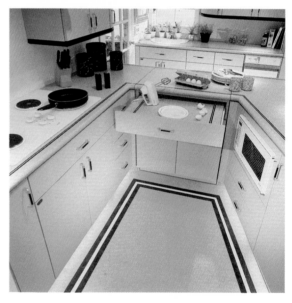

This cooking area is easily used by someone in a wheelchair. The pull-out solid surfacing work surface has a cutout for a recessed mixing bowl. It is part of a roll-out cart that can be located anywhere in the room, turning the peninsula into an island. The microwave is located down low. The black heating elements on the cooktop contrast with the white background. Burners are staggered, and controls placed in front to increase safety. For increased visibility, the toekick is illuminated and the edges of both floor and counter highlighted with dark strips of inlaid solid surfacing.

A baking area with low-mounted ovens, a mixer mounted on an elevator shelf, and a semicircular storage cabinet with a sliding door.

A second prep area with an icemaker, here used for potting plants. Notice the metal-lined drawers for storing flour or potting soil, the "touchless" faucet with an infrared sensor that automatically turns on the water to a preset temperature, and the large drawer pulls in contrasting colors so they can be located easily by someone with poor vision.

This very traditional-looking kitchen features an island and second work surface at the right height for someone in a wheelchair. Notice the ample appliance garages concealed behind the tamboured doors.

House" used Glenn Berger's kitchen design firm on our Concord barn project and on our Jamaica Plain triple decker, with good results.[*]

Another source of help is a custom-cabinet shop. Good ones may handle the entire design process, and at a considerably lower cost than an architect.

In our opinion, using either a kitchen store or a cabinet shop to design your project is fine, provided you have looked at representative examples or their design *and* construction work and have checked their references. By the nature of their business, cabinetmakers and kitchen stores run the risk of looking at the kitchen mainly from the standpoint of how many cabinets the homeowners want and where they want them — possibly overlooking imaginative solutions regarding light, views, circulation, and other architectural considerations. But some homeowners, having lived in and thought about their kitchens, know just what they want done. For those of you in this situation, a cabinetmaker or a kitchen store may be an excellent choice.

If you know just what you want, you may turn to a skilled carpenter. In addition to building much of the project, he may be able to offer good advice on whom to hire for plumbing, heating, and electrical. For a fee, he may be willing to act as the general contractor. Try to find a carpenter who specializes in kitchens; look at his work, and interview his references.

A general contractor, like a carpenter, can supervise the project and can also recommend cabinetmakers and other craftsmen, sometimes even designers or architects. While some contractors may have a lot of experience with kitchens, many have concentrated on other types of construction projects and therefore don't have the background required for a major kitchen design.

The general point here is that the scope of the project goes a long way toward indicating where to turn for help. You should get from the various sources the things they're best able to provide. A carpenter is an excellent person to ask about construction possibilities such as removing bearing walls, but may not be a good person to consult for the actual kitchen layout. A contractor can organize the job and quote a price, but for designing the room you are better off with an architect.

---

[*] If you have trouble finding kitchen designers, the National Kitchen and Bath Association (124 Main St., Hackettstown, N.J. 07840) can provide a free directory of member firms that design, supply, and install residential kitchens and bathrooms. Some experienced kitchen designers who are members of the association and who have received instruction in kitchen topics are known as Certified Kitchen Designers; they display the initials CKD after their names. The association can also provide a list of Certified Kitchen Designers.

I'd call this one the epitome of the "most for the least." Meticulous planning turned an urban closet into a functional kitchen. Twin under-counter refrigerators free up invaluable counter space, the sink on the diagonal utilizes what might have been a dead corner, pots and pans hang above, cookbooks occupy a shelf over the cabinets, and the butcher block provides a separate work area. The mirrors along the backsplash expand the sense of space.

This kitchen has everything for two cooks — right down to a triple sink with two spigots and separate stovetops with storage on either side for each cook's favorite utensils and appliances. The lower level of the range allows for improved sightlines over the shoulders of the other cook and into his or her pots.

Because of the high cost of kitchen renovations, homeowners sometimes decide to hire workers with lower qualifications than we are recommending. If you decide to go this route, recognize the potential drawbacks and compensate for them as much as possible. If you give your kitchen project to a contractor or carpenter rather than a design professional, spend some time learning about the aspects of the kitchen these tradespeople are not trained in. Study up on lighting design and fixtures; read about critical design considerations such as how to achieve comfortable circulation patterns.

In my own kitchen renovations, my personal investment of time and effort early in the design phase has been consistently rewarding. In one small house, we needed to renovate the entire first floor: kitchen, living room, and dining room. I dreamed up the ideal kitchen and drew it in scale on graph paper. Then I took my design, with its neatly drawn plans, measurements, and elevations, to Marilyn, who politely but firmly ripped it to shreds. She took a piece of tracing paper, laid it over the floor plan, and proceeded to move the kitchen to the living room, open it onto the dining room, then move the living room to the kitchen. She so thoroughly revised my drawings that there was not one element left unchanged. Yet, my work had not been wasted. I instantly saw the singular elegance of her design because I had spent so much time groping for a solution. I could enter into her logic and aesthetic because I had immersed myself in the problem. Ironically, that design, about which I was all wrong, is still one of the most satisfying I've been involved with.

There's no "best" way to do things. Your method should suit your needs and finances. But no matter what route you choose, be prepared to get involved. The most satisfying kitchens spring from the energy of the people who use them.

●

When a friend who had just renovated her kitchen saw this photo, she gasped: "Please don't show it to my husband! All he wanted was a kitchen like this!" The room radiates the American ideal of "kitchenness" with its grand cherry table, ample work island, separate baking area, and glass cupboards. The photo got me into some trouble, too, for when my wife saw it she wanted one as well!

Design

I was always amazed at how rapidly Marilyn seemed to solve design problems. Granted, she had known my wife, Evy, for twenty years and known us as a couple for nearly ten, so she could dispense with the rounds of questions a designer would usually have to ask, but still, her solutions came quickly. She simply "saw" the finished product, she told me, and her first conceptualizations were usually her best.

When Marilyn first walked through our unrenovated 1836 Colonial Revival, she swept away three bearing walls, a fireplace and chimney, a staircase to the second floor, a bulkhead to the basement, and the whole back wall with a wave of her hand and the pronouncement "All this can go." Thus, our kitchen was born. After plans were drawn, we modified them very little, adding the fireplace and a skylighted niche — we had neither time nor money to examine many alternatives. Besides, Marilyn's initial vision was surprisingly accurate, that is, coherent, appropriate, you might even say *robust*.

There is no such thing as the "ultimate" kitchen, especially in a rehab. Nor is committing the time and money to the pursuit of the ultimate a particularly good way to come up with the robust. When I told him about Marilyn's design style, Jock Gifford commented, "Successful kitchen renovations are inspired by limitations," of budget, space, design, and construction timetables. These constraints inspire the designer, contractor, and client to focus on the essential and leave aside the superfluous.

In planning and executing my own renovations, I've always had to work hard to get the greatest effect for the least money. The best way to achieve this is through elegant design. I use the word in the scientific sense: finding the simplest solution to the problem.

In this chapter we start with general design considerations, your kitchen's relation to the outdoors and to the rest of your house, then work through increasingly specific design problems: handling traffic flows, planning the work centers, placing the appliances, organizing cabinets and storage, providing for eating and entertaining in the kitchen, considerations regarding an office, stereo, and television, and finally general considerations of style.

A simple table by large windows makes a corner into a gracious place to dine or plan your garden.

Orientation

If you're lucky enough to be able to choose which direction your kitchen will face, consider orienting it toward the east or southeast, where the rising sun will fill the room with light. It's wonderful to prepare breakfast in a sun-filled kitchen. In a "This Old House" project a few years ago, we removed the dilapidated back portion of an 1850s Greek Revival home in Arlington, Massachusetts, and built in its place a big new kitchen and sitting area. It faced southeast, so we took every advantage of the exposure by installing glass doors and skylights. We painted the walls and ceiling white and used red Saltillo tile on the floor. The white walls made the room bright and the red tiles not only absorbed the sun's warmth but provided a water-resistant surface on which to place big potted plants. We revisited the house recently and were happy to hear that the room worked out just as planned.

Besides the psychological lift a sunny kitchen gives in the morning (especially during the dark, cold months of winter), a room oriented to the south or southeast can be designed as a solar collec-

A greenhouse addition gave this traditional house a sunny breakfast room as well as opening the family room onto the garden. The brick floor, laid in a basket-weave pattern, echoes the brick of the courtyard outside.

tor, pumping heat into the house and lowering utility bills. You may also be able to capture wonderful views of your garden.

To me, the ideal kitchen would open onto a protected southeast patio, for in all but the coldest weather, I love to sit outside for morning coffee. I would also have a small patio facing southwest for evening entertaining.

Unfortunately, in a rehab, choosing the southeast orientation is not always possible, although we think it's worth working hard to achieve. If it simply can't be done, orienting the kitchen to the south or southwest is a good second choice (in northern latitudes, anyway). If you go this route, provide some means of shading the room from the hot summer sun, with deciduous trees or shrubs, awnings or overhangs above the windows, or even with good window blinds.

Orientation is important, but how the kitchen blends with its ancillary areas — driveway, entrances, mudroom, halls, and staircases — is critical. In a detached house, there's much to be said for positioning the kitchen on the side closest to the driveway. A house is not an island; it requires frequent contact with the outside world, most

Before

In order to illustrate the kinds of trade-offs typically encountered in kitchen renovation, architect Chris Dallmus (at Design Associates), illustrator John Murphy, and I created this imaginary project. It is based on a real house, the front rooms of which date from the late 1700s. The back rooms were added on later.

Our house had some big advantages. It is structurally sound, and the front and side façades still retain their historic charm — something that we wanted to preserve in our renovation. Also, it is ideally oriented: the front to the north and the kitchen to the south, something we wanted to take advantage of.

We worked through the various options as if it were to be a real project. I considered it my house, and scrutinized each possibility as if I was going to pay for and build the project. We rejected some early sketches that placed the new fireplace and sitting area in what is now the kitchen because we favored a plan that located the kitchen to service easily both dining room and breakfast area. We also rejected as uneconomical a scheme that extended the south wall of the house beyond its current boundaries.

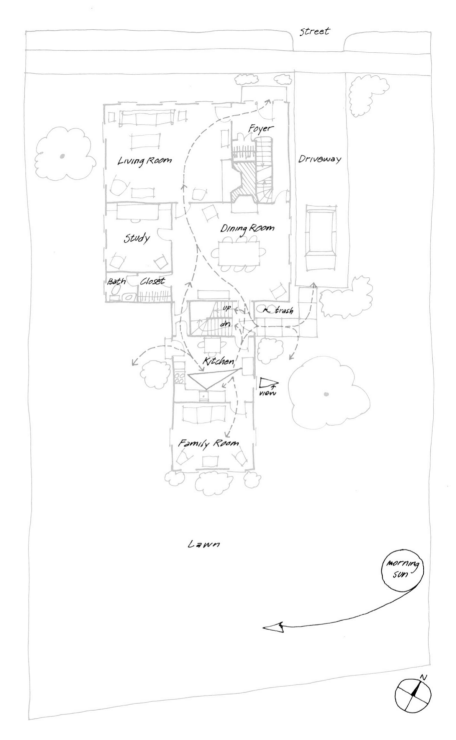

After

In the end we came up with what we consider four viable plans, which cover, but by no means exhaust, the range of possibilities both in terms of scope and cost of renovation. Each scheme has advantages and disadvantages, a fact we like because it illustrates the nature of design: balancing trade-offs.

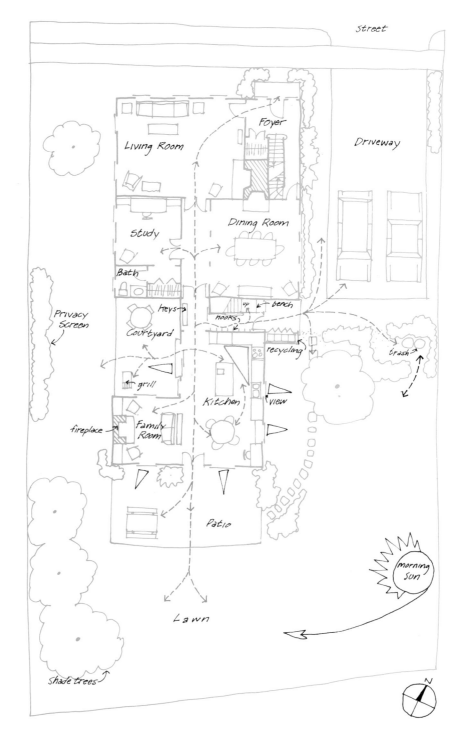

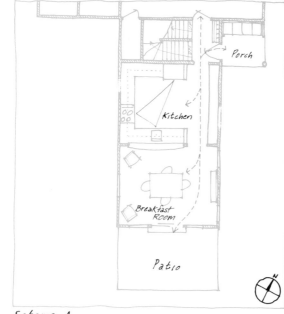

Scheme A

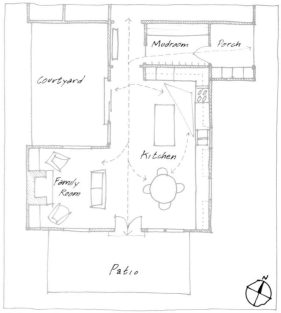

Scheme B

Scheme A

"Minimal Renovation" Offers the greatest impact for the least money.

Features:
- Retain existing counters and appliances.
- Remove partition wall between den and kitchen to create one space.
- Place new counters at NW corner to isolate work triangle from main traffic spine.
- Add small entry porch for recyclables, strollers, and other items. This porch is inexpensively built because it is not heated or finished inside and because it needs no continuous foundation.
- Add bench and hooks inside the door.
- Add windows to east wall of kitchen for morning light. Counter and storage under. Option of second sink above.
- Add patio doors to access small patio.

Advantages:
- Minimal cost yet overcomes many of our objections to the space. If I was going to stay in this house for five years or less, I would build this plan.

Disadvantages:
- Tight mudroom space.
- Circulation bottleneck at the entry/stairs.
- Routes traffic through the dining room, effectively making it a hall.
- No family room.

Scheme B

Features:
- Eliminates stairs to create large mudroom with seating, hooks, and closet.
- Entry porch as in Scheme A.
- Reorients kitchen to east wall creating a circulation spine through the center of the house. This eliminates the bottleneck at the back entry.
- Creates western courtyard accessed by sliding doors for evening entertaining or grilling in an area separate from entertaining areas.
- New family room with fireplace.

Disadvantages:
- Eliminates the back stairs to the second floor, something I have in my house and find very handy.

Scheme C

Features:
- Eliminate basement stair, but retain flight to second floor.
- Place a heated, finished mudroom on site of entry porch.
- Open kitchen onto stairs.
- Peninsula separates kitchen from eating area.

Disadvantages:
- No wall to separate kitchen from the entry. Island becomes the staging area for articles going into and out of the house: purses, briefcases, lunchboxes, and so on.
- Finished mudroom adds to overall project cost.

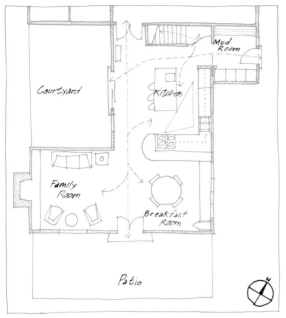

Scheme C

Scheme D

Scheme D

Features:

- **A synthesis of A, B, and C. We like separating the kitchen from the entry to provide a sense of transition and to discourage the use of the island as a staging area. We used Scheme B kitchen, family room, and outdoor spaces.**
- **Retain second floor stairs.**
- **Use covered porch concept to lower costs.**
- **Eliminating basement stairs gives adequate, if not generous, mudroom space. We added a pocket door to close it off when cold or messy.**
- **Excellent circulation from family room all the way to the living room, which does not interfere with breakfast area, family room, kitchen, or dining room.**

- **Places sink on east wall for morning light and views of "big tree."**

- **Provides a built-in work area in the breakfast area.**

- **Retains the private, western courtyard.**

of which is accomplished by car. An attached garage closely adjoining the kitchen will reduce the burden of carrying groceries in and returnable bottles out. Considering the number of grocery bags that must be brought in after a trip to the supermarket, you will appreciate a quick and convenient route between car and kitchen every time you use it.

The door to the kitchen need not be part of the kitchen itself; in fact, it's preferable if it's not. In a big turn-of-the-century home "This Old House" did in Boston, for example, we eliminated the exterior door in the corner of the kitchen, as it would have taken a big bite out of an area we wanted to use for cabinets and counters. The door also let in frigid blasts of air all winter long and threatened to send traffic through the cook's work area. Instead, we funneled traffic from the kitchen into a center hall, through which people could enter and leave the house. This added a few feet to the route from kitchen to car, but our homeowners recently told us that the sacrifice was well worth it. The kitchen now stays warmer in winter, the work space layout is more efficient, and the new traffic pattern makes it easier for people to circulate throughout the house and outdoors without passing through the kitchen. There was even an unanticipated advantage to this design change. The new entrance path outside is close enough to the kitchen so that our homeowners can see who is arriving, giving them some advance notice before the doorbell actually rings.

This major improvement in circulation and access was accomplished by a single, elegant design insight. But if, in your kitchen, the problems are not so easily solved, we suggest carving out space for, or even adding on, what New Englanders call a mudroom.

The Mudroom

At "This Old House" we've become believers in this enclosed porch–*cum*-pantry-*cum*-closet area. Ideally, it is placed between kitchen and driveway, where, with a door at either end, it buffers the kitchen from cold blasts of winter air. It has storage for hats, coats, boots, and mittens; a bench on which to sit down and pull off your boots and to put on and remove kids' outerwear. It could have pantry storage for bulky or heavy canned and bottled goods you don't need in the kitchen right away and stowage for paper products, returnable bottles and recyclable goods, dry cleaning on its way out or back in, as well as a staging area for the numerous other articles brought into and taken out of the house. I'd include a table or chest on which to place car keys, briefcases, a telephone, the family calendar, and a notepad for messages.

My wife and I wanted a mudroom when we renovated our house, but there simply wasn't space given that we also wanted eating and sitting areas in the kitchen. But now, having lived with the design, we sorely miss a mudroom and are considering adding on a small one. All of us at "This Old House" feel that a mudroom is highly desirable in New England, and very useful in other parts of the country.

The Work Triangle

For most of this century, kitchens have been organized around what's called the work triangle — the geometry determined by sink, range, and refrigerator. Since most kitchen work is a dance among all three appliances, the design objective is to make the distances between them comfortable. If the distances are too short, the work area will be cramped; if too far, the cook will become worn out trotting between them. The rule of thumb is that the three legs of the triangle should add up to between 12 and 26 feet (although some authorities feel the maximum should be 21 feet).

You can determine what's comfortable for you by experimenting in your own kitchen. Go through the motions of, say, making an omelet, which involves the retrieval of eggs and vegetables from the refrigerator, washing the vegetables in the sink, chopping them

This small but well-organized mudroom holds winter boots and jackets as well as toys, bottles, and recyclables. The ideal mudroom would be much larger, and we think it's worth adding one on, as we did in our project here.

on a work surface, and cooking the whole thing on the stove. Ask yourself if you need more or less space on each leg of the triangle. Measure distances and record the data. You will use it later when you start sketching ideas for your new kitchen.

●

There are three basic layouts for the work triangle: U-shaped, galley, and L-shaped. In the U-shaped kitchen there's a triangular path from the sink along one wall to the range along another, to the refrigerator

Typical Work Triangle Configurations

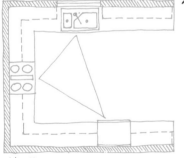

U-Shape

L-Shape

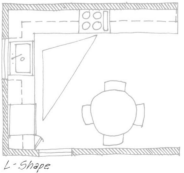

L-Shape with island

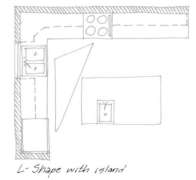

Galley ~ two sided

Galley ~ one sided

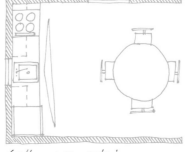

L-Shape with penninsula

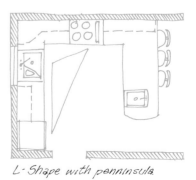

The galley aboard the ketch *Sunrise.* **Notice the diesel cook stove and charcoal heating stove, both of which drive away the chill of those stolen late-autumn days on the water. You'd be amazed at how efficiently you can cook in such an arrangement.**

along a third. For a lone cook it is a highly efficient design. In an L-shaped kitchen one element of the work triangle is against one wall with the other two along another. In very tight circumstances, such as a small urban apartment, all three points are arranged along the same wall. The cooking facilities on older yachts were set up like this, thus the name "galley" kitchen.

Ideally, the work triangle should be situated so that no traffic passes through it. Nothing is more irritating than having people crash into you when you're trying to whip the egg whites for your soufflé. If there's going to be an island or table in the room, it should be placed where it will neither obstruct the work triangle nor be too far from it to be a useful work station itself. If there must be an exterior door in the kitchen, try to locate it well out of the work triangle. This is sometimes difficult to achieve, but it's worth spending the time to get it right.

Keep in mind that people not directly involved in the cooking often need access to the kitchen. If yours is a typical household, the appliance most frequented is the refrigerator, for drinks, ice cubes, and snacks. Of the three components of the work triangle, the refrigerator should be located at the triangle's outer corner. Make it as easy as possible for noncooks to get in and out without causing disruption. The sink also draws traffic and thus should be accessible as well. But the cooking surface ought to be as protected as possible and therefore should be positioned at the most remote point of the work triangle. An integrated range, with burners on top and oven below, is still the most economical way to meet the kitchen's cooking needs, but you can gain a bit more design flexibility (at greater expense) by specifying a separate cooktop and oven, or ovens. With this arrangement, locate the cooktop in the work triangle and protect it from intrusion. Where you place the oven is much less critical since, in most homes, it is used far less than the cooktop, and when in use requires less tending.

The microwave oven, too, can be placed away from the work triangle, since it is most frequently used for preparing snacks (or re-heating Chinese takeout). Even when it is used in full meal preparation, the time spent tending it is short. Some designers cluster the microwave with a coffee maker and toaster in a "snack node" in one part of the kitchen. Ideally the snack node would not be too far from the sink and refrigerator, since snacks often entail the use of these, but not so close to the primary work triangle to cause conflict.

The work triangle evolved at a time when one person did all the cooking. But times have changed, and in many homes today two or more people pitch in for meal preparation. (Our young son loves to chop vegetables, crack eggs, and beat pancake batter.) If this is true in your house, your design might incorporate two or more overlapping work triangles. The main work triangle could be the refrigerator, sink, and cooktop, while the secondary work triangle could be the refrigerator, sink, and work surface. When two cooks are working in the kitchen, it's very helpful to have a second sink, since the sink is a primary point of conflict; then the two work triangles would overlap only at the refrigerator. My wife and I have found that the small prep sink we installed on the island is too small. Had we to do it over again, we would use a full-sized, single-bowl sink.

●

To function well, the sink, cooktop, and refrigerator each need to be surrounded with a certain amount of both floor and counter space. The refrigerator door needs a clear swing and, if possible, enough

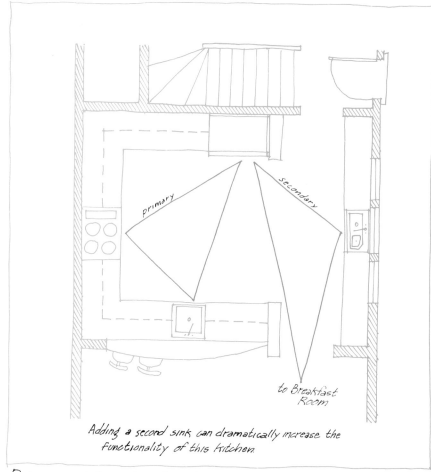

Adding a second sink can dramatically increase the functionality of this kitchen.

Primary and Secondary Circulation

room for two people to reach in simultaneously. The doors of any cabinets around the refrigerator should not conflict with the refrigerator door. The refrigerator also needs a patch of counter as a staging area for foods going into or coming out of it. An eighteen-inch run of counter is considered minimum. Clearly, the bigger the staging area, the easier the task of stocking the refrigerator after a shopping trip will be.

The sink and the cooktop most heavily influence the kitchen's organization. By custom, the sink is placed beneath a window, both to provide daylight for chores done there and to give one a view outdoors. I suppose this custom derives from the days before dishwashers, when the task of washing-up was a tedious affair done by hand. Yet working at a sink with a window is still much more pleasant than

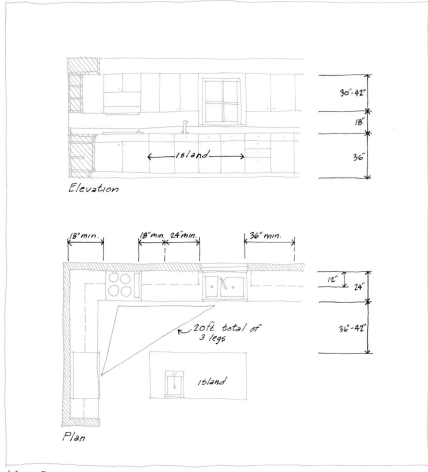

Key Dimensions

working at a sink without one. Designers often place the sink first, and lay out the rest of the work triangle from there.

However, placing the sink under a window is not always possible. In a "This Old House" project in Arlington, Massachusetts, the logical wall on which to place the sink had to remain windowless because it enclosed a stairway to a second-floor apartment. Instead the sink was located on a peninsula running perpendicular to this wall, where it looks over an open office to a window about eight feet beyond. The homeowners are very pleased with this solution. We've increasingly seen sinks installed on peninsulas facing a social area, so that whoever is working there can still participate in the conversation. But even in this arrangement, it's a good idea to try to provide a window somewhere beyond the sink so you can see outside. (If you go this route, consider raising the level of the counter around the sink to hide it from the social area.)

The sink might be equipped with a built-in drainboard or a second bowl large enough to hold a drying rack to facilitate drip-drying pots, pans, and dishes without messing up the counter. We've even seen industrial-style stainless-steel drainboards used in residential applications. They are not particularly elegant but are undeniably effective. Minimum counter lengths are considered to be thirty-six inches on one side of the sink and twenty-four on the other. This will give you a staging area for dirty dishes on one side and a drying area on the other. When not used for dishes, this area becomes a work surface for the preparation of meals.

It seems logical to locate the greatest expanse of counter on the side of the sink closest to the cooktop, since that is where most foods prepared at the sink are destined. This might also be a good place for a built-in chopping block if you want one, although for sanitary reasons most cooks now prefer to use a plastic chopping board that can be washed in the dishwasher.

If you plan to install a dishwasher, it should be placed near the sink, perhaps just to the right or left. Where you choose to put it might depend on whether you're right- or left-handed and on the path the dishes are likely to take when cleared from the table. Also consider the choreography of two people loading and unloading the machine.

There are a lot of other things that need to live near the sink: sponges, brushes, scouring pads, hand and dish soap, dishwasher detergent, towels, garbage bags, and so on. Glassware and dishes should be stored in cabinets or on shelves near the sink; and frequently used pots and pans could be stowed between the sink and cooktop, or from a rack hanging from the ceiling, placing them a

Many cooks find that a small workshop is very easy to work in. Everything is close at hand and refrigerator raiders are easily kept at bay at the gates. Good, compact design features are evident everywhere, especially in the dishwasher located directly beneath the sink, but the real secret to this design is the pavilion that separates the kitchen from the eating area and provides storage for both kitchen and dining implements.

short reach from either work center. Professional cooks, who spend a great deal of time in their kitchen workshops, often prefer to have their utensils in easy reach. Julia Child stows her knives above her sink in a very utilitarian fashion — nails support the handles and a magnetic strip holds the blades.

Consider locating the silverware drawers close to the drying rack or dishwasher — but somewhere outside the primary work triangle so that one can set the table without disrupting the cook. You might place drawers for small utensils like measuring cups, wooden spoons, spatulas, French whips, and so on between dishwasher and

An island with lots of storage. Painted wire recycling bins roll out for easy use. Notice the wire door shelves and general organization of the pantry unit beyond.

cooktop, although many cooks find it convenient to put spoons, spatulas, and the like in a sturdy crock on the counter within easy reach of the stove. Articles that get only occasional use, such as special serving dishes, large soup pots, and turkey roasters can be stored in more remote cabinets without causing inconvenience.

One kitchen necessity that deserves more attention than it usually gets is the garbage container. Ordinarily it's placed behind a door under the sink where, to throw anything away, you have to bark the shins (and incur the wrath) of whoever is working there. Consider locating the garbage container a step or two from the sink, perhaps underneath one end of the island. You can place it in a cabinet without doors, making access easy, or install a device that allows the garbage container to slide out when needed. Another solution to the problem is to install a garbage compactor. My wife eventually insisted that we have one; I agreed, under protest, but have come to respect its usefulness. I particularly like the fact that you can open the sliding garbage drawer with your foot.

In many communities, recycling programs are, or will soon become, mandatory. Often these programs require the homeowner to separate glass, metal, paper, and other materials, so consider allocating enough space for this when choosing a place for the garbage.

●

Now let's look at the design considerations that affect the third of the kitchen's major work centers, the cooktop. The optimum location for this appliance is along an exterior wall, rather than on an island or peninsula (even though this is sometimes tough to accomplish in today's open-plan kitchens). With the stove on an outside wall, it is easy to install an effective hood and ventilation system, which we consider essential to capture and expel the grease, smoke, and (in a gas range) combustion gases.

If your kitchen layout demands that the stove be placed on a peninsula or an interior wall, it is still possible to install a hood and vent it to the outside by running the ductwork through overhead cabinetry, tucking it into the ceiling, or even venting it straight out through the roof.

The stove or cooktop needs enough overhead clearance so that the cook can readily see and get at pots on the rear burners. In one "This Old House" project we used a range unit that featured a built-in microwave and vent system above the cooktop. We found, to our chagrin, that there was not enough vertical clearance to get at the back burners. Twenty-one to thirty inches of vertical clearance between the cooktop and the bottom of the ventilation hood is considered high enough to allow the cook easy access to the back burners

The standard L-shaped configuration puts the refrigerator at one end and the ovens at the other. This one was clearly designed with a baker in mind — notice the double warming ovens in addition to the standard double ovens. The granite-topped island has two elevations: the standard 36-inch surface, which holds a second sink, and the 30-inch-high snack bar, which doubles as a place to roll out dough.

while still low enough that the ventilation system can function efficiently. (For more on ventilation systems, see chapter 7.)

In my own kitchen I used a gas-fired, downdraft-ventilated cooktop, installed on the peninsula. The fan is powerful, if noisy, and it can handle the smoke and steam generated by all but the most ambitious Chinese stir-frys. A downdraft-ventilated stove may be a good choice if your design mitigates against any overhead hood and ventilation system, but choose your model carefully, as some do not work well in the presence of cross-drafts, especially in summer when the windows are open. Still, if you are a devoted cook, you will probably want to consider a restaurant-type range and hood.

The cooktop also requires a lot of counter space — at least sixteen or eighteen inches on either side, more if you can find it. It's better to have counter space on both sides rather than concentrate it all on one side. If there's to be a special place for baking, it might be near the cooktop or oven. Many people like the baking center to be at a lower height — 30 to 33 inches — so that they can more comfortably exert downward pressure while kneading dough.

Shelves or a wall cabinet above the cooktop could hold foods that aren't affected by warmth, such as pasta, rice, and breakfast cereals. Usually there's room enough to build a shallow shelf below the cabinets as a handy place for cooking supplies and implements. It is sometimes possible to build a drawer or a shallow tilt-out hamper beneath the cooktop, which is handy for odds and ends. In professional kitchens we typically see a restaurant-type range topped with a generous hood. On open shelves below the hood we find a timer, hotpads, salt and pepper shakers, a sugar container, a big can of olive oil, and a crock or other container holding wooden spoons, large forks, whisks, basting brushes, and so on. Nearby is a well-stocked spice rack. This "workshop"-type cooking area is not only charming to look at, but great to work in.

Islands

A well-designed center island can serve several functions at once: lower storage, a good work area, a table for informal meals, and a congenial setting for socializing. The island can match the height of the counters (standard height 36 inches) or be higher or lower. Specify a lower height if you expect to use the counter for baking, a taller height if you're a tall person. You can also split the island into areas of more than one height.

If you plan to sit at the island, you will undoubtedly use stools, since, at standard counter height, the surface will be too lofty for ordinary chairs. When "This Old House" converted the H. H. Richardson–designed Bigelow estate into condominiums, we specified a large island in one of the kitchens with seating on three sides. We even installed a footrest to make sitting there more comfortable. This feature has been so successful that the current owners complain that they can't get people away from the island.

If an island is to accommodate stools, it will need ample overhangs. Twelve inches is considered minimum. An overhang gives you a place for your knees while seated and also offers stowage for the stools when not in use. If people can sit along at least two sides of the island, conversation seems to flow more naturally. The sides of the island intended as work space may or may not have overhangs, depending on whether you like to stand or sit while working. If you put storage beneath the island, be careful about placement of drawers and doors. Those on the "work" side will be easy to use (if there's no overhang); those on the "sitting" side very difficult. Either forgo access to storage on this side or use this space for seldom-needed articles. Most islands are rectangular, but if you're thinking of a large one (3 by 6 feet, for example), consider angling one or more corners to facilitate circulation.

This impressive split-level island was created by mitering the edges of ¾-inch Athenian verde marble and assembling them to make the slab look thicker. The kitchen is filled with natural materials: glazed ceramic tile floor, tile counters, and the massive Douglas fir roof truss. The greenhouse window on the back wall floods the room with light.

When sizing your island, remember that larger is not necessarily better, especially if it chokes general circulation in the kitchen. The aisle between island and base counters should be wide enough to allow two people to pass easily, but not so wide that it's uncomfortable to pivot between them while cooking. Aisles are generally specified at 42 to 54 inches wide, although in my own kitchen I squeezed by with 35-inch aisles, which works adequately.

On any "sitting" side of the island there should be 54 to 60 inches of aisle between island and counters. The more people you anticipate will use and pass through the kitchen, the more important becomes clearance in the aisles. The island should not block the route between sink and cooktop or between cooktop and refrigerator. If there's a dishwasher or range in the island (not an option we like), make sure its door does not conflict with an appliance or cabinet door along the room's perimeter.

An old butcher block serves as island, cutting board, and one of this kitchen's thematic elements.

Home design magazines love to show islands with sinks, cooktops, and barbecues mounted in them. These islands look alluring and purposeful, but it's been our experience that placing the main sink in an island is usually a mistake. For the sink to be functional it must have an area on one side where things wait to be washed, and an area on the other side where they dry or wait to be put away. This takes up a lot of counter space, which would destroy an island's function as a central work surface. Also, it is only in the magazine photographs that the sink is an object of beauty. In real life, the sink catches grease and food remnants, and is often cluttered with dirty dishes, smudged glasses, and dirty pots. Why design this as the focal point of your kitchen?

For these same reasons we advise against island-mounted cooktops and grills. They are a source of much grease and smoke and are hard to ventilate properly. If a hood is installed, it will block

eye contact across the island. Downdraft systems are an alternative but, again, they may be overwhelmed by cross-drafts unless surrounded by a raised edge to create a pocket of still air.

Perhaps some of the fascination with island cooktops comes from cooking shows, in which the chef presides behind an island. But these are specialized studio props, designed primarily to allow the cook to face the camera. Julia Child entertains a great deal when not on camera. It is instructive that in her own kitchen she has located the range and grill along the perimeter, where they can be easily ventilated to the outside and where the inherent mess of using them won't dominate the center of her room.

Peninsulas

A peninsula can serve many of the same functions as an island, and many of the same design considerations apply.

In an open-plan kitchen the peninsula is sometimes the only place where you can locate the sink or cooktop. The disadvantages of doing so are the same as in an island but, as we suggested above, can be mitigated somewhat by locating it behind a "step" or raised

The small kitchen in this converted New York City industrial loft is defined by the peninsula, but the "industrial" look of the design and materials unites it with the whole space. The poured concrete counters, brushed steel corner posts, toekick and light fixture resonate with the brick, but the roughness of these surfaces is balanced by the stained oak floor and glazed ash cabinets.

A well-used pantry cabinet. I like the adjustable wire-grid shelves on the doors.

platform on the "social" side of the peninsula. An elevation difference of just four to six inches helps hide the clutter and also defines the boundary between kitchen and social area. Even if there is seating on the social side of the peninsula, the slight difference in height is not uncomfortable.

Hoods and ventilation ducts above a peninsula must be deftly designed if they are not to destroy the openness the peninsula was intended to create in the first place. If you absolutely do not want an overhead hood, a downdraft cooktop is a tolerable compromise. If you go this route, spend the extra money for a high quality unit that can tolerate cross-drafts.

Cabinetry and Storage

As we incorporate more and more appliances into our kitchens and buy groceries in larger quantities, the size and functionality of our cabinets becomes increasingly important. Although we later devote a whole chapter to cabinets, it's useful here to review a few key points that affect kitchen design.

First, the base cabinets, those which sit on the floor, commonly measure 25 inches deep and 36 inches high, including countertop. The standard dimensions of the wall cabinets, which hang on the wall above the base cabinets, is 12 inches deep by 30 inches high. The standard clearance between countertop and wall cabinets is 18 inches.

Second, bear in mind that you can use the cabinetry to hide good task lighting. We install thin fluorescent or incandescent lighting fixtures beneath the bottom of the wall cabinets to illuminate the counters. Similar fixtures can be installed on top of the wall cabinets to "wash" the ceiling, filling the room with pleasant, indirect light.

Third, cabinetry presents some of its most difficult problems at corners. L-shaped and U-shaped runs of cabinets result in "dead" corners — corner cabinets that are hard to reach into. A lazy Susan or a new device called a "half Susan" can help utilize this dead space, but it's still a good idea to try to eliminate any unnecessary corners.

Fourth, cabinets are not the only place to put things. A large volume of kitchen goods can be stowed in a pantry, an efficient, relatively inexpensive means of storage. Since a pantry is essentially a closet lined with shelves, it's easy on the budget; the only surface that needs to be of high quality is the door. Also plan for a utility closet, perhaps as part of a pantry or incorporated elsewhere into the cabinetry. It is very useful to have storage for brooms, mops, and cleaning supplies in or near the kitchen.

Office, Phone, and Electronics

If you want a desk or office area in your kitchen you may want to integrate its design with the rest of the cabinetry. The office area should certainly be located outside any work triangles, in a relatively quiet corner of the room. In it, you might store your cookbooks and recipe files, plan menus, make up shopping lists, go through the mail, pay bills, make phone calls, and leave messages. You might also want to plan a space for a personal computer, or incorporate storage for briefcase, car keys, and other articles you need when leaving the house.

Desk area or not, plan the location of your telephone (don't forget an electric outlet for the base unit of a cordless phone if you use one). It is very convenient to have a phone book nearby, an area for messages, and perhaps a tack board on which to post school announcements, party invitations, cleaning slips, video rental receipts, unpaid parking tickets, and the many other miscellaneous pieces of paper that have insinuated themselves into our lives.

Another thing to consider as you plan your cabinets is an entertainment area — a place for the television, stereo, compact disk player, tape recorder, and other electronic gear. If you want music in the kitchen (for some of us, listening to the Rolling Stones at full volume is the only way to clear up after a party), you might incorporate places for speakers into the cabinet design. If you have, or intend to install, an intercom system, you should plan the kitchen unit's location in concert with your cabinets. And finally, we see an increasing number of "intelligent house" systems being installed as a matter of course in high-end renovations and new homes. These computer systems monitor security, fire, temperature, and other house functions from a single video display terminal. If you are considering one of these systems, you may want to hide it, with the rest of the electronic gear, behind a cabinet door — unless you want your kitchen to look like a set from *The Empire Strikes Back*.

The Kitchen Table

There's probably nothing homier or more intimate than sitting down at the kitchen table, sipping a cup of tea or glass of wine and chatting with the cook while dinner is being prepared. This is what I love about my friend Françoise's kitchen — it somehow contains the essence of what a kitchen ought to be.

If you're thinking about placing a table in your kitchen, here are some basic physical parameters: A rectangular table with a seating capacity of four to six should measure 2½ by 5 to 5½ feet. You'll need 2½ to 3 feet clearance all around for chairs and adequate circu-

A work area can be as small as a simply designed end of a counter. Supplies can be tucked away behind the tamboured door.

An entertainment center adjacent to the kitchen encourages lounging — when the homework is done or the bills paid, that is.

This desk offers a telephone, a rolling file cabinet, and shelves for books or storage above. I love the full-length chalkboard on pantry door.

lation, although you could squeeze by with a clearance of 2 feet. A round table takes up less space, yet can accommodate a crowd when the occasion arises. If a round table suits your needs, remember that a small increase in radius makes for a big increase in the circumference of the table and therefore the floor space it will command.

In very small kitchens we've seen hinged tables that fold down when not in use, and in one of my own kitchens I built a small (2 by 3 feet) counter-height peninsula table supported by a single leg at the "seaward" end. With stools for seating and a paper lantern suspended above for illumination, the table made a cozy place to sit, work, or dine.

Whatever type of table you choose, be sure to equip it with a lighting arrangement that can be brightened to provide task lighting when the table is used as a work surface and dimmed when it is used for dining.

You might also consider a skylight to bring natural light into the center of the kitchen. When "This Old House" remodeled an adobe house in Santa Fe, New Mexico, we installed in the kitchen a large, 6 by 6–foot skylight that flooded the room with natural light. Natural light is perhaps the most comfortable to work under, so if your kitchen communicates with the roof above it, installing skylights is worth considering. To control the quantity and intensity of light coming through the openings, most manufacturers can supply adjustable blinds or louvers. In hot, sunny climates like the Southwest, skylights are often sheathed in frosted glass, which transmits light without admitting the direct rays of the sun.

One last thing to consider: the very charm of a table in the kitchen can be a drawback. Very often, once guests are settled in at the table they will not leave. In my own kitchen, friends establish themselves and, despite the fireplace and more luxurious furnishings of the living room, they will not abide being moved in there, and when they are, they soon find an excuse to drift back to the kitchen. Friends of ours, now retired, recently renovated their second home located in Santa Fe. They told me they intentionally made their new kitchen compact, Spartan, and lacking a place to sit, because they wanted to discourage their guests from remaining there. Their plan worked, for we conducted this conversation while happily ensconced before a piñon log fire in the living room, with no thought of returning to the kitchen.

A Sitting Area

The warning about a table in the kitchen applies to sitting areas as well. The prominent Italian designer Ettore Sottsass is vigorously op-

What could give you the sense of hearth and home more than the kids drawing pictures at the kitchen table? This table as well as the one in Julia Child's kitchen (opposite) evokes a sense of well-being and belonging. If you want family and friends out of the kitchen, don't make room for a table!

I myself would trade a year of Sottsass's "ritual meals" for just one of Julia Child's — but only if I could eat it at this table in her kitchen. Julia's kitchen was never "designed" — it developed over the years until now it is an extension of her mind and personality.

posed to large eat-in kitchens. "Cooking and eating lose all sense of ritual and concentration," he laments. "They cease being special moments set apart from the rest of the day." This objection may be worth heeding if incorporating a sitting area in the greater kitchen would leave the house devoid of any separate social area for relaxing. When "This Old House" has built sitting areas in kitchens, it has been in houses with a living room or den elsewhere in the home. It is always preferable to have this choice of atmosphere. Even if your guests refuse to leave your kitchen, *you* can escape once they've gone home.

Sottsass's lament notwithstanding, the instinct to socialize in the kitchen is so strong that sitting areas sometimes come into being without conscious planning. In one of the condominiums we carved out of the Bigelow House, we built a large room that we envisioned as

Our own kitchen represents a series of compromises. My wife, our friend and designer Marilyn Ruben, and I all felt strongly that we needed kitchen, dining, and sitting spaces that opened onto our spacious backyard. Because we are in a historic district, and for budget reasons, we had to stay within the building's existing footprint. On top of it all, we had to design and build fast, because we'd sold our condominium and were living in a one-room loft apartment. The fireplace niche is lit from above by skylights during the day and by wall washers at night. I ran heating tubes under the slate hearth to warm it during the winter, which makes it comfortable for lounging before the fire. The sitting area is a great place to view the garden or talk with the cook. We briefly discussed placing the kitchen in what is now the dining area in order to make space for a large mudroom, but Marilyn felt strongly (and I think correctly) to the contrary. On the down side, all traffic to and from the driveway (on the sink wall) and the backyard goes through the kitchen area, which at 14 feet by 15 feet is not very large.

half kitchen and half dining room. But the new owner furnished the "dining room" as an informal living area, and this is where guests generally prefer to remain, even though the apartment boasts a spacious living room with a fireplace.

There are a few drawbacks to consider before deciding to open the kitchen to a sitting area. First: odors. An exhaust vent can remove most cooking smells, but some odors will inevitably pervade the sitting area. Since you will certainly want to cook and socialize at the same time, you might upgrade your ventilation system to one that is efficient and yet quiet enough that the fan noise is not intrusive.

The same point is to be made for the other noise-producing appliances like the refrigerator, dishwasher, garbage disposal, and trash compactor. The general noise level can be kept at a minimum by choosing higher-quality appliances and by furnishing the kitchen with materials and textures that absorb rather than reflect sound.

The third issue is visual. From the sitting area you and your guests are going to look right into the kitchen. This has implications for your choice of materials, appliances, and grade of cabinetry (which, in turn, has implications for your budget). Major appliances can be oriented in such a way that they don't dominate the view from the sitting area. Some refrigerators, like the Sub Zero and GE Monogram Series, are only 24 inches deep instead of the standard 31 inches and thus install flush with the base cabinets. Their doors can be faced with the same material as the cabinet doors, which blends them in with the cabinetry. These refrigerators, while more expensive than standard units, also tend to be quieter. It's worth considering separate cooktop and ovens, since, while costlier than an integrated range, these blend in with their surroundings better.

In the kitchens in the Bigelow House, cabinetmaker Jack Cronin built the casework as a handsome backdrop to the kitchen sitting areas. In one kitchen he used oak, in another cherry, and in a third butternut, which imparts a beautiful, mellow glow that the homeowner is so taken with that he polishes the cabinets with lemon oil once a month.

Style

How you tackle these design elements has much to do with the style of your kitchen and of the rest of your house. If you've been thinking about your new kitchen for some time, you probably have a certain style in mind. Whether it is the informal look of a country kitchen, the seamless lines of a European kitchen, or something unusual and avant-garde, it is the style of the casework that will establish the basic look of your kitchen. While most designers feel that the cabinetry should be consistent throughout, pulling the room together with long, unbroken runs, there is a contrary school of thought. David Leonard of the Kennebec Company, which built the Shaker-style cabinets we used in the Weatherbee Farm in Westwood, Massachusetts, tries to avoid what he calls the "fitted look" of integrated cabinets. "We prefer the breaking of planes, the look of individual pieces," he says. "We like the kitchen to look as if the pieces have been added over the years."

Keep in mind, while you're still in the design phase, the practical implications of the style you choose. Informal styles, like the country look, can tolerate a good deal of the clutter that is a natural part of kitchen activities. Sleeker or more formal styles require much more diligent housekeeping to look presentable. Be realistic about the style that will best suit you.

Regardless of style, your kitchen will make more of an impression if it reflects your own personality. Perhaps it features those handcrafted tiles you've found in your travels through Mexico, or a collection of antique cookie jars, or salt and pepper shakers, or those beautiful copper pots and pans you bought at Dehillerin's on your honeymoon in Paris. Modern kitchens necessarily rely on a great number of machines, appliances, and other manufactured items, but the really rewarding kitchens rise above the anonymous look of standardization to achieve a look of individuality — a feeling that the kitchen *belongs* to someone.

What Next?

What we've laid out so far in this chapter should help in the important work that comes next: identifying the specific needs and goals of your own kitchen renovation. If you've already done some design work on your kitchen, you might want to take a second look at your sketches. If you haven't started yet, it's time to go through the "predesign" exercises outlined in chapter 1.

Identify what you dislike about your current kitchen. Is it too dark? Are the cabinets beat up? Is there insufficient counter space? Make a list. Everyone in the household should contribute to it. Include *every* negative point you can think of.

Next, start a "wish list" of features you would like to have in your new kitchen. You might want a kitchen that gives guests a comfortable place to sit and talk while you're preparing dinner. You might want to establish a certain mood once dinner is on the table. Your list might be very specific, down to the type of flooring or the features of the range. Think practically. If the children are expected to set the table, for instance, you might specify that the drawers for

Meredith Moses's art gallery specializes in emerging artists. She gave two young designers a free hand, resulting in this geometric exploration of light, form, and space. Dishes are housed in the rectangle above the sink. The refrigerator is on the far left, behind vase. Contrast this look with that of Julia Child's kitchen.

(Right) Everything you can think of to say about your kitchen is useful, especially strong likes and dislikes. This is the time to state your mind.

Dear Mr. Dallmus:

Here is our wish list.

The kitchen is used primarily by me, Jack (who likes to cook on weekends), and the kids. They can prepare their own snacks, lunch and breakfast. They are messy. I am neat. Jack uses a lot of pots and pans when he cooks. I try to keep the kitchen well organized so everyone can find what they need, and to encourage everyone to participate in the preparation and the cleanup.

We like to entertain on weekends, and also host a lot of family events. My sisters always pitch in with the cooking and cleaning when they visit. The kitchen is definitely the center of our daily life. We would prefer a more formal dining room for entertaining (one that doesn't feel like a hallway), and would use the backyard a lot more if there was a patio or a deck, and some nice trees. We're not big gardeners, although Jack grows herbs in pots by the side door.

We'd like to stay here if we can get more mileage out of the house. The main problem with the kitchen is that everyone (kids) is constantly going through it to the family room. I'm always sideswiped when I'm at the sink. I also can't really see into the yard. It feels claustrophobic.

Other thoughts:

Could use a small desk area with a phone.

A small sunny breakfast nook?
Kitchen should feel welcoming--colorful, not sterile.

I'd love to incorporate more of my basket and textile collection in the kitchen.

We shop once a week and need a pantry.

Can you get a bar sink near the seating area?

Do we have room for a place where the kids' sports stuff can be stashed? All the bats and balls and skateboards end up lying at the top of the basement stairs.

Appliances include:
gas cooktop
dishwasher
microwave
separate wall oven
sub zero refrigerator and freezer

Thanks for your help, sincerely,

Pam

This kitchen is self-contained but without walls. The refrigerator, on the back wall, is painted to look like a screen door. The surrounding counter is high enough to hide the clutter of food preparation, but not the cook. In filming our "This Old House" Concord barn project, we looked at a similar kitchen in a converted barn. That kitchen's owner — also the designer — reported that the arrangement worked very well. Notice the placement of the microwave and oven in the vestibule entry.

silverware, napkins, and placemats be accessible to them. Much of your list could be based on the subjects of the chapters of this book — cabinets, counters, lighting, appliances, and so on — to the extent that you know what you want in each category. You might also begin to define the style you want, if you haven't already done so.

Finally, your list should indicate how you and your family use or want to use the kitchen. How many of you cook? Do you cook together? Do you bake or can or make big batches of soups and sauces for the freezer? Do you frequently make snacks, and does their preparation typically get in the way of general cooking? When, and how, do you prepare school lunches? Are children or guests welcome to help with meal preparation, or are they kept on the sidelines? What noncooking activities take place in the kitchen? Do your children do their homework at the kitchen table? Do you pay bills or maintain your correspondence in the kitchen? This kind of information, when compiled and prioritized as a requirement list, will help you see more clearly what you want your kitchen project to accomplish.

Turning Your Wishes into a Design

Once your list or statement has been developed, there are several things you could do next. You could consult an architect or designer (how your prospective design professional responds to the issues on your list can help you evaluate whether this is the right person for you). He or she would then help steer you through the rest of the design and construction of the project. An alternative course would be for you to start conceptualizing the design yourself. This is easiest to do when your kitchen is going to keep its current size and shape, as is usually the case in budget-oriented renovations.

Get yourself some graph paper and, using a scale of six inches to the square, draw the outline of the kitchen. On this floor plan, draw walls, doors, and windows in their current locations. Cut out pieces of paper or cardboard to scale, representing the refrigerator, sink, and cooktop, and begin arranging them into a work triangle that seems to meet your needs. Locate the rest of the major kitchen elements — counters, cabinets, dining table, island, peninsula, pantry, and whatever else you think your kitchen should have. Place a sheet of tracing paper over the graph paper and draw the emerging floor plan on it in bold lines, so you can really see it.

If you have access to a personal computer you might do your layout with one of the software programs written for just this purpose. The basic ones are inexpensive, easy to use, and contain libraries of the shapes and sizes of appliances and furniture as well as architectural symbols.

The owners of this 1930s kitchen loved everything about it but the low ceiling and the lack of light. The solution was to blow out the existing roof and replace it with this dramatic vaulted skylight structure. Notice the childproof locking doors fitted to cover the oven and burner knobs of the restaurant range.

Most likely, while you're working on this first tentative floor plan, you will start to see alternatives. Some of these may be variations of the same basic plan — switching stove and refrigerator or moving the island. Draw each variation on tracing paper and number them. The paper cutouts for the various kitchen components (or the symbol library in the design software) will make it easier for you to move things around and get a sense of how they fit together. To help free up your thinking, try developing a radically different floor plan. Explore its variations as you did with your initial floor plan.

During your investigations you may decide you want to see how relocating walls and windows affects the kitchen. If a bearing wall (a wall that carries some of the house's weight) stands in the way, it can be removed. "Homeowners tend to be more intimidated by bearing walls than they should be," says master carpenter Norm Abram. "In a multistory building, it may be difficult or impossible to remove a bearing wall, but in a house it's not the big deal it once was." A steel or laminated wood beam can be installed to carry the load of the unwanted wall without looking obtrusive. In most cases, it is a routine operation that any experienced carpenter can do, so the expense will probably not be prohibitive. Anyway, right now it's only costing you the price of tracing paper, so go ahead and take a look at what this would do to the design.

You might also spend an hour or two building a little model of your design. This can be easily accomplished by drawing each wall (called an *elevation*) in scale, showing a front view of cabinets, stove, hood, ovens, and so on. Tape the drawing to cardboard or foamboard (available at any art supply store) and join the "walls" together at the corners with tape. Stand it up on the edge of a table and look into it from the perspective you would have if you were actually in the room. We used this technique while designing the Sante Fe kitchen and were amazed at how realistically we could visualize the space. "It's surprisingly satisfying to make a model," Jock says. "Once household members can *see* the new kitchen, they will start asking questions. Then the design process really gathers momentum and becomes a lot of fun."

Making a model can have implications for your project's ultimate cost, as well as contributing to its design. I met a woman who built a model of her architect's first conception of her new house. The model showed her that the house was far larger than she and her husband needed. As a result, they down-sized the plans considerably, saving themselves a lot of money.

When you get tired, let your designs rest. Resume work when everyone is fresh. Sometimes good solutions spring to mind when you are not concentrating on the problem.

If you've been doing your work well, you will come to the point when you can't decide between two or more equally good plans. This is your assurance that you're on the right track. "It is also the point in the design process when things really get interesting," claims Gifford. Struggling with several good plans forces you to ask hard questions about your design goals. Often what results is a design synthesis that's better than the sum of its component plans. Gifford habitually draws three or four plans, the first being the most conservative and the last being the most daring.

Eventually the time will come to show your sketches to an architect or designer. If you want to keep the design fees to a minimum,

The kitchen in this tiny Martha's Vineyard house shows what can be done with simple materials and attentive design. The open shelves and wood-paneled island are fully in tune with the house and the summer island.

you might work up the design yourself, and then pay a designer to spend a couple of hours discussing its flaws and suggesting improvements. That might be enough to ensure you don't make any big mistakes or miss some golden opportunity.

Even if you hire someone else to produce the design, you will still want to be involved. The architect may propose solutions, but it will be up to you to tell him why a particular design element does or does not appeal to you. As the design work moves along, you and the designer will hone your understanding of your design objectives. This process usually takes time, energy, patience, and insight on the part of both designer and client.

After the design is refined, you will want to remain involved because there are so many options in cabinetry, materials, finishes, and detailing that it would be foolish to leave these choices entirely to someone else.

Another thing you might want to do as the design process evolves is to track the cost of the various options under consideration. Ellen Cheever of the National Kitchen and Bath Association suggests asking your designer to provide multiple choices for products and materials, labeled "good," "better," "best," and "ultimate." That will indicate where you can scale the project back to control costs, and help you see some of the possible trade-offs. You might decide to cut back on the quality of the flooring, for instance, and use the savings on really fine countertops.

You might also consider controlling costs by doing the project in phases. We've seen people live with their plywood subfloor for a year or so until they could afford to install the finish floor they most wanted.

But the best way to control costs is right up front in the design phase. We've seen basic, cost-effective materials turned into wonderful kitchens through elegant, inspired design. You will spend a great deal of time in your new kitchen, so while it is costing you only time and paper, have some fun with it.

●

3 Contracts

The owners of this house first drew up a rough floor plan, then met with a designer. Instead of hiring the designer, however, they decided they would act as both their own designer and general contractor. But the key to this renovation was their discovery of a good local carpenter who had never built a kitchen from scratch before. Far from seeing this as a liability, the owners felt they got an excellent craftsman who was free from preconceived notions about what a kitchen should look like. The three fashioned the renovation, making decisions as they went, and the result is an unusual room well suited to the owners' lifestyle.

Being your own designer or contractor will give you a highly personalized renovation, but you need to be a good decision-maker, and have ample time.

If you choose to go this route with a carpenter, be sure your contract is flexible enough to account for your inevitable change-orders without either of you feeling cheated.

Unless you're planning to tackle your kitchen project singlehandedly, you'll need to reach agreement with an architect and general contractor or, in the case you're the general contractor, any number of subcontractors. In this chapter, we look at some of the considerations your contracts should address to facilitate a smooth and successful project.

Let's start with the fundamental question: Do you really need a written contract? We've found quite a few architects, interior designers, and contractors who work without a contract. They feel they have more flexibility this way and argue, justifiably, that no contract can eliminate every conceivable problem. They'd rather spend their time building or designing rather than thrashing out legal paperwork. Recently, a Boston designer told us: "I work on the basis of a handshake, and I've been working that way for twenty-five years. If I don't have enough confidence in a client to proceed on a handshake, I don't take the job." He said this so imperiously that by the time our conversation ended, we wondered if he sometimes used the absence of a contract to intimidate strong-willed homeowners.

Some homeowners go through sizable projects without a contract and have only good experiences. If you're one of these, count yourself lucky. The fact is, a contractor knows a lot more about renovation than most homeowners, and a dishonest one can use his knowledge to take advantage of you. "There are still a lot of unscrupulous people in the home-improvement field," observes Jeffrey Locke, a general contractor in New Haven, Connecticut. "In my state, the only field that has a bigger incidence of consumer complaints is automotive sales. People know better than to buy cars on the basis of a handshake; they should exercise the same caution toward their home-improvement projects." Unless you've worked previously with your contractor or subcontractors, we consider a well-written contract to be essential. Even with familiar tradespeople, a contract is desirable.

The act of drafting a contract forces you and your contractor to be clear about what the project does and doesn't entail. Often people are so eager to get started on a kitchen renovation that they fail to anticipate the pitfalls. Misunderstandings can often be avoided if the homeowner and contractor take time to negotiate a written agreement which accurately represents their expectations and responsibilities. The final revised and dated drawings should become part of the contract, and these drawings updated to reflect all changes.

If problems do emerge after the project has begun, the contract will be useful because of the guidance it provides; it specifies which responsibilities are borne by the various parties, and lays out certain deadlines, materials, and methods of construction. The stipulations in the contract make it more likely that disputes can be settled in an orderly manner, preventing relations between you and your contractor from turning sour. A well-written contract is more a route marker on a highway you've never taken; it identifies the path you're on and helps you avoid wrong turns. It also helps protect you when others fail to live up to their promises.

Here are several important questions that should be answered during the process of negotiating a contract:

- Does the contractor have insurance to cover any damage or accidents that take place at the project site?
- What warranties will be provided on the work?
- Whose responsibility is it to supply building permits and other needed documents?
- What is the starting date for the project?
- What is the anticipated completion date? Is this date firm or only an approximation of the deadline by which the work must be done?
- What happens if the completion date is not met? Are penalties to be assessed? If so, how much will they be?
- Is it all right for the contractor to start work and then go elsewhere to work on another job, or is he expected to work without interruption on your project until completion?
- After the contractor submits an estimate or bid, how long does that figure remain binding in the absence of a signed contract?
- What is the project's cost, and who is to cover any increases in the prices of materials and supplies after the project has begun?
- If conditions are encountered that increase the project's cost, as, for instance, when the opening up of old walls reveals rotten timbers, and these conditions could not reasonably have been foreseen, who bears the expense of the remedy?
- Will the work be paid for in installments? How much will each be, and when will they be due?

- Who will clean up the job site? Will cleanup be required at the end of each workday?

Insurance, Warranties, and Building Permits

The question of insurance should be raised early in the process. If your prospective contractor doesn't carry insurance, you, the homeowner, are at risk in the case of injury or damage. The contractor should carry three different forms of insurance. First, he should be enrolled in a workmen's compensation program to cover any injuries to himself and his employees. If he is not, and an accident occurs, you may be judged to be the employer and held responsible for compensating the injured worker. Ask the contractor for his workmen's compensation number or other proof of coverage.

Second, the contractor should have personal liability insurance to cover injuries suffered by anyone else at the job site. Otherwise, you, as the property owner, may be liable.

Third, the contractor should have property damage insurance to cover any damage to the homeowner's property. Many contractors have a certificate of insurance that they show homeowners to demonstrate that they're covered. If your prospective contractor claims to have insurance but cannot produce a certificate, you should ask for the name of his insurance carrier and verify his coverage.

In most states, contractors' work is required by law to carry a limited warranty, referred to as an "implied limited warranty," even if it's not explicitly discussed in the contract. Usually this warranty covers all the contractor's work for one year after completion of the job. In a few states, the warranty — which mandates replacement, repair, or a refund for defective work or products —continues for a longer period. The warranty is good only as long as the contractor stays in business. A few contractors offer ten-year protection through the Home Owners Warranty program of the National Association of Home Builders in Washington, D.C. Whatever type of warranty the contractor claims to have, it's important to get the name and address of whoever will be responsible for claims — be it a contractor, manufacturer, or distributor.

In most municipalities, a building permit is required if structural work is to be undertaken or the living area is to be expanded. Obtaining the permit is the contractor's job and should be indicated as such in the contract. "If a contractor asks the homeowner to get the building permit, that's a bad sign," warns Bryan Patchan, executive director of the Remodelers' Association of the National Association of Home Builders. "It may mean that the contractor is not licensed.

Whoever gets the permit is responsible for the work and would be held accountable for any violations that occur on the job."

A fundamental principle to follow is that anything agreed upon should be written down, and copies of these stipulations should be provided to all the affected parties. Jock Gifford follows up each meeting with clients by writing a summary of the meeting and giving the clients a copy. "People have selective memories. With a written summary, they're reminded of facts they may have overlooked. If there's a mistake, it can be rectified before problems arise," he says.

Methods of Paying Architects

Methods of payment vary among contractors, kitchen designers, and architects. Architects typically work under one of three different schemes. (The one you and your architect choose should be spelled out in your contract.) The first calls for the architect to be paid a percentage of the construction cost, which may vary according to the scope of the job. Typically, the smaller the job, the larger the percentage. For designing an entire house, a "name" architect might charge 15 percent of the cost of construction and of items ordered by the architect, such as major appliances. For a design-intensive project like a kitchen remodel, the percentage may be higher. Architects with less renown (and lower overhead) may charge a lower percentage. Yet, along with many architects, we consider the percentage method of payment undesirable. It not only penalizes the architect for finding ways to economize, but also leaves everyone uncertain what the total fee will be. On some big jobs, neither architect nor homeowner has a reliable projection of the project's ultimate cost, and when this is so, the architect may demand a high percentage just to protect himself.

A second payment scheme is a fixed fee, also called a "stipulated sum." This arrangement often works well with homeowners and architects who have worked together in the past or with homeowners with experience using architectural services. Its big advantage is that it specifies a definite figure for design. In return for committing to a set fee, the architect may insist on a contractual provision that either limits the client to no more than a couple of major revisions or that limits the number of hours he or she will devote to the job. Without such a provision, the architect's profit could be eaten up by extra hours at the drawing board.

The contract should specify how much involvement the architect will have in overseeing construction. It's usually a good idea to have him visit the site at least weekly, to ensure that everything is being built according to plan. If the contractor knows the architect will periodically inspect his work, he's less apt to substitute materials

The owner of this house had been piling up building material for years, hoping to one day incorporate them all into a house. The result is a new structure with a sense of age and belonging that would have been impossible to achieve with new materials. Note the salvaged beams, barnboard soffits, and bluestone fireplace.

Working with salvaged materials, however, takes far longer than with new. Before they could begin, the stonemasons first had to sort and grade the enormous pile of bluestone. (Normally the material comes sorted by quality and graded by size.) The carpenters faced the same task with the pile of barnboard. Since no one could tell in advance how much time this would take, a contingency clause was written into the contract.

or deviate from the specifications. The contract may state how many site visits the architect must make. If you want him or her to supervise construction actively, rather than simply making an occasional visit, a higher architectural fee is justified.

A third scheme is payment on an hourly basis. This method is especially well suited to homeowners starting with vague notions of how large or costly their project might be. In most instances, the architect will hold at least one initial meeting with you at no charge, to assess your goals and determine whether you'll be comfortable working together. Once work on the design actually begins, the clock

Scheme A

Computer-aided design (CAD) is now powerful and cheap enough to be used by many architects and kitchen designers. To give three-dimensional reality to the design schemes of our prototype house, Greg Conyingham (of Design Associates) and I designed a computer model to see what our kitchen would look like. Modeling of the surfaces is surprisingly realistic. The computer takes into account natural as well as artificial light.

Scheme A

Scheme D

Even as professionals, accustomed to rendering floor plans into three dimensions mentally, we found the reality of these computer-generated images extremely compelling. We both immediately saw the flaws in scheme C and D: C exposes the stairway to view, and denies the kitchen an inside corner; D exposes the workings of the kitchen too much. After seeing these images, we would put scheme D's peninsula onto scheme C.

In the future we expect CAD to become a powerful and much-used design tool. It can help architects, contractors, and homeowners exert more control and precision in all phases of renovation — from design to construction.

Scheme C

Scheme C

Scheme D

starts running. Unless contractually specified, this method allows either of you to back out at any point — a desirable option if you are uncertain whether you will ultimately build the project.

When purchasing architectural services on an hourly basis, ask to be billed frequently. This will help avoid the shock of a bigger bill than anticipated and allows you to resolve any disputes as they arise. If you are eager to keep architectural expenses down, you may sometimes do so by doing your own research on appliances, sinks, faucets, and other items. Many architects are happy to delegate these tasks to the homeowners. As Jock Gifford says, "I encourage my clients to do the legwork and I make myself available for phone consultations. It saves them money, keeps them involved in the design, and frees me up for the more 'architectural' aspects of the job."

Methods of Paying Kitchen Designers

Kitchen designers also get paid under several different schemes. Most work for kitchen stores, which make their income chiefly by selling cabinets and major appliances. It's common for a store to charge a set fee for the design work, which can then be credited toward the price of goods bought from the store. If the fee is on the low side (say, $100), the store may insist that the plans remain the store's property until you order your cabinetry and place a deposit. This method is often termed a "design retainer."

Alternately, the store may allow you unrestricted use of the floor plans, drawings, and other materials if you pay a substantially higher fee for design services. One Boston kitchen store we've dealt with charges $450 for design services if the customer wants to keep the drawings and use them to solicit bids from other suppliers. This method is usually called a "design fee."

Kitchen designers not affiliated with a store either charge an hourly rate ($25 to $100 per hour) or a flat fee, generally accompanied by a limit on the number of redesigns or hours the designer will work.

Most kitchen stores adhere to payment terms recommended by the National Kitchen and Bath Association: a 50 percent payment when you order your cabinets, 40 percent upon delivery, and 10 percent upon installation. If you install the cabinets yourself, or hire a contractor, 50 percent is required upon ordering and the balance upon delivery.

Methods of Working with General Contractors

Once you've got your kitchen designed, you'll need to get it built. Most homeowners have neither the time nor the skills for this, and thus turn to a general contractor. It's wise to solicit bids from a num-

Details are what make the difference between the ordinary and the artistic — but they do raise the price tag. Each detail in this photograph — the glass panel in the drawer, the carefully selected rhythms of beechwood grains and patterns, and the counter-edge profile and graceful end-detail had to be designed, cost-estimated, and built to the specifications. The more detail, the more time-consuming the construction phase, but, if well done, the richer the kitchen.

ber of them, because competitive bidding will help you get a solid, cost-effective price. But for a successful bid competition, you must have complete and detailed specifications. "You've got to be sure everybody is bidding on exactly the same project," Norm Abram cautions. "The more decisions you make about materials, finishes, and detailing before asking for bids, the easier it will be to select a contractor and the fewer problems you will have once he begins the job."

If you haven't specified all of the materials, expect the contractor to insert an "allowance" in the contract — a specified sum of money or price per square foot — to cover unspecified material. If you haven't decided whether to use wood, vinyl, or ceramic tile on the floor, for instance, that line item could be omitted from the contract. But then you would have no idea of the flooring's impact on the overall budget. Thus both contractors and clients usually decide that it's better to include an approximate figure than none at all. The contractor would then put in an allowance for oak flooring at, say, $4.50 per square foot. If you ultimately decide that oak is to be used, $4.50 would be the price. But if you specified a different material, the budget would be adjusted upward or downward to reflect the cost of that choice. You would also have the option of hiring a different contractor to install the flooring or postpone it altogether. As a general rule, remember Norm's advice: A contract with many allowances is a weak one.

●

Upon receiving bids from contractors, you should ask for an explanation of anything that's unclear. If there are wide disparities in bids, ask the bidders why their prices are low or high. It may turn out that the high bidder is offering superior quality of workmanship or materials or that the low bidder has little idea what he's bidding on.

If you have a particular contractor you like to work with, you may skip the bid process altogether; and if you feel comfortable committing yourself to a contractor before he has enough information to give you a definite price, you can "fast track" the construction process. Your contractor can start building your job before the drawings and specifications have been finalized, just as long as he knows that the detailed information he needs will arrive in time. Since good contractors usually have work lined up for months in advance, this arrangement can significantly shorten your project's time frame.

If you've already hired an architect, he or she may be able to recommend a good contractor. If, however, you've started with a contractor, he may recommend an architect. There can be an advantage to using people who have worked together; the architect will know how much detail he or she must include in the drawings and

Handcrafted touches like these ceramic columns and cornices can make a kitchen unique. Keep in mind, though, they should be incorporated into the design in the early stages. Just like any other subcontractor whose work must fit into the enterprise as a whole, craftsmen and artists should be part of the design process and subsequent communications loop, and must be able to meet production schedules to keep the renovation on track. A contract with an artisan should satisfy the same requirements as those with the other trades on the job.

the contractor will know how the architect wants the plans built.

When a contractor bids a project, his price generally stands for a limited time only, typically thirty to sixty days. If a contract is not signed within that period, he is under no obligation to stick to that price.

You should also know that in many parts of the country there are laws or ordinances guaranteeing a three-day cooling-off period during which you can cancel the contract without obligation. These laws, which generally apply to contracts signed in your home rather than in a business establishment, were designed to thwart high-pressure sales tactics. Some standard contracts notify the customer of this right, but others do not. If you don't know whether the cooling-off period applies in your area, call the consumer affairs office in your municipal, county, or state government office, or talk to your attorney.

If the cost of materials changes after the contract has been signed, the contractor must absorb price increases or benefit from reductions. You pay the amount specified in the contract. If he made mistakes calculating his bid, this is also his responsibility. If he breaks something, such as a window, it's up to him to pay for the repair or replacement.

Often the contractor shields himself from unpredictable situations by including a contingency in his calculations. Let's say he estimates a project's cost at $10,000. If it is a straightforward job he may feel a 10 percent contingency is sufficient, and thus would add it to his estimate, producing a total of $11,000, which would become the bid. Naturally a contractor is reluctant to divulge the amount of the contingency, for it is the cushion to protect him from losing money. The more uncertainty there is in the project, the higher the contingency will be.

In many projects, especially in older homes, unexpected difficulties are often encountered. The crew opens up a wall, for instance, and finds rotten sills that must be replaced. Complications that could not have been easily anticipated are usually your responsibility unless the contract states otherwise. Thus you should have your own contingency of at least 25 percent to cope with unforeseen problems — or even 50 percent, because there is a tendency to expand the project as you go along.

Prior to signing the contract, it's a good idea to discuss with the contractor which problems he will cover at no extra cost and which will be your responsibility. Assume nothing. He may have different expectations than those we've laid out here, or you may want to try to get him to accept greater responsibility for unexpected problems. The more that's spelled out in the contract, the more smoothly the project will run. Here's an example of a contract clause that limits the contractor's liability. It's found in the contracts of Cox Kitchen and Baths in Baltimore, Maryland:

> Correction of hidden, unknown damage or building code violations, or damaged pipes, faulty wiring or weak structural parts, the relocation or alteration of concealed obstructions of wiring, piping or supporting of structural members, or the repair or replacement of rot or decay in the structure or parts will be done in addition to this agreement and will be billed to the purchasers at actual cost plus 20% overhead, such work and estimated cost to be specified in writing and signed by both parties prior to the commencement of the work.

If you request a change in your project after the contract has been signed, you must pay for it. "The cost may be substantial," warns Norm Abram. "Extras are always marked up more than things that were in the contract at the start. I advise you to make your initial decisions carefully." This underscores the importance of good design and planning.

Whenever a change is made it should be written as a "change order" and attached to the contract. Typically, this is a simple form that tells you what aspect of the job is being changed and at what cost. The contract should be kept up to date to avoid misunderstandings, and a nasty shock from a big bill at the end. It will also avert arguments between parties who have conflicting recollections about what was agreed upon.

Many homeowners are afraid to take issues directly to the contractor, and approach a member of the construction crew instead. This puts the worker on the spot and undermines the contractor's position. There is a chain of command in a contractor's operation and you are obligated to take your requests directly to him. In general, if you treat him with respect, he will return the courtesy and the job will go smoothly.

Office supply stores sell standard forms of contracts. Many of these are one-page documents, much too short to cover the variety of situations that arise in the course of a kitchen renovation. More detailed contracts for use with an architect or contractor are available from the American Institute of Architects for a small charge. Both the AIA's headquarters in Washington, D.C., and its chapters throughout the United States distribute them. Standard AIA contracts, although regarded as cumbersome by many contractors, may be beneficial from your point of view, since they give you a control over the contractor that the typical one-page document doesn't.

Many contracts list a date by which the project is to be completed. If enforced, a deadline is valuable, because an extra week of living with the kitchen torn apart (or in larger jobs, the whole house) can seem an eternity. Penalties for failure to meet deadlines can be specified in the agreement. If you don't want the contractor to start your project and then take care of other work before returning to finish yours, this should be discussed during negotiations; any understanding can be included in the contract.

Payments for a construction or renovation project can be scheduled in whatever way you and the contractor prefer. There's no universally accepted method. Some contractors push "front-loaded" contracts, which require you to make a large payment upon signing the agreement. Swindlers use such tactics to collect money on projects they never intend to carry out. If you're asked to make a payment before work has begun, you're entitled to an explanation of why any money has to change hands so early. Not every request for a payment before commencement of construction is suspect, however. Sometimes the contractor has to make major purchases of materials before he can begin the job and it's reasonable for him to request a substantial up-front payment. It's not uncommon for the first payment, perhaps 20 percent, to be due when materials arrive at the job site. Alternatively, the first payment could be due when work starts, although many excellent contractors are willing to wait until they've been at the site a week or two. Subsequent payments may also be tied to specific stages of the work. It's a good idea to specify that the final payment will be released only after the entire project has been inspected and any defects remedied. The final payment might be 10 percent, a sum that gives the contractor strong incentive to finish the "punchlist," that is, all the little details that need final attention. "You're holding the contractor's profit," says Norm. "If the final payment is much less than 10 percent, some contractors might be slow to 'punch out.' " In any event, the contract should say what action you can take to recover some money if the contractor doesn't complete the job satisfactorily.

Some homeowners act as their own general contractor and save perhaps 20 percent of the cost of the project. With a few exceptions, they earn it. Getting all the subcontractors — carpenters, plumbers, electricians, masons, drywallers, and so on — to show up when they're wanted is a challenge, even for a general contractor who's been in business for years. For you as a homeowner, it's a tough assignment because the "subs" usually don't know you. What they do know is that you can offer only a one-time job, while a con-

tractor can offer steady work in the future. This is why "subs" may ig-
nore your plea and work instead on another project. Still, a lot of
homeowners have succeeded at managing their own projects. It
saves money and yields great satisfaction, but requires persistence
and professionalism.

　　One job that homeowners often take on is the demolition and
removal of everything that has to go in order for the construction project to begin. Demolition is dirty work, but it has its rewards. One
woman we know ripped the thin 1960s paneling off one of the walls of
her kitchen to find wainscoting that had been on the walls since the

**This barn was moved
to a new location, and
the "house" shoe-
horned into it. For this
kind of job you want
resourceful problem-
solvers for both your
designer and contrac-
tor. Avoid anyone
whose experience is
primarily with new
buildings or stock ren-
ovations.**

house was built in 1910. She carefully removed it, and had a carpenter reinstall it on another wall. As a result, she gave her new kitchen some of its original character, while saving money. The homeowner, because he can take time to do the demolition slowly and meticulously, can undertake this kind of salvage work better than a contractor. Economics force a contractor to get it done fast; he just hasn't time to salvage and reuse materials.

Many contractors are wary of letting the homeowner take the responsibility for demolition for fear that it will not be completed by the time his tradesmen are due to begin their part of the job. If you have the time and aren't afraid of getting dirty, we think you can handle the job. But treat it as a serious obligation, doing everything you've promised on time. You should also be aware of the presence of potential hazards, such as asbestos tiles, insulation, or lead paint, which require special permits and professional removal and disposal.

Another job you can take on is purchasing the materials. "If the customer can chase down tile, fixtures, and other things himself," Norm says, he can do fairly well financially, "because many home centers sell at low prices." If the contractor does all the purchasing, he will buy from his usual suppliers and may add a percentage for overhead and profit. A homeowner can take the time to search for discounts or sales. Some contractors are reluctant to participate in such an arrangement because they lose the markup on materials, or because they're afraid the homeowner will get the wrong products, in the wrong quantities, or make other errors. Delays in getting materials to the job site could mean his men are idle, and that costs him money. If you take on this job, treat it seriously. "It can't be done at the homeowner's convenience," says Tom Silva, who, with his brothers, has done several "This Old House" projects. He points out that many items must be ordered in advance, so you must think well ahead and in concert with your construction schedule.

As important as a contract is, your biggest asset in your project is your relationship with your contractor. Many contractors are craftsmen who build for the satisfaction of a job well done. If you're lucky enough to find one, it's important for you, as the client, to recognize, appreciate, and respect his talent and abilities. Such a craftsman will often go out of his way to improve the job, at no additional cost, because it's the right thing to do.

●

Sometimes you have to do a little more demolition than you first anticipated. . . . When "This Old House" renovated an 1850s barn in Concord, Massachusetts, our initial thought was to pull off the siding and sheathing, dismantle the post-and-beam structure, repair or replace any timbers that needed it, and reassemble the building on the original foundation. After we skinned it, though, we found that the powder post beetles had so eaten the wood that it was just not worth saving.

In renovating older homes — and even some new ones — you often run into unexpected structural damage that can increase the scope and therefore the cost of the job. A responsible contractor will leave open a part of his bid until after the demolition, when he can assess the cost of any unforeseen structural problems.

4 Demolition and Framing

Once the plans are drawn and the contracts signed, you have arrived at the moment of truth. You can still back out, you know — perhaps just paint the kitchen, buy some new appliances, and use the rest of the money for a nice long vacation in Bali. If you have any lingering doubts about forging ahead, consider them well, for the next step is demolition, the point of no return.

I have always enjoyed demolition. I used to love it for the brute satisfaction of legitimized destruction, but now I enjoy the challenge of figuring out the fastest and cleanest way to go about the task. I always experience a curious mixture of emotions as demolition begins. First there is a twinge of sadness that the old, however dreadful, must now be swept away; next is a sense of crossing roads never to be recrossed, for once the kitchen is destroyed it must be rebuilt; finally there is a sense of commitment to the enterprise of the new, and a drive to get on with the project as directly and efficiently as possible.

●

The general contractor usually does the demolition to ensure that his project moves forward on schedule. But some homeowners love to tackle this part of their job, even though it's tough, messy work. To these folks, ripping out ceilings and walls, cabinets and windows is pure joy, not to mention the source of savings.

No matter who is doing the demolition, the first rule is to remove or protect any old features that you want to incorporate into your renovation. There is a lot of rough treatment during a construction project, and it's easy for old work to be damaged. The second rule is to keep the site as clean and orderly as possible. We've seen projects where so much debris was scattered about that workers had trouble finding their tools. These conditions are dangerous for both workers and homeowners. Even if the contractor is contractually responsible for cleaning the site at the end of each workday, you will gain a lot of respect if you make it your business to keep the job picked up. For this, you'll need a pair of thick work boots; you'll thank yourself for buying them the first time you step on a nail.

●

If you're doing the demolition yourself, proceed in an orderly manner. Many amateur renovators crash through their demolition with a crowbar and sledgehammer like Livingston slashing through the jungle with his machete. When I did the "demo" on my house, my two assistants, Yavina, from the New Guinea Highlands, and Pierre, a Frenchman visiting relatives before returning to France to join the *Army de l'air*, blew through the back ell in just this way. It all came down quickly, but afterward the place looked like London during the Blitz and took just about as long to clear out.

In demolition, framing, and drywall you will see the most dramatic transformations of your project. Work moves very fast in these phases, and so it should. Don't be distressed if progress seems to slow down later with the details of installing cabinets, floors, counters, and finishing.

If you proceed in an organized fashion, the demolition will be cleaner, faster, and safer yet will lose none of its cathartic qualities. First, pull out old cabinets, plumbing fixtures, iron radiators, and appliances and dispose of them. If you have gypsum board on the walls, pull that off in sections and load it into the dump truck or Dumpster. If you have old horsehair plaster walls, skim the plaster off the lath with a garden spade and shovel it off the floor. Then pull the lath off the studs and tape or tie it into manageable bundles. If you pull both lath and plaster down in a frenzy, the lath will become jumbled like pick-up-sticks and will take forever to clear out. When the lath and plaster or gypsum board is removed, you can proceed with the demolition of walls. It goes without saying that you should wear work boots and a dusk mask.

Dust will inevitably drift into the portions of the house not under construction. To keep this to a minimum, take some time before you begin to seal off your site with sheets of polyethylene taped to the walls with duct tape. Polyethylene is cheap and is available in large rolls from home centers or lumberyards. If your kitchen has an exterior door, use only that for access. Despite all your precautions, if you are pulling down old horsehair plaster walls and ceilings, the dust will get through anything you hang in the way and settle on every horizontal surface in your house.

New framing within an old shell: After I did the demolition in my own house I discovered a crumbling foundation, rotten sills, and under-size framing members of junk lumber (evidently salvaged from an old outbuilding). Since, for historic and financial reasons, I couldn't demolish the back ell, even if only to replicate it, the only solution was to shore the building up and re-frame from the inside — long and backbreaking work.

Some of the stuff you are tearing out has value. Old brass and copper pipes and iron radiators, for instance, may be sold to scrap dealers. But most of the debris must be hauled away. In most communities, construction rubble is not accepted for routine municipal trash removal, so you'll have to hire a dump truck or a Dumpster. In the Boston area, a 30-cubic-yard Dumpster costs more than $600 per load, so it pays to pack it densely — no sense paying to remove air pockets. Put no garbage in the Dumpster, for it may sit there for weeks attracting insects and rodents.

Framing

Once demolition is complete, you or your carpenter can start the framing of any floor decks, ceilings, and new or modified walls. In large projects, like an entire house, the framing is sometimes done by a specialized subcontractor. But on small projects, like a kitchen renovation, the contractor or carpenter will generally do all aspects of woodworking, from framing through finish work.

The frame provides both the structure for the house, and the substrate for the finish materials — the gypsum board or plaster ceil-

ings and walls and the wood, carpet, vinyl, or tile floors. The framing layout is organized according to a fairly standardized scheme: for walls, 2x4 or 2x6 boards or *studs* are set vertically on 16- or 24-inch *centers,* that is, the distance from the center of one stud to the center of the next. Ceilings are attached to undersides of horizontal framing members called *ceiling joists* (which have first been cross-strapped with 1x3 wood strapping) or to the roof *rafters.* Floors are attached to the top face of the *floor joists.*

The ends of the joists must connect to *bearing walls,* that is, walls which carry the house's load to the foundation. This connection can be made in several ways. The joists may tie into a *joist header* — a horizontal framing member at a right angle to the joists and nailed into the studs. The joist header may be a beam (an especially strong, load-bearing horizontal member), or the joists may rest on a *sill,* a horizontal member directly on top of the foundation, or on a *plate,* the horizontal member on top of the wall. As an alternative, the ends of the joists may rest on a *girder,* which in turn rests on *posts.* Joists,

This extension, though not large, is just enough to house the real work part of the work triangle, providing more room for the kitchen's preparation and entertaining areas. The designer preserved a farmhouse feel by using oversize double-hung windows above the sink and echoing the grid pattern with a deft blend of glass block, clear glass, and tile. The result is a sense of light and air but on a very human scale.

To create this kitchen–family area, the walls were knocked down and the support posts trimmed out as pillars. The kitchen space is still clearly delineated from the rest of the house but enjoys the light and vistas to the outdoors.

headers, sills, and beams are all horizontal in their long dimension; posts are vertical. Some of the construction terminology may be confusing at first, but the basic principles are quite simple; the structure is made up for the most part of horizontal and vertical pieces of lumber, which carry and transfer loads to the foundations, footings, and finally the earth itself. (See diagram.)

●

The framing crew uses various techniques to strengthen and stiffen the frame. Wooden *blocking* or wooden or metal *bridging* extends from the side of one joist to the side of the next, taking the bounce out of the floor. *Sisters* — wooden members that are attached alongside the joists — may be used to add strength to joists. *Sistering* is done in both old and new buildings, in areas where rot or cuts in the wood have weakened the structure or where joists have been deliberately removed to allow for stairways, doors, skylights, and so on.

The frame is the skeleton of the house and it must remain stable despite windstorms, snow loads, and other challenges to its integrity. If it shifts, walls will crack, floors will sag, and windows and doors will become hard to open and close. Extreme shifting may indicate major structural flaws in the building. In some old houses the structure has crept out of *square* (no longer coming together at 90-degree angles); windows that started out perfectly rectangular have over the years become distorted into parallelograms.

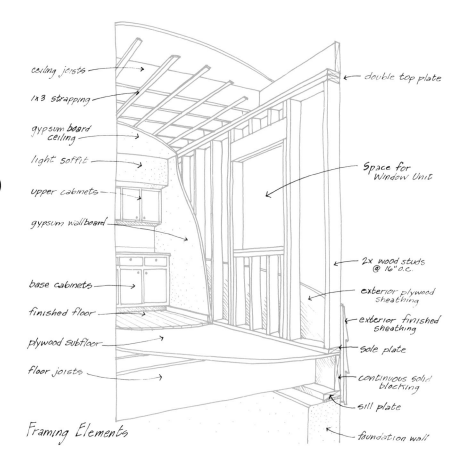

ceiling joists

1x3 strapping

gypsum board ceiling

light soffit

upper cabinets

gypsum wallboard

base cabinets

finished floor

plywood subfloor

floor joists

double top plate

Space for Window Unit

2x wood studs @ 16" o.c.

exterior plywood sheathing

exterior finished sheathing

sole plate

continuous solid blocking

sill plate

foundation wall

Framing Elements

For many homeowners, one of the most anxiety-producing issues in renovation is the removal of walls. A wall can be either *bearing*, which means it helps to support the structure and its contents, or *nonbearing*, also called a partition wall, which means it merely separates one space from another. Before removing any part of a wall, you must determine which type it is. Examine the joists wherever they're exposed, such as in the basement or attic. If the joists run in the same direction as the wall, it's probably nonbearing and can safely be removed. If the joists run perpendicular to the wall, it's probably a bearing wall and can be removed only with the proper techniques.

Some houses have neither basement nor attic, so examining the joists is a bit more difficult. Sometimes you can remove a piece of molding, making it possible to explore the building without doing harm. Or you can drill a series of small holes at 2-inch intervals until you hit a joist. Then, if you drive nails at 16-inch intervals and make contact with joists, the wall is probably bearing. If you don't make contact with joists, it's most likely a nonbearing wall. The locations of the joists may also be identified by using an electronic stud sensor.

All the loads in a structure, the weight of the building, its contents, and people, must be transferred through the structure to the earth itself. This can be done with posts and beams made of timber or steel, or with *bearing walls*, constructed of 2 × 4 or 2 × 6 lumber. In this house, the outside walls are load bearing, as are the walls running down the middle, which transfer the weight of the attic joists and the first and second floors to the earth via the beam, columns, and concrete footings in the basement. Moving these interior bearing walls would require installing a beam large enough to carry the loads of the floors above it.

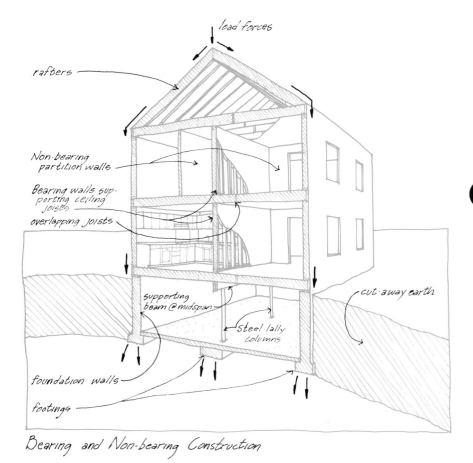

load forces

rafters

Non-bearing partition walls

Bearing walls supporting ceiling joists

overlapping joists

supporting beam @ midspan

steel lally columns

cut-away earth

foundation walls

footings

Bearing and Non-bearing Construction

In very old homes, such as my own, which have been modified again and again over the years, it is sometimes impossible to figure out the framing details using these standard techniques. Occasionally I cut a 4-inch-diameter hole in a wall or ceiling with a hole saw to have a peek inside, but sometimes the wall or ceiling surface must be removed before you can plan your framing scheme. The special problems encountered in historic houses drive up the cost of renovating them.

Removing a Bearing Wall

"Today just about any wall can be removed if you take the right precautions," says Norm Abram. The load that's been carried by the studs can be carried instead by a beam. The beam will then pass its load to posts, beefed-up studs, or other framing members. Beams are available in steel, solid wood, or laminated wood. Steel is heavy and difficult to attach wood to, but is very strong and thus can be sized to be easily concealed in a wall or ceiling. "Steel is cheaper than wood, but more expensive to work with," Norm says. Solid wood beams, on the other hand, need to be sized very large to carry a heavy load or accommodate a long span. Laminated beams are made of many thin

layers of wood glued together. They are very strong yet can be worked with standard woodworking tools. Joists can be attached directly to them via metal joist hangers. Laminated beams can be ordered in several wood species. They are *prestressed*, that is, the top curves upward to counteract the downward pressure of the building weight, and come marked "top" and "bottom." Before removing a bearing wall, it's necessary first to build temporary walls, or shoring, to carry the load until the new beam and other supporting members are installed. The size and placement of temporary walls as well as beams and other framing components should be specified by an experienced carpenter or structural engineer. If you're tackling a project like this for the first time, seek the advice of a professional.

Framing around Windows

Windows make their own demands on the structure. Unless a window is very narrow, about 14 inches or less, it will interrupt the wall studs, and thus the framing members around it need to be bolstered. The usual way to do this is by installing a *header* over the window, which is supported by *jack studs*. Short studs, called *cripples*, are installed under the window to provide necessary support.

   Sheathing of plywood or *oriented-strand board* (OSB) is nailed to the exterior of the frame, and areas where windows and doors will be installed are cut out. To the exterior of the sheathing we apply an air-infiltration barrier of *spun-bonded polyester* (trade

Pocket door and pocket window keep noise and odors in the kitchen without shutting it off visually. The pocket door is a good choice here, for it disappears when open. The glass terrarium on the pass-through lets the gerbils see what you're serving for dinner.

names: Tyvek, Typar, and Bear Wrap). This helps prevent wind and moisture from infiltrating the house while still letting the walls breathe. The siding, usually clapboards or shingles, is nailed right over this.

Selecting Doors and Windows

Doors are available in a number of materials, including wood, metal, glass, and fiberglass. Some of them feature a core of insulating material to stop heat flow and integral weather stripping to prevent drafts. Metal-clad doors are the easiest to maintain because there's no danger that they will warp or pull apart, as sometimes happens with wood doors (although manufacturers still have trouble getting the windows in these units to look good). While we've had good luck with fiberglass doors, wood doors look more elegant and have a nicer feel. Glass doors are made of tempered glass, which will reduce the hazard of flying glass if accidentally broken. We no longer install glass doors with an aluminum frame, as aluminum conducts cold, on which moisture condenses. Instead, we use glass doors framed with wood, which look more attractive and perform better in our cold New England weather.

Windows are available in many shapes, styles, and materials. *Bay* windows are most commonly available with a center *light*, or pane of glass, parallel to the wall, and two sidelights. A *bow* window follows a gently scribed arc. Both bays and bows can bring more

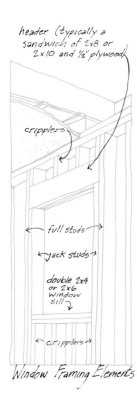

header (typically a sandwich of 2x8 or 2x10 and ½" plywood)

cripplers

full studs

jack studs

double 2x4 or 2x6 window sill

cripplers

Window Framing Elements

Window Types

Fixed Ribbon

Casement

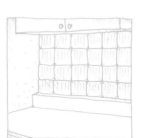

Glassblock

Awning

Full Height Double Hung

Bow

Hopper

Slider

A handsome kitchen drawn with a strong hand. The choice of windows here reinforces the room's sense of assuredness. These windows pivot horizontally to open both at top and bottom. This allows for good ventilation and easy cleaning of the outside, but they cannot be fitted with insect screens.

Round

Palladian Top

Bay

Double Hung

light into the kitchen while providing a nice area for plants. Some of the lights in a bay or bow may be fixed, while others operate.

Casement windows are hinged outward like a door. They are operated with a crank mechanism and generally require less effort to open and close then *double-hung* windows, which slide up and down. When the window is over a kitchen counter, it's easier to crank a casement open and closed than to lean forward to heft a double-hung window up or down. But because casements swing out they are more exposed to the weather than are double-hung windows, and are thus apt to require more maintenance. Another choice is an *awning* window, which hinges at the top and opens outward, and is also operated with a crank. Awning-type windows are easy to operate and are less exposed to the weather than casements but do not admit as much air as either a casement or a double-hung.

If the windows are to be installed in an older house, it's important to consider how they'll complement the house's appearance; often it's inappropriate to replace an old window with a new one of a different shape or style.

●

Double-pane windows — two panes with an air space in between — have been on the market for years. These may be a good, low-cost choice for temperate climates, but for more demanding applications we use the new crop of technologically advanced windows. "Low-E" or *low-emissivity* windows (typically dual-pane) have a metallic film on one pane, which helps to reflect radiant energy, keeping the sun's heat out in the summer, yet retaining the warmth generated by the heating system in the winter. The windows are called low-E because glass with this treatment emits little radiant energy. An inert gas such as argon is sometimes used to fill the void between the panes, further improving the window's insulating value. A side benefit of low-E glass is that it cuts the transmission of ultraviolet light, reducing the fading of carpets, fabrics, and wallpaper. An even more advanced technology, called "Heat Mirror," involves suspending a low-E plastic film between two panes of glass, creating a triple-glazing effect. Some manufacturers of these windows make the spacer between the panes of glass from an insulating material, further cutting the transmission of cold into the house. The most advanced windows now achieve an insulating rate (or R rating) of 5.5, a figure unheard of ten years ago. By comparison, three inches of fiberglass insulation gives an R value of about nine.

Skylights, like windows, have improved dramatically in design and performance in the last few years. In the old days, they leaked or became covered with condensation, which then dripped on

Skylights with built-in
blinds are banked to-
gether to create the
sense of an atrium.
Large shade trees keep
the room cool in sum-
mer. What makes this
design is the rhythm of
the upper and lower
cupboards in relation to
the skylights.

walls and ceilings. They were difficult to open and close, lacked an insect screen, and came with no prefabricated flashing system — the "L" section plastic or metal material that makes a watertight joint between the roof and the skylight's curb — which made the units tricky to install. But technology has solved the condensation problem by using insulating and low-E glass, and excellent factory-supplied flashing kits make the new units straightforward to install and virtually leakproof. Many skylights on the market can be opened and closed without moving the insect screen, some by automatic or remote controls. You can even install sensors to open your skylights automatically in hot weather and close them when it rains.

Place your skylight carefully, considering where the sunlight will fall in the room. A basic mistake (one that we made in our first project in Dorchester, Massachusetts) is to install the skylight so that sunshine falls directly on the refrigerator. You might consider orienting your skylight to the north. Artists' studios have long been lit from above with north light, which is diffuse and of a constant color. If you live in a hot climate, northern orientation for your skylights will keep the room cooler. Sometimes a frosted panel is used on the skylights, which admits light but not the direct rays of the sun. If you're installing a skylight on a pitched or cathedral ceiling, consider installing a horizontal soffit and a vertical sill, a detail that we think looks better and will distribute the light more widely into the room.

Insulation

After the windows and doors have been installed, the next step is the rough plumbing and electrical installation, followed by insulation. Since we devote the whole next chapter to plumbing and electrical "rough-in," let's discuss insulation here.

Our customary technique at "This Old House," now fairly standard, is to fill the cavities between studs of an exterior wall with unfaced fiberglass batts (the thicker the better). We then pull 4- or 6-mil-thick polyethylene sheeting across the whole wall, cutting openings for doors, windows, and electrical boxes. The polyethylene film serves as a *vapor barrier*, sealing out drafts and preventing moisture in the house from penetrating the walls and condensing on the insulation (destroying its effectiveness) and possibly causing the wood to rot. A vapor barrier increases the comfort of a heated house, since the higher the humidity, the warmer a given temperature feels to the human body. Another alternative is to use fiberglass insulation with a foil facing on one side. The foil serves both as a vapor barrier and to reflect some radiant heat back into the room. This *foil-backed* insula-

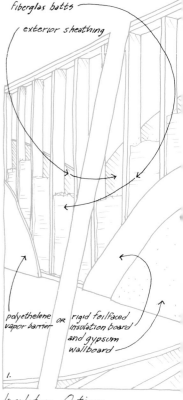

fiberglas batts

exterior sheathing

polyethelene vapor barrier or rigid foilfaced insulation board and gypsum wallboard

1.

Insulation Options

tion is installed with the foil toward the heated interior of the house. However, we've found it faster and cheaper to use unfaced fiberglass with the polyethylene sheet.

We, and many builders, have begun to take this concept a step further by replacing the polyethylene vapor barrier with rigid foil-backed foamboard. Sold under various trade names, the board comes up to an inch thick. With an R value of 7.5 per inch in thickness, the foamboard adds considerable insulating value to the wall, which is unbroken by the studs, which serve to transmit cold from the exterior to the interior of the building. The board's foil backing both reflects radiant heat back into the room and acts as a vapor barrier. At around $15 per 4x8-foot sheet, this sytem is expensive but it is sometimes the most effective way to retrofit an old house with energy-efficient walls.

This stairway-countertop turned an architectural liability into an asset. The design preserves the light and access afforded by the french doors on the left while increasing both the counter acreage and storage in the form of bookshelves accessed from the stairwell. Note that the butcher-block counter becomes the handrail.

Plywood

In an old kitchen with irregular walls, or even a new kitchen in which you plan to install many wall-hung cabinets, consider first sheathing the interior walls with ½-inch plywood. This will serve both to straighten small irregularities in the walls that will later make installing counters and backsplash more difficult, and to give solid anchorage for wall cabinets. The gypsum board would then be installed over the plywood.

Wall Materials   *Drywall and Blueboard*

Decades ago, builders used to nail thin, narrow strips of wood, called lath, to the studs, which were covered with three coats of plaster. This time-consuming operation has long been superseded by quicker techniques. Today, the typical wall surface is gypsum board — large

Different framing materials have different architectural properties. A wooden support post could have been used here (wood is very strong in compression, i.e., when used as a post) but a slim steel column was used instead, to bring out the salvaged wooden beams as the dominant visual feature.

flat panels made of gypsum, a chalky substance quarried from the earth, sandwiched between reinforcing layers of paper. The gypsum board panels, typically ½ or ⅝ inch thick, are installed over the vapor barrier and secured to the studs with screws. On ceilings we screw the gypsum board to strapping, generally 1x3 boards or strips of expanded metal, which we attach perpendicular to the joists on 16-inch centers. Holes are then cut in the gypsum board for windows, doors, and electrical boxes.

There are a number of different products composed of gypsum board: drywall, blueboard, and fire-resistant board. The difference between these products is the type of paper that coats them and some additives to the gypsum.

Drywall is the most commonly used product for wall surfacing. After installation, the joints between the panels are covered with paper or fiberglass-mesh tape, which is then coated with drywall compound, or "mud." Since the compound shrinks as it dries, three coats are usually necessary. When dry, the final coat is sanded smooth, and can then be painted or papered. Drywall comes in a fire-resistant version for use in multifamily dwellings and other areas where the building code requires it.

This existing pantry was redesigned to house the refrigerator and ovens. The window was moved from the left wall to the center, panels of glass block added to either side. The framed header was installed to sharpen the distinction between kitchen and pantry and to provide visual continuity with the dark wood of the doors and windows.

Blueboard gets its name from the blue color of its paper covering. It installs just like drywall but is finished differently. It has a tough, waterproof paper specially formulated to bond to "veneer" plaster. The joints between panels are taped with fiberglass mesh tape, and the whole surface skimmed with a thin coat of plaster. The result is a clean, smooth, hard surface that closely resembles the old lath-and-plaster finish.

Veneer plaster is a job for professionals, but it has particular advantages for renovation. It easily hides any uneven meeting of old and new walls and ceilings, and because veneer plaster is a one-step process, as compared to drywall's three-step process, the plasterers are in and out much faster, making way for the subcontractors who follow. Blueboard and veneer plaster is a common technique here in New England and is competitive in cost with drywall. But this is not the case in other parts of the country. Older plasterers tell us that veneer plastering is an evolution of the old lath-and-plaster techniques that were once universally practiced. In New England, workmen never lost their skills, whereas in other parts of the country, lath and plaster was abandoned for drywall. This shortage of skilled labor may make skim-coat prohibitively expensive outside of New England.

We have found exceptions, however. When "This Old House" did our adobe house in Santa Fe, New Mexico, we found superb lath-and-plaster jobs still being done by highly skilled native New Mexican tradesmen.

Wood Paneling

Wood can give a kitchen tremendous warmth and character. Matched fir is one species we've used, tongue-and-groove pine is another choice, as is painted beadboard, pine with small beading every two or four inches. Beadboard is fairly cost-effective in comparison to veneer plaster. It is often milled from common pine, with knots, but also comes "clear," that is, without knots.

Because wood does not absorb moisture as much as gypsum board, we've seen it used in houses that are directly on the water in places like Cape Cod and the Pacific Northwest. For the same reason, it is also well suited for a vacation or ski house that will be unheated when unoccupied.

An advantage of wood is that you can stain it before it goes up, eliminating a messy job when your kitchen is nearing completion. If you plan to paint it, we recommend you prime before installation. Many people prefer merely to seal the wood and let the grain make its own design statement. Both satin and gloss polyurethane varnish is available; use whichever one suits your tastes. Gloss is

(Above) Tile makes a big statement about who you are and what you want your kitchen to be. Here the two tile types, maroon on the wall and off-white on the counter, are both handmade. Their color, texture, and light-reflecting qualities work nicely with the cherry cabinetry.

(Above right) The simple pattern on these tiles creates an unfussy atmosphere in this small kitchen.

(Left) A spacious pre-war apartment kitchen combines wood wainscoting with classic black and white tiled walls. The black border helps visually to lower the very high ceilings.

more durable than satin, but for walls we think the difference is negligible.

Keep in mind that unpainted wood will grow darker as it ages, and dark wood tends to make a room look smaller. The treatment of the wood needs to suit the overall appearance of the room. In a room with lots of things out in the open and competing for the eye's attention, wood may make the room look too busy, whereas in a room decorated in a simple, spare manner, natural wood may be just the thing to make the kitchen homey and inviting.

Tile

Tile is often the wall-covering of choice for commercial kitchens. It is hard, eminently cleanable, and very durable. Installation on walls is not as demanding as on the floor or countertop. In a dry location, the tiles can be glued directly to drywall with *mastic,* a gooey organic adhesive that is applied with a notched trowel. In wet locations you should use the *thin-set mortar* method, in which mortar is applied to a cementitious backer board and then covered with tile. (Tile installation methods, mortars and grouts are discussed in detail in chapter 12.)

There is an extensive variety of colors and finishes available in wall tile. Because the wall will not see anywhere near the abuse that a floor will, you can use a shiny glazed tile without worrying that it will get scratched. We would tend to choose large tiles to minimize the number of grout lines to be cleaned, but there are no general aesthetic rules regarding this. I have seen whole walls covered with 2x2-inch speckled dark gray tiles grouted in white. It may sound terrible, but the effect was beautiful.

5 Plumbing and Electrical Rough-in

Thoughtful planning for your electrical and plumbing needs will provide the infrastructure for all those wonderful gadgets and appliances you will want in your new kitchen.

Every building or renovation project has certain phases when the work seems to progress rapidly, and others when it seems to creep along. Demolition and framing are usually fast and, as the old space gives way to the new, one sees dramatic changes nearly every day. But then the job enters what you might call the infrastructure phase, and the work seems to slow down. Pipes and wiring are no less important than demolition and framing, their installation is just less dramatic.

You will see your plumber and electrician on two phases of your renovation: installing the pipes and wires — which is called "rough-in" — and finishing the job by installing the fixtures and electrical devices. Rough-in takes place after the walls have been framed and closed in with exterior sheathing, windows, and doors, but before the installation of the insulation, vapor barrier, and gypsum board. Since every plumbing or electrical device you plan to use in your kitchen will need pipes or wires run to it at rough-in, careful planning is critical. Also, since pipe is bigger and less flexible than wire, it is not a bad idea to schedule the plumber on the job before the electrician, and, unless you're gutting your kitchen, you may want to consult with both tradesmen about how much of the old walls, ceiling, or floor must be removed.

Plumbing Rough-in

When your plumber arrives to do the rough-in, he will lay out his runs of pipe from his set of your kitchen's plans. These are the same plans used to construct a bid on your job, and, presumably, they list the specific type (down to the model number) and location of every water– and natural gas–using device.

It used to be that plumbing a kitchen required only water and waste pipes to the sink and dishwasher, and a natural gas pipe to the range. Now, kitchens often have a second sink (both with garbage disposals) and even a second dishwasher, a hot-water dispenser, perhaps a water-purification system, an icemaker, a gas grill, or even a gas-fired wok. We review kitchen fixtures in chapter 10, so suffice it to say here that long before your plumber first arrives, you should decide exactly what you want and where it will be placed.

If your project is a minor rather than a major renovation, you may try to limit your plumbing costs by keeping the sink where it is and clustering any additional water-using devices close together. But before letting the sink determine your whole layout, consider that it can often be moved a few feet without too much cost or difficulty. "If the new sink is within, say, five feet of the old one, there shouldn't be much of a problem," advises "This Old House" plumbing and heating expert Richard Trethewey. "Your plumber can run the pipes horizontally behind or, if he must, within the new cabinets." Five feet is the limit for an easy changeover. Beyond that, a new vent (see below) will be required, which may mean opening up more walls, because the vent typically runs up through the wall cavities and out the roof.

But more important, keep in mind that a kitchen layout dictated solely by the existing plumbing may be at odds with the kitchen's ultimate workability. Although plumbing is not inexpensive, it is not so dear that it should prevent you from getting the kitchen you want. We think it is preferable to fit the plumbing costs into the budget rather than to make do with an awkward layout.

One way to plan for a more elaborate kitchen without building it all at once is to have the plumber run rough plumbing to the future sites of, say, a bar sink or an icemaker. He can then cap, or "stub out," these pipes, making it easy and relatively inexpensive to install those fixtures at some future date.

The main thing to keep in mind is that with today's plumbing and construction techniques, water-using devices can be installed just about anywhere, so don't let any preconceptions you might have about plumbing restrict your design.

●

The average residential plumbing system can be broken down into three subsystems: *supply lines,* which deliver hot and cold water throughout the house; *drainage and waste lines,* which convey contaminated water to the sewer or septic system; and *vent pipes,* which allow gases in the waste lines to escape to the atmosphere. (Your plumber will also install any gas piping your kitchen needs.)

For every sink or appliance, *shutoff valves* for the hot and cold water supply should be provided, each in a location where it can readily be reached — these will come in handy during any future repair work. If your kitchen is not on the ground floor, or if your renovation encompasses more than just the kitchen, it is generally a good idea to engineer into your design a *plumbing chase,* a clear, unobstructed shaft through which pipes, vents, and wires can be run from floor to floor. A chase is of great use later on when you want to do further plumbing or electrical work on the house. In a region with

Moving plumbing five feet in either direction from existing fixtures is not costly or difficult. However, putting a sink in an island implies more extensive construction, because the vent line needs to run to and up an outside wall. A bow vent is important here because it helps compensate for the longer distance the vented air has to run, and helps eliminate backup.

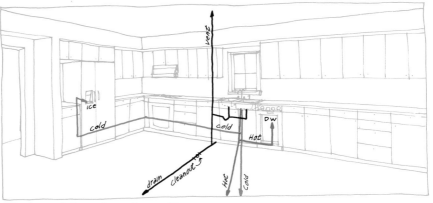

Plumbing at typical counter condition.

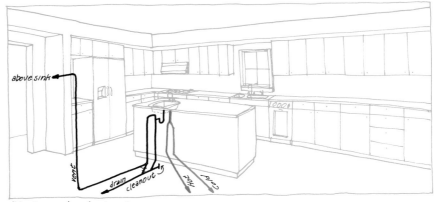

Plumbing at island sink.

cold winters, like New England, we keep the water supply pipes out of exterior walls, because it takes just a small draft to make a pipe freeze and burst during a January cold snap. If the design or framing structure forces you to run supply lines in an exterior wall, insulate them thoroughly or take the precaution of wrapping the pipes with heat cables.

The word *plumbing* comes from the Latin word for lead, since early pipework was fabricated of that metal. Up until the turn of the century, lead was still used for piping, and many cities, Boston among them, still have miles of lead water mains buried beneath the streets. (If your house has lead pipes you may want to replace them.) Other materials like cast iron, galvanized steel, and brass have also been used for piping. Now, copper tubing is the standard material for water feed lines. It is light, nontoxic (in contrast to lead), relatively easy to work with, and long-lived.

For waste lines cast iron was the standard until recently, but plastic pipe made of PVC (polyvinyl chloride) or ABS (Acrylonitrile butadiene styrene) is now almost universally used; very few jurisdictions do not allow it. PVC and ABS are light, strong, and can be

These "roughed-in" bathrooms in a "This Old House" project are piped back to back to keep all the plumbing in one "wet wall." Notice the copper feed pipes for hot and cold water, capped and ready for pressure-testing, and the PVC waste and vent lines, also capped.

quickly and easily cut and glued together with simple tools. The interior of the pipe is more slippery than cast iron, which helps prevent clogging.

"In the future I think we'll see plastic pipe start to displace copper for the water supply lines as well," predicts Trethewey. Already polybutylene, or PB, tubing is accepted for drinking water in many jurisdictions, as is chlorinated polyvinyl chloride, or CPVC, and cross-linked polyethylene, or PEX. PEX is now widely used in Europe for drinking water, and "This Old House" has been using the material in the radiant-floor-heating systems of which we have become so fond (more about this in the next chapter).

If you find this plethora of acronyms confusing, if not downright threatening, you may take some heart from the fact that plumbing, like electrical work, is highly regulated by state and local codes, which, together with the regularly scheduled inspections of your job by your local plumbing inspector, should ensure that your system will be safe, dependable, and built of tested and approved materials.

Water Treatment

The plumbing codes govern the quality of our residential plumbing systems but unfortunately have little to do with the quality of the water that flows through them. Problems with water quality range from the presence of relatively innocuous minerals like calcium and magnesium, which cause "hard" water, to contamination by bacteria and industrial and agricultural chemicals, which may present a serious health hazard. Municipal water plants are very well monitored, Trethewey tells us, and instances of these plants delivering tainted water are rare.

But impurities or pollutants can find their way into the pipes at any stage along the water's journey from the municipal plant to your tap: in the water mains, in the supply line from the main to the house, or in your house's plumbing system. While a private well is much more vulnerable to pollution from local agricultural or industrial activities, there have been some cases (such as in Love Canal, New York, and Woburn, Massachusetts) in which toxic wastes had contaminated municipal water wells. The local water plant unknowingly pumped this contaminated water into the local water system.

Trethewey recommends that if you have *any* question about the quality of your water, have it tested by an independent lab bearing the stamp of the Water Quality Association (Naperville Road, Lisle, IL 60532). A water test may cost from $25 to $200. The results of the test will help you select the right treatment for your water's specific problem.

There are two general strategies for treating your domestic water. A whole-house treatment, as the name suggests, treats all the water coming into the house from your well or the city's mains. Water containing excessive amounts of minerals or dissolved iron are typical candidates for whole-house treatment. But the average American household uses 293 gallons of water per day, so treating all your water can be a big job. Thus, for water problems such as poor taste or odor, the presence of chemicals or bacteria, a point-of-use treatment is best.

Whole-House Treatment

High levels of dissolved iron or manganese in the water, while presenting no health risk, will cause stains in bathtubs and sinks and shorten the service life of water heaters, washing machines, dishwashers, and toilet tanks. A whole-house iron-removal system is thus in order. These devices work in two stages. First, the water is swirled in a tank exposing it to air, where oxygen causes the dissolved iron to oxidize, that is, rust. In the second stage, a filter of either diatomaceous earth or a granular resin removes the rust, leaving iron-free water.

Another problem demanding a whole-house approach is excessive sand or dirt particles in the water. Trethewey recommends a sediment filter. One type is a cartridge filter, similar to your automobile's oil filter, which is composed of a woven fabric that simply traps or nets the sand or sediment. When the filter becomes filled to capacity, it must be replaced with a fresh one. A second type is a fine stainless-steel mesh filter that traps the sediment. This type is called "backflushable" because when the mesh becomes clogged with particles it can be cleaned by reversing the flow of water through it.

Hard Water

One of the most common water-quality problems is "hardness," that is, the presence of dissolved calcium and magnesium in the water, which forms spots on glassware, leaves a film on the bathtub, and generally makes cleaning and laundering more difficult. The solution is to install a water softener, a tank containing sodium chloride in the form of rock salt that removes the calcium and magnesium. People with high blood pressure may want to avoid drinking softened water because it contains higher levels of sodium. A more expensive alternative is to use potassium chloride as the softening agent.

Another common water problem is bad taste, accompanied perhaps with a slight odor. Water is a nearly universal solvent, with the ability to dissolve and absorb literally thousands of different compounds and bacteria, many combinations of which can produce bad taste or odor. The presence of taste or odor does not of itself indicate a health hazard, but if in doubt the water should be tested.

Granulated Activated-Carbon Filters (GAC)

The point-of-use treatment we see most often is a granulated activated-carbon (GAC) filter installed at the sink. It is a cartridge-type system in which loose grains of activated carbon — that is, carbon chemically treated to absorb many different compounds and bacteria — are held within a woven fiber shell. The water passes into the cartridge, through the woven outer shell, and is then cleansed by the activated carbon. This activated carbon core must be replaced periodically, usually after 1,000 gallons. A variation of this filter, which restrains the carbon with a ceramic plate instead of woven fiber, can be removed, cleaned with a common abrasive pad, and reinstalled.

Ultraviolet Light Filters

To kill bacteria in addition to filtering impurities, some manufacturers combine a standard GAC filter with a strong source of ultraviolet light. Water first passes through the activated-carbon filter, and then through a clear tube similar to a neon tube, where it is bombarded with ultraviolet radiation.

Reverse Osmosis

This and the next type of filter offer the most complete filtration of any on the residential market.

Reverse-osmosis filters force water through an extremely fine membrane, removing all impurities down to a microscopic level. To keep the membrane clean, a significant amount of water must wash past it. Reverse-osmosis units, in fact, consume six gallons of water for every gallon of filtered water they produce. Because of low output, these units are suitable only for limited point-of-use applications.

Distillation

Distillation-type filtration units achieve similar levels of purity and output. Simply put, these units boil tap water to produce steam, which is then condensed, leaving pure water. Because of their low output, distillation units are intended for low-volume applications. Some people complain that distilled water is tasteless.

Which Type Do You Need?

"It is cheap insurance," says Richard Trethewey, "to install a granulated activated-carbon filter for your sources of cooking and drinking water. Your water may be fine, but like I say, it's insurance." Aside from this, if you have any reason to believe your water has problems, you must begin your filter decision process with a water test. The cure will be dictated by the laboratory analysis.

Dissolved Lead and Heavy Metals

Serious health consequences may result from ingesting dissolved heavy metals — lead, cadmium, mercury — in your drinking water. The presence of lead in the human body may cause irreversible brain damage, especially in children under the age of six. Since the middle of the nineteenth century, lead water mains have rarely been installed in municipal water systems, but even so, miles of lead pipe are still in the ground and in use. Until recently, lead pipe was used to connect individual houses to the water mains, and lead-based solder was used to make up the connections in copper supply pipes within the house. The use of lead-based solder was banned in the early 1980s.

Before you get alarmed, you should know that dissolved oxygen in the water rapidly oxidizes the lead, which gives the inside of the pipe a protective sheathing that prevents the water from becoming contaminated. Still, you can alleviate any danger by running your tap for at least thirty seconds to flush standing water out of the system. If there is a possibility of serious lead contamination, you may have to install a distillation filter, a reverse-osmosis unit, or a granulated activated-carbon filter augmented with an *ion-exchange resin* filter, which, through molecular attraction, traps and retains the heavy metals.

●

Discussing potentially health-threatening water problems is disturbing. Should we be worried? "Yes and no," answers Trethewey. "We have always been confident that the water from our tap is pure — and in the overwhelming majority of cases it still is. But with the recent instances of undetected contamination in our water supplies, I think it is only prudent to be skeptical. When in doubt, have your water tested by an independent water analysis company."

Low Water Pressure

If you're having problems with low water pressure, don't assume the installation of your new kitchen plumbing will overcome it. The problem might be corrosion in the public water system's line from the water main to your house. You can ask your water company to test the pressure in this line, and if faulty, you can request it be replaced. Fees, permits, and even the timing of the work (some cities do not allow the street to be dug up in winter, as it hinders the removal of snow) vary from municipality to municipality, so check with your local public works department. If the problem is in your house's water lines, then it is, of course, entirely your responsibility. In an extreme case it may be necessary to replace all the supply pipes from the water main to your faucets.

"There's no point in trying to save money by tolerating inadequate water pressure," advises Richard Trethewey, "or by such other seeming economies as getting an undersize hot water tank. There are places where you can save money in a renovation project, but plumbing isn't one of them. You want to make sure that you'll have a system that will give good service for a long time."

Electrical Rough-in

Electrical design may not be the most glamorous element of your project but, like plumbing, electrical rough-in comes early in the renovation process and requires careful planning. The nature and design of the wiring you install now will determine your finished system later; how lights are switched and what circuits they are on will greatly affect both the aesthetic and functional qualities of the room.

Electrical work is tightly governed by standards laid out in the National Electrical Code, which is embodied in federal law. State or local codes may impose additional requirements. Local building inspectors are responsible for determining if the work meets the standards. The system of inspections and approvals by local building inspectors sees to it that an electrical installation is safe and functional. It is foolish to try to skirt code requirements or avoid inspection. For the price of a permit, the code operates to your benefit, ruling out substandard work.

●

Electricity reaches your house from the local power grid via a *service line*, which is made up of heavy strands of copper or aluminum wire. The power passes through the electric meter and then to a *main disconnect switch*, usually located on the *service panel*, which is equipped with circuit breakers or, in older systems, fuses. The panel distributes power throughout the house in *circuits*, which carry either 110 volts or 220 volts. In the United States and Canada, 110 volts is standard for lighting, outlets, and most household appliances (overseas, 220 volts is standard), but electrical devices requiring a lot of power, such as electric hot water heaters, clothes dryers, ranges, and water pumps run more efficiently on 220 volts.

Whereas *voltage* is roughly analogous to the *pressure* of water in a hose, *amperage* is analogous to the *volume* of the flow. The total volume of electricity a house can draw from the grid is regulated by the main circuit breaker or fuse. It used to be that 60 amps was considered an adequate capacity for homes, and in many older houses you still see what is called a 60 amp service panel — that is, a main disconnect switch that will allow only 60 amps to flow into the house. Now, with the number and variety of electrical appliances 100 amps is considered minimum and it is not uncommon to see a 200 or even 400 amp service panel. If you still have an old 60 amp panel, upgrading to a 100 or 200 amp service panel may be a necessary part of your kitchen renovation.

Electricity is distributed throughout the house in circuits — loops of wire that originate at a circuit breaker in the service panel and deliver electricity to a number of lights or outlets. The thicker the individual wire, the greater the amperage it can handle. If a wire's rated amperage is exceeded, it will overheat, with the risk of fire. Thus, each circuit is protected by a circuit breaker, which, just like the

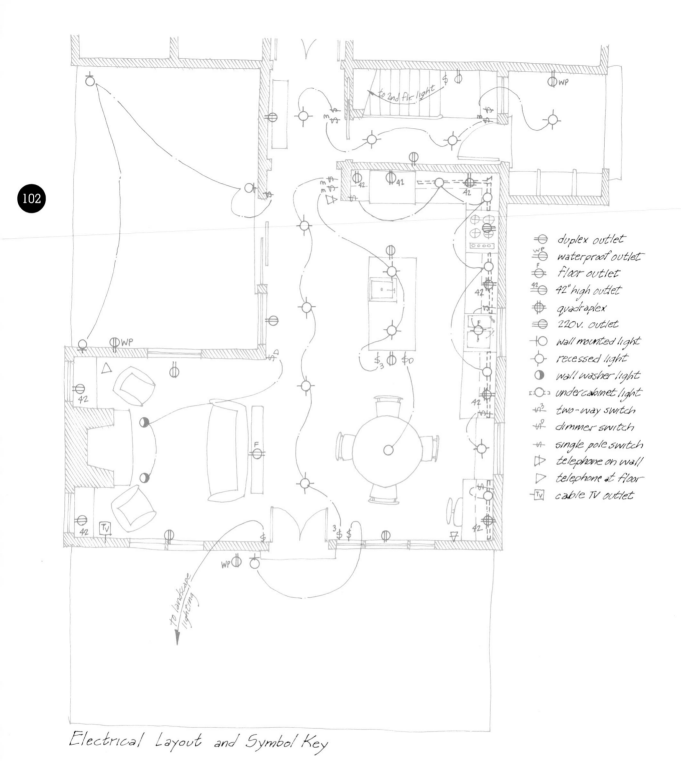

to 2nd flr. light

to landscape lighting

⊖	duplex outlet
⊖WP	waterproof outlet
⊖F	floor outlet
⊖⁴²	42" high outlet
⊕	quadraplex
⊖	220v. outlet
⊢○	wall mounted light
⊹	recessed light
◑	wall washer light
⊏○⊐	undercabinet light
⊣A³	two-way switch
⊣Aᴰ	dimmer switch
⊣A	single pole switch
▷	telephone on wall
▽	telephone at floor
⊣TV	cable TV outlet

Electrical Layout and Symbol Key

Your electrical contractor will both bid and wire your job on the basis of an electrical plan such as this one, so it's a good idea to become familiar with the symbology. The plan compresses all levels of the room into one — ceiling lights and outlets near the floor are all represented on the same plane. The lines connecting the lighting fixtures show circuits, not necessarily the routes the wires will follow.

main service disconnect, will shut the circuit down if the electrical demand is too great. A common 110 volt circuit for lights and outlets is usually rated at 15 amps. Kitchen circuits which service the outlets above the counter are usually 20 amps. It is common practice to provide each major kitchen appliance like the refrigerator and microwave oven with its own 20 amp circuit. Electric ranges and ovens are fed by an individual 30 or 50 amp 220 volt circuit. Any competent electrician can advise you on the number, size, and design of electrical circuits.

●

Usually your electrician will both formulate his bid and wire your job on the basis of an *electrical plan* that shows the location of all electrical components — appliances, switches, lights, and outlets. If you've designed your kitchen with an architect or designer, an electrical plan will probably be included in your set of drawings. If not, you'll need one. Think carefully about where you want your outlets and switches and whether you want dimmers, three- or four-way switches, track or recessed lighting. Also consider the style and mounting detail of the electrical devices. In the absence of a detailed plan, your electrician will probably follow his customary practice. Your kitchen could end up with what you consider an ineffective switching system or electrical outlets installed vertically instead of horizontally or in the wrong places. Details like this can make a surprising difference. (For more discussion of light switches, see chapter 8.)

●

Outlets within six feet of a sink are required by code to be equipped with a *ground fault interrupter,* or GFI. This device senses a "ground fault" or short circuit, and will shut the circuit down to prevent electrical shock. These devices work very well and it makes no sense to try to save money by skirting the code and not installing them. The best testimony to their effectiveness, and to the seriousness of electrical shock, is to be found at the ends of many tradesmen's extension cords, where they have installed electrical boxes containing GFIs to protect them and their employees from electrocution.

●

If your kitchen contains old wiring, we tend to accept the electrician's judgment as to whether it needs to be replaced or not. Old wiring should pose no safety problem as long as the insulating sheath is intact and the connections are still strong. Older houses were commonly wired with armored cable, a flexible cable composed of two rubber-insulated wires bound together with tape and enclosed in a conduit of interlocking spirals of steel strand. Your elec-

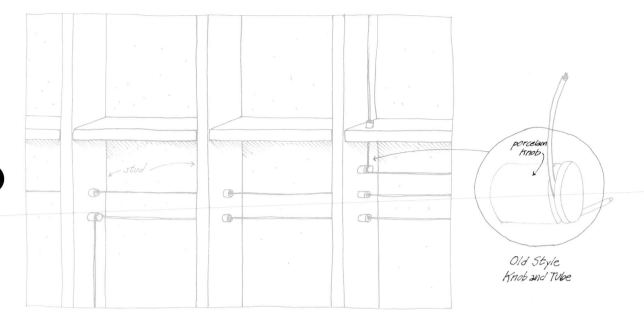

stud

porcelain
knob

Old Style
Knob and Tube

trician can judge whether the cladding is in satisfactory condition and if the insulation around the wires themselves is still intact. If armored cable appears deteriorated, most electricians prefer to replace it all, for a short circuit within can make the metal cladding the conductor!

The earliest method of residential electrical wiring is called *knob and tube*. Individual strands of insulated wire were run throughout the house suspended on ceramic insulators, or knobs. Where the wire had to penetrate a beam, joist or plate it would run through a porcelain tube. If knob-and-tube wiring is still in good shape, it is perfectly safe. Electricians claim that it is even safer than modern wiring, as the two halves of the circuit, the positive and the neutral, are kept separate. My own Greek Revival was wired with knob and tube, and when I suggested it should be replaced, my electrician would have none of it. Again, a qualified electrician can determine if the knob-and-tube wiring in your home is still safe.

In recent years the standard material for residential wiring has become nonmetallic sheathed cable. This cable contains two or more conducting wires and one ground wire, each sheathed in plastic insulation and wrapped together with strands of tough paper in a plastic cover that resists fire and moisture.

In commercial work and residential wiring in some jurisdictions, steel conduit or electro-metallic tubing (EMT) will be required. In a conduit job the EMT is first installed and connected to the various electrical switch and junction boxes and then single-strand insulated wire is fished through it. In most residential work, conduit is used only in exterior locations, basements, or other places where the wiring cannot be concealed and protected within a wall.

●

Copper has long been the preferred material for the conducting part of the wire itself. For a number of years aluminum wiring was used until it was discovered that the different expansion rates of aluminum and copper loosened the splices and connections, posing a potential fire hazard. Another fire hazard resulted when the aluminum oxidized and formed a resistant film, which caused the wire to heat up. If you have aluminum wiring in your house, it warrants close inspection. Codes allow the aluminum to remain, if switches, outlets, and service panels are made of a compatible material. "Compatible with aluminum" or some such indication should be stamped or printed on the device. While in some jurisdictions aluminum wiring is still permitted, we, along with the majority of electricians, feel that copper is a safer, though more expensive, choice.

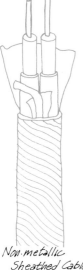

Aluminum is still employed, though, in the form of large cables such as the service cable, which conducts the electricity from the *weather cap*, where your house wiring ties into the power grid, to the service panel, and from the service panel to major appliances or *sub panels*, smaller panels that service a discrete area of the house or a shop or garage. Like aluminum wire, aluminum cable requires the use of special aluminum connectors and other hardware. If properly installed, it is considered perfectly safe, although a minority of electricians refuse to use it at all.

●

If you are planning a sophisticated, multicircuit lighting system, you may want *low-voltage* wiring for that purpose. This type of lighting requires only 12 or 24 volts, instead of the usual 110 volts, and is cheaper to operate. However, low-voltage systems also require special transformers, switches, and fixtures, so such systems carry much higher up-front costs.

●

We cannot overemphasize the importance of a methodical review — well before the electrical work actually starts — of all the electrical devices you want in your new kitchen. When the walls are open, wiring is cheap and easy. After the walls are closed in, it's more difficult and costly.

As you consider your electrical plan, don't forget to wire for telephones, cable television, sound systems, security systems, and even a local area computer network. As more and more people move their offices into their homes, the demand for domestic computer and communication systems grows, and wiring for these needs becomes

Armored Cable

Non-metallic Sheathed Cable

Electro-metallic Tubing (EMT)

Planning for small appliances when you do your electrical layout is critical. This lovely prep area would have been rendered useless without good electrical planning in the design phase. Notice the four-gang outlet and switch on the right wall, another outlet for the toaster on the left, and above, in the shelves, an outlet and a cable jack for the television.

something to think about. My own office is in my house, and as I added a fax machine, a local area computer network, and a telephone system, I quickly exceeded the capabilities of the wiring I had installed during the renovation.

●

Sometimes, especially in restorations of buildings which have historic or architectural value, your wiring options may be limited. Some electricians are wizards at snaking wires through the walls of the old eighteenth- and nineteenth-century timber-frame structures commonly found here in New England, but in some masonry buildings you may have to resort to a surface wiring system of either EMT or a *wiremold raceway,* a surface-mounted, low-profile metal channel that protects and hides electrical wiring. In an historic structure in which the goal is to make as few intrusions into the walls as possible, you may even have to choose between desirable electrical improvements, but not those essential for safety or required by code, and the character of the existing walls.

It is up to you, not your contractor, to strike the right balance between improved plumbing and electrical systems and competing historical and aesthetic considerations. As in every other aspect of your kitchen renovation, the more informed and involved you are in the process, the better your renovation will reflect your dreams and requirements.

●

6 Heating

Up until a hundred years ago, heating and cooking used virtually the same equipment. This magnificent wood stove still does its job, filling the large old country kitchen with plenty of heat while the stew simmers and the bread bakes.

One of the most desired qualities in a kitchen is coziness, and since it's hard to feel cozy in a cold, drafty room, the design of your kitchen's heating system is very important.

In most households, the kitchen is the busiest room of the house. It is used from early in the morning, for quick breakfasts while on the way to work, to late in the evening for a midnight snack or a cup of tea. Moreover, the kitchen is a room you and your family will visit in all states of dress and undress. At "This Old House," we've found that the kitchen demands more heating capability per square foot than any other room in the house — with the exception of the bath, which shares the same problems and requirements.

And yet, the kitchen is also the most difficult room to heat. Cabinets, cupboards, and appliances command much of the wall and floor space, making it a challenge to find real estate for vents, ducts, and baseboard heating units.

A variety of manuals will tell you how to calculate your kitchens's heating requirements. One of the liveliest is *Manual J*, published by the Air Conditioning Contractors of America. It sells for about $16 and makes Kant's *Critique of Pure Reason* read like a bedtime story. Fortunately, your architect, plumbing and heating contractor, or supplier will do the calculations so you don't have to make *Manual J* part of your library.

All methods used to determine the kitchen's heating requirements will factor in variables such as square footage, window area, the R value of the insulation, and the material of the wall and exterior siding.

Your choice of a heating system depends to some extent on whether you are renovating an old kitchen, adding a new kitchen, or building an entire house. For a new house you can select whatever heating system you want. But in renovation, there is money to be saved by adapting your existing heating plant to serve the needs of the renovated kitchen. Let's look at the options.

Forced Hot Air

Forced hot air is the most common kind of heat in the United States, and furnaces are available that run on every type of fuel: wood, coal, oil, natural gas, propane, and electricity. Forced hot air furnaces employ a large blower that draws cold air from the house, pushes it through a plenum, or heat-exchanger, which transfers the heat from the firebox, burner, or heating coils to the air, where it is then conducted throughout the house by large pipes, or *ducts.*

Nearly every model of furnace is equipped with a replaceable fiberglass filter that can trap some dust, lint, and pollen, but one of the most common complaints about forced hot air is that it stirs up a lot of dust and particulates. A new breed of filter, called *electronic air cleaners,* or EACs, are now available; these scrub the air extremely clean using the principle of electrostatic precipitation. Particles in the air become positively charged as they pass through a network of wires within the unit. These particles are then attracted to and trapped by negatively charged collector plates. EACs remove tobacco smoke, airborne bacteria, and particulate fumes in addition to dust and pollen.

Forced hot air systems tend to be noisy with the sound of the fan and the air issuing from the registers. Also, the heated air can be exceedingly dry, all the moisture having been baked out by the furnace. Fortunately, most systems can be fitted with a humidifier, which replaces the moisture, and the noise can be reduced by good system design.

A problem yet to be overcome is that forced hot air may impart less comfort than its temperature might lead you to expect. Plumbing and heating specialist Richard Trethewey tells us that a forced hot air system introduces heat into the room very suddenly when the blower and furnace first start up. If the thermostat is set at 70°, the system tends to overshoot and bring the room's temperature up to 72° or 74° before it shuts off. Then, as the room temperature drops down a bit, you feel cold, even at 70°. This is known in the trade as the "cold seventy" phenomenon. The cycling of the furnace and the fact that moving air — even warm moving air — tends to chill the human body is the chief cause of this discomfort.

But forced hot air has some strong advantages as well. One is that the system is economical to install. Another is that it can easily accept piggybacked central air conditioning, which utilizes the existing ductwork. A third advantage, important for our purposes, is that a forced hot air system can generally be extended to serve a new or renovated kitchen. All that is necessary, in most instances, is to add some new runs of ductwork, one or more registers to deliver warm air, and perhaps a duct to return cold air to the furnace.

Ideally, the registers should be installed low in the wall to in-

Forced Hot Air Flow

troduce warmth near the floor, where cold air collects. A register installed in the kitchen floor is inadvisable, since it will accumulate all manner of dirt, objects, and debris.

Hydronic Systems

Steam and hot water baseboard and radiator systems are collectively called *hydronic systems* as they use water or steam instead of air as the medium for conducting heat from furnace to house. The advantages of hydronic systems over forced hot air are that they do not produce drafts, so exposed skin is not as readily chilled, and dust is not stirred up and circulated throughout the house. Because water is circulated throughout the pipes by means of a small pump, hydronic systems are quiet; and because water cools much more slowly than air, the temperature remains much steadier in the house, reducing the "cold seventy" phenomenon. You feel comfortable at cooler temperatures.

Whereas a forced hot air system can be *balanced* by adjusting dampers that regulate the volume of air going to various rooms, a hydronic system can be *zoned.* The hot water can be routed to a number of discrete subsystems, each independently controlled by its own thermostat. This means that the kitchen zone, for instance, could be kept at 70° while the rest of the house was at 65°. If you have a steam system, or a hot water system with cast-iron radiators, your plumber may not be able to create a separate zone for the kitchen, and he may need to use a similar type of cast-iron radiator in the new or renovated room to balance the heat throughout the house.

Some elderly hydronic systems, mainly found in very cold climates, use steam. The boiler brings water to the temperature at which it vaporizes, and the resulting steam gives off a great deal of energy as it passes through cast-iron radiators or baseboard heating elements. A steam system responds quickly to the thermostat's call for heat, but this can be a mixed blessing. It can mean wide temperature swings, producing the same "cold seventy" phenomenon as with forced hot air. Steam systems are rarely installed these days.

Radiators and Baseboard Units

In older hot water and steam systems, the device that did the actual heating of the room was the familiar radiator. These cast-iron contrivances were big, heavy, ugly, got in the way of furniture, intruded on the room's general decor, and in steam systems could get hot enough to actually burn an unwary child.

If the principal disadvantage with the old cast-iron radiators is that they are ugly, there is a new breed of radiators, which are slimmer and very attractive. In a "This Old House" project in Arlington, Massachusetts, we installed sleek steel radiators made by Runtal. Finished in a crisp white, they blended well with the contemporary decor of the kitchen and solarium/dining area we added. Equally attractive radiators manufactured by the Italian firm DeLonghi and the French firm Acova are now available in a variety of colors and sizes, from long, thin units that can fit along a wall or under a window, to high, vertical units to fit next to a counter or pantry cabinet, or even under the overhang of an island sitting area where it will warm the center of the room. But beware, beauty has its price; these units are expensive.

Old-fashioned radiators are rarely used these days; most hot

These radiators provide a lot of heat, take up little space, and are very nice to look at. There are several companies who manufacture very pretty radiators that can be incorporated into a renovation without detracting from the design.

water systems use baseboard heating units, which are installed around the perimeter of the room. Known generically as *fin-tube* or copper-fin baseboard, these units are so termed because they consist of a copper pipe, or tube, to which rows of aluminum plates or fins are attached. The fins draw the heat from the hot water running in the pipe and disperse it into the room. The actual tube and fins are concealed behind a steel housing, aerodynamically designed to allow the heated air to rise through the fins and then up the wall and into the room. Baseboard units are equipped with a damper that can be closed to choke the flow of air around the fins, thus regulating the heat output of the unit.

If you already have a fin-tube radiator system, it should be a fairly easy task for a plumber to extend the system to a new or renovated kitchen. Although it may cost a bit extra, we think it an excellent idea to put the kitchen on a separate heating zone, complete with its own thermostat, independent of the rest of the house.

Some old houses have what is called a *gravity hot water* sys-

Fin / Tube

Forced Hot Air at Toekick

Radiator at window

Radiant Panel at Toekick

Cast Iron Baseboard

Radiant Panel Baseboard

tem. As the water is heated, it rises gradually throughout the house without the aid of pumps. After it gives off its heat in the various rooms, it cools and sinks back down to the boiler. A system of this kind is often incapable of being expanded without adding a circulating pump. This will be particularly true if the new kitchen is a long distance from the boiler.

•

Even with a standard hot water system utilizing fin-tube baseboard units, simply finding enough wall space on which to mount them can be problematic. Modern kitchens demand the maximum possible runs of counter and cabinet, which leaves little free wall on which to mount baseboard units. One tactic used to overcome this difficulty is to have your cabinetmaker create an "open kickspace," which conducts cool air from the floor to a fin-tube unit mounted along the wall behind the counter. A 1½- or 2-inch space behind the backsplash allows the heated air to flow into the room.

Another strategy is to install what is called a kickspace heater. These units are designed to fit in the void space under the cabinet bases. They operate similarly to your automobile's radiator: hot water circulates through a very compact fin-tube unit, which gives off its heat to a fan-induced stream of air. The fan speed can be regulated with a rheostat.

For their size, kickspace heaters produce a lot of heat. However, the fans create drafts and noise. Because kickspace heaters require the ministrations of two trades to install — a plumber for the pipes and an electrician to wire the fan — they can get expensive. Yet, because of their high heat output, kickspace heaters are sometimes the only effective way to heat the kitchen. Because my own kitchen has a great expanse of north-facing glass *and* a long run of cabinets and counters, I had to install two kickspace heaters. They kept the room warm but were so noisy and drafty that I soon began to contemplate, and eventually converted to, a different principle in heating, called radiant heat.

Radiant Heat

This system has become our favorite way of heating the kitchen. Simply put, warm water is circulated through plastic tubes under the floor. The whole floor then becomes the radiator, giving off a gentle, even heat throughout the room.

Radiant heat is not a new concept. Roman builders devised a system to circulate geothermal steam through passages beneath the floors of their baths to warm the stone. In this century the principle has been used by no less an architect than Frank Lloyd Wright. Twenty or thirty years ago, New England builders used a form of the system that entailed laying copper tubing in a concrete slab. But a chemical reaction occurred between the concrete and the copper, which degraded the copper and caused leaks. Apparently leaks were also created as the copper heated up, expanded, and strained the joints and unions against the more rigid concrete. Radiant floor heat still has a bad reputation in conservative New England.

This looks as if it will change, though. A few state-of-the-art plumbing contractors are using a new radiant floor heating system that employs a high-tech plastic tubing instead of copper pipe, and control equipment that closely regulates the temperature of the water flowing through it.

The system has several big advantages over other systems.

First, it is the most comfortable heat we have experienced. The whole floor reaches a temperature of 75° or 80°, radiating its heat into the room much as a stone wall warmed all day by the sun gives off its heat at night. There are neither hot nor cold spots, nor are there fan-induced drafts to chill the skin. Because the entire mass of the floor is heated, the temperature swings are kept to a minimum, avoiding the "cold seventy" phenomenon. The system also makes it easy to get enough heat into a room with wall space too limited to accommodate baseboard or cast-iron radiation.

Radiant heat counteracts the natural tendency of cold air to settle, chilling the feet. When your feet are warm, your whole body feels warm and comfortable even if the air temperature is slightly lower than normal — I can now speak from firsthand experience. After having seen the radiant floor installation "This Old House" did in our Concord barn project, and in our Santa Fe, New Mexico, project, and having enjoyed the comfort of the system in the concrete floor of the New Yankee Workshop, I decided to install it in my kitchen. It is a great pleasure to come home from a cold day of shooting "This Old House," pull off my boots, and feel that nice warm floor beneath my bare feet.

●

The principal disadvantage of radiant floor heat is its high cost — at least *double* a standard fin-tube radiation. This is mitigated somewhat by the fact that the system is more efficient to operate than a standard system. With the price of energy certain to rise, the payback period for this equipment becomes shorter and shorter.

A second disadvantage is that radiant floor heat is the most difficult system to retrofit, and specifying it is bound to increase the level of difficulty of the job. Because the equipment is fairly new in this country (although not in Europe), it may be difficult to find a plumber familiar with the installation procedures and an electrician willing to tackle hooking up the computer and control equipment.

●

There exist electric radiant systems consisting of electrical cables embedded in the floor. Also available are radiant ceiling panels that heat the top of your head while leaving your feet to chill. But the electric systems tend to have high operating costs, so we prefer hot water systems.

Hydronic radiant floor heating can be driven by a boiler using any type of fuel: propane, natural gas, oil, electricity, wood, coal, or solar. A radiant floor zone can, in most cases, be added to your existing boiler.

Three methods of installing radiant floor heating tubes:

Tubing is laid on the concrete slab or wooden subfloor and encased in lightweight concrete.

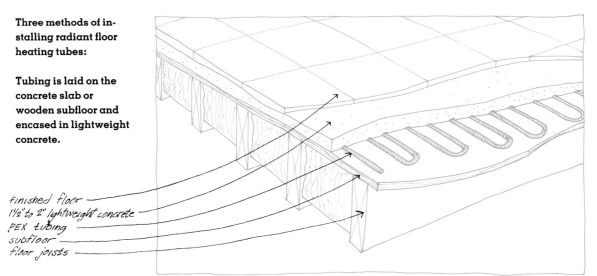

finished floor
1½" to 2" lightweight concrete
PEX tubing
subfloor
floor joists

Radiant Floor : New Floor

Tubing is laid between sleepers on slab or wooden subfloor and wood plank or strip floor installed above.

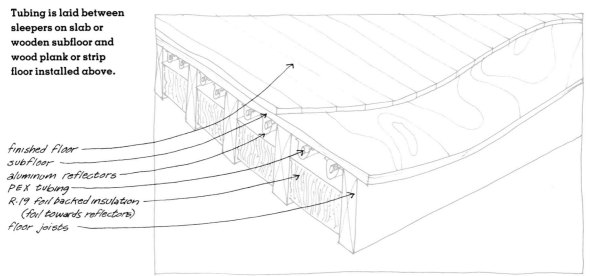

finished floor
subfloor
aluminum reflectors
PEX tubing
R-19 foil backed insulation
 (foil towards reflectors)
floor joists

Radiant Floor : Retrofit to Existing Floor

Tubing is installed beneath the wooden subfloor with aluminum reflectors and then insulated.

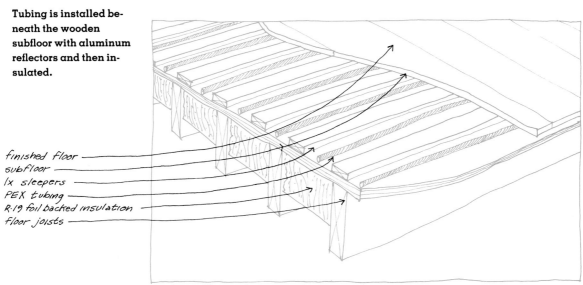

finished floor
subfloor
1x sleepers
PEX tubing
R-19 foil backed insulation
floor joists

Radiant Floor : between sleepers

The control equipment for the systems we have used on "This Old House" monitors the outdoor temperature with a sensor, then, by means of a small computer, calculates the water temperature the system requires in order to maintain the indoor temperature at 68°. This heating curve can be adjusted to match the thermal characteristics of each house. In my house, if the outside temperature is 0°, the computer will order the boiler to bring the water up to 180°. But if the outside temperature is only 35°, the computer will order the boiler to make only 120° water. Since it takes much less fuel to heat water to 120° than to 180°, this control equipment alone will save on fuel costs.

Normally it is the thermostat that activates both the boiler and the circulation pumps. When the temperature of the room has reached that set-point on the thermostat, the boiler and the pumps shut down. Thus, even in a standard fin-tube baseboard heating system you get a bit of the "cold seventy" effect. When I retrofitted my existing gas boiler with the radiant zone, the computer took control of the whole house. The computer now tells the boiler when to fire up, and since the heated water circulates constantly, my house stays at a steady 67°. Because there is virtually no "cold seventy" effect, I find this temperature very pleasant.

Variations of this type of control equipment, called *weather-responsive controls,* can be installed on any hydronic system. You do not need to convert to radiant floor heating to enjoy the comfort and economy these controls can provide.

●

Although some copper tube radiant systems are still installed, predominantly in the Southwest (encased in sand rather than concrete and with brick, tile, or flagstone placed on top), most systems now use either plastic or rubber tubing. Richard Trethewey warns that the rubber tubing is unproven and cautions that it should be avoided. Some systems use a plastic called polybutylene, or PB. This material is cost-effective, but has the disadvantage that oxygen can diffuse through the wall of the tube to be absorbed by the water circulating through it. The more enriched with oxygen the heating water becomes, the more "aggressive" it is, causing corrosion in valves, pumps, and the boiler. Some boiler manufacturers will not warrant their boilers if used with any plastic or rubber tubing that lacks an oxygen barrier.

The tubing we have been using on "This Old House" is called electronically cross-linked polyethylene (PEX). It has been vigorously tested and rated at a 200-year life. The tubing has a special coating that prevents the migration of oxygen through the walls, thus preventing the boiler, valves and fittings, and pumps from rusting.

●

There are several ways to install the tubing in the floor. The preferred method is to lay the tubing in a predetermined pattern directly on a concrete slab or plywood subfloor, securing it to a plastic grid with wire-ties. (You can also use a special waffle-panel substrate which the tubing snaps into.) Once the tubing is down, it is covered with 2 inches or so of lightweight concrete, which not only makes an ideal heat-sink but also a perfect base for a finish floor of tile, slate, flagstone, terra cotta, carpet, or a laminated wood "floating" floor, so called because it is not secured to the subfloor. (See chapter 9 for more information on floating floors.) Of all the materials and installation methods we will describe, the concrete base finished in masonry best transfers heat into the room.

    To accommodate the radiant floor system to a standard hardwood floor, you can first place on the subfloor parallel rows of "sleepers" made from either common lumber or a specially manufactured aluminum/particle board composite, and then weave the tubing around them. The finish flooring is then laid on, and fastened to, the

Radiant floor heat installed in our "This Old House" Santa Fe, New Mexico, project. The blue plastic waffle panels were first secured to the concrete slab with concrete nails, and the PEX tubing snapped into place. Here self-leveling, lightweight concrete is being pumped into place.

sleepers. This was the method Trethewey successfully used for our Weatherbee Farm project in Westwood, Massachusetts. The only disadvantage with the system is that, for obvious reasons, extreme care must be taken when nailing-off the finish floor.

In a situation such as my own kitchen, where the finish floor was already down and I had no intention of ripping it up, you can run the tubing on the *underside* of the subfloor, weaving it in the bays between the floor joists. The tubing is secured with aluminum reflectors stapled (with an electric staple gun) into the subfloor, and otherwise held by a series of special plastic cleats. After installing the tubing, you must insulate the joist bays with 6-inch foil-backed insulation to reflect the heat up into the floor. It took my friend and plumber Rich Bilo and me three days to install this system in my kitchen, so you can see it is labor-intensive.

Most of the radiant floor heating systems now available have been developed in Europe. The reason for this is simple: over 90 percent of European heating systems are hydronic, compared with less than 10 percent in the United States. This, combined with consistently higher energy costs in Europe, has driven the demand for innovation there. But radiant floor heating systems are generating tremendous interest here in the United States, despite their high initial price tag, because of their comfort and lower operating costs. As more companies enter the marketplace with new products, and as more plumbers become qualified to install these systems, we would expect the range of choices to increase and the price of the systems to drop.

●

Ventilation

The design of this hood creates a focused cooking environment. It defines the cooking area architecturally, is fitted with good lighting, and ventilates very effectively. Note the stone tiles on top of the backsplash. The back of the stove is lined with this same stone to buffer the eating island from heat.

Bob Walsh, a colleague of my wife's, is a brilliant software engineer able to solve complex computer problems with elegance, if not élan. In his spare time he is an impassioned and restless experimenter in Indian and Szechuan cooking. My wife and I, often among the first victims, would trudge up the stairs to Bob and his wife Alice's third-floor apartment (which they'd occupied since college days) and into the fog created by his latest tandoori, poori, or vindaloo. At the top landing Bob's parrot would screech and Alice's cat skitter off into the shadows as we made our way through the smoke into the closet-sized kitchen. There, above the tiny, unvented stove and a patch of counter that could barely hold an open copy of the *Boston Globe*, was a bank of stereo speakers, pots and pans, hanging baskets filled with multi-colored chilis and strings of garlic. There was also a battery of electric fans, the arrangement of which looked as if it had been engineered by the Cat in the Hat. Some fans blew the smoke from the stove over to other fans at the window, which were to exhaust it outside, but since a contrary wind was blowing, most of it was coming back in. Yet more fans were were focused upon the hanging carcass of a plucked duck, glazed with beer and honey and awaiting preparation Peking-style for tomorrow's dinner.

When Bob finished preparing the meal, the fog cleared and one by one the fans were switched off (except those required by the duck). With Bob and Alice, the fellowship was always wonderful and the food sensational — and for a week afterward, you would recall the evening every time you smelled the tandoori in your coat and scarf.

●

A proper ventilation system is one piece of infrastructure often over-looked in kitchen renovations. Developers trying to save a few dollars will install a ductless fan unit that filters the air before expelling it back into the room, and we've seen some homeowners who install no fan at all.

In the 1940s and 50s, kitchen ventilation frequently consisted of only a single extractor fan stuck in the wall or ceiling above the stove. Kitchens then were small, utilitarian spaces relatively isolated from the rest of the living areas. Houses were not as weathertight as they are now, and the air infiltration through loose-fitting window sashes, poorly sealed electrical boxes, and small cracks in the exterior sheathing was all that was needed to ventilate the smoke, steam, and combustion gases generated in the kitchen. But new building techniques such as the use of a vapor barrier and new products like spun-bonded polyethylene sheeting and high-efficiency windows have cut air infiltration to a minimum. Also, the kitchen is no longer removed from the rest of the house and often serves as family and living room. Even though the combination of hood, fan, and ductwork represents a significant investment in both machinery and design and installation time, we feel it is as indispensable as heating, plumbing, and electricity.

An old-fashioned wall fan works best in a semienclosed area like this. Make sure the walls are covered by a surface that is easily cleaned.

Types of Systems

There are two basic types of systems: a *ductless* or *recirculating* system, which filters the smoke and pumps the air back into the room, and a *ducted* system, which conducts the smoke and fumes outside. Sometimes, in an apartment or condominium, it is impossible to install a ducted system. We'll discuss ductless systems a bit later, but if you've ever seen a recirculating system trying to cope with the onslaught of smoke generated while cooking the spice base of Pla Num, or Thai fish in red sauce, you'll see why we prefer a ducted system.

There are two general types of ducted systems: a hood-type with either an internal fan mounted inside the hood or an external fan mounted outside the house, and a downdraft system, which sucks the steam and smoke through a grill or vent mounted at cooktop level. Both systems expel the dirty air outdoors through the roof, eaves, or wall via aluminum or galvanized steel ducting. (Plastic ducting should not be used as it will burn in the unlikely event of a grease fire within the ductwork.) To trap grease, there is usually an aluminum mesh screen in the air intake. This screen should be removed and washed periodically.

Most exhaust hoods are equipped with a spring-loaded flap to prevent outside air from coming into the house through the ducting. Sometimes these flaps cannot cope with strong winds. If at all possible, locate the exhaust hood in an unexposed location, so the flap mechanism can work as it should.

Effectiveness

Three factors determine the effectiveness of the ventilation system. First is the sheer power of the vent fan or blower. This is easy to determine. Manufacturers label their equipment in terms of how many

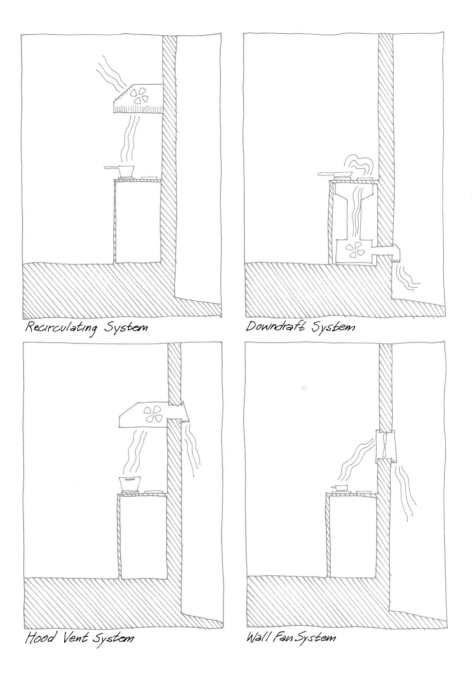

Recirculating System

Downdraft System

Hood Vent System

Wall Fan System

cubic feet per minute, or CFM, the fan will draw. Second is the length, size, and directness of the duct system. (Short, straight duct runs are most effective. The longer or more sinuous the run, the larger the diameter of the ducting should be.) Third is the location and size of the hood or grill that collects the dirty air.

Testing at the Minnesota Cold Climate Building Research Center at the University of Minnesota demonstrates what common sense suggests — that the most effective collection device is a hood located over the cooktop. The best location for the cooktop and hood, moreover, is along a wall, where cross-currents will be less likely to compete with the ventilator.

The hood should be mounted directly over the cooktop, high enough that it doesn't block the cook's ability to tend tall pots on the rear burners, but not so high as to be ineffective in collecting vapor. The Center's tests found the optimum distance to be 21 to 30 inches from the bottom of the hood to the cooking surface. The projection of the hood from the wall also influences its performance. The broader and deeper, the better. While a projection of 20 inches is considered minimum, the ideal is to have the hood project as far from the wall (and extend as far in width) as the cooking surface itself.

●

It's much harder to ventilate a cooktop on a peninsula or island. The most effective device is a hood or canopy mounted no more than 30 inches above the cooking surface. But a hood will block sightlines, and taller people will have to stoop to maintain eye contact with those across the island or peninsula. The hood can be raised higher, but then it will require a more powerful fan, a matter of some concern when it is drawing a lot of household air that you've paid to heat or cool; even at that, a high hood will not be as effective as one mounted lower.

The alternative for islands and peninsulas is a downdraft system, which, as we've explained, sucks the exhaust air downward and then out of the house. Some cooks love these systems; others are disappointed in their performance. The Minnesota research shows that a downdraft system works well only when the vent and cooktop are installed against a wall and the cooking is done in low pans. (Tall pots and pans issue much of their vapor into the room.) In these conditions, cross-currents will not disrupt the vent's ability to pull gases downward. The system loses some of its effectiveness when mounted on an island or peninsula, but you can overcome the problem of cross-currents by building a lip several inches high around the cooktop.

●

There are differing designs for downdraft systems. One design locates the vent at the rear of the cooking surface. It is electrically controlled so that when switched on, it rises a few inches above the cooktop; when switched off, it retracts out of sight. The Minnesota research found this system works well for the rear burners but is ineffective for the front.

Other downdraft systems locate the vent in the center of the cooktop. This location may be adequate when cooking food on a grill

A hood over a peninsula like this needs to be mounted higher than the recommended 30 inches so it doesn't obstruct sightlines. Be sure the fan is powerful enough to compensate for increased distance between stove and hood.

or griddle or in low pans but works poorly with tall pots. Hot air's natural tendency is to rise, and a downdraft system must overcome the laws of physics to be effective. The Minnesota study concluded: "Select a downdraft unit only if the majority of cooking consists of grilling, frying, or cooking in low pans."

Still, finding a place for a wall-mounted hood and cooktop is impossible in some kitchen renovations, especially where an open plan is desired. I faced this problem in my own kitchen and accepted the compromise of a peninsula-mounted, downdraft cooktop. The unit does indeed give the room clean sight-lines but fails to collect the smoke and steam resulting from my more ambitious experiments in Indonesian cookery. Even though I consider this a serious drawback, had I the kitchen to do over again, I believe I would make the same choice, considering the constraints of the room.

An "industrial strength" hood does not have to look like an industrial machine. This stainless hood is proportioned to fit very well with the cabinets around it.

Another vent system that is fairly common is a combination microwave oven, range, and ventilation system. The vent is intended to remove exhaust air from both appliances while taking up little space. But the path from cooking surface to vent is fairly long and indirect, pulling grease and steam-laden air across the front of the microwave. "This Old House" used one of these units in a project in Arlington, Massachusetts. Our homeowners complain that the vent works poorly and that grease accumulates on the doors of wall cabinets in the vicinity of the cooktop. A variation of this product, a hood and vent system attached to the bottom of the microwave, also functions poorly. The tests in Minnesota confirm our experience, showing that a "microwave hood" performed inadequately. Varying the height of the hood beneath the microwave made little difference. Whether it was 15 or 21 inches above the cooktop, the vent was ineffective.

●

This straightforward treatment of the ventilation lets the ductwork speak for itself. The design is part of a conscious balance of horizontal and vertical elements, which is seen throughout the kitchen and surrounding rooms.

Let's return to our discussion of the ductless, or recirculating, systems. As we said, these units pull the air from the cooktop through one or more filters and then send it back into the room. It should properly be called a filtration system rather than a ventilation system. Although these units are very efficient in terms of energy conservation, because they don't expel heated or air-conditioned air from the house, we recommend them only for a very light-duty kitchen. Both water vapor and combustion gases (in the case of a gas stove) remain in the house, and the units are less effective at dealing with grease, smoke, and odors than a ducted system. Many ductless hoods combine a metal mesh screen for capturing grease with a charcoal filter for removing odors. The mesh screen should be removed regularly and washed (if it has been manufactured to allow such washing — some are not), and it's also important to replace the charcoal filter periodically (some manufacturers recommend annually), otherwise it will become clogged and lose whatever effectiveness it had.

The latest generation of ductless systems features additional filters to trap more grease and remove more smoke and odors from the air. If it is impossible to install a ducted system in your kitchen, as is the case in many apartment buildings, a high-quality ductless system will help. If you can vent to the outdoors, we think ducted ventilation systems are worth the investment.

Finding the Right Look

Some people don't want a hood and vent system because they object to the hood's appearance. This is a legitimate concern, but keep in mind that a hood can actually improve the kitchen's appearance and help to establish its character. We've seen slick, white enameled hoods in urban kitchens, funky hoods covered in hand-painted tiles in southwestern kitchens, and industrial-looking stainless-steel hoods in loft kitchens.

Some manufacturers offer minimalist-styled hoods that will do the job without making a big design statement. Both Broan and Gaggenau make glass "hoods" (Broan calls its product a "glass drawer"), which slide out from the bottom of the wall cabinet directly above the cooktop. The fan unit is mounted inside the cabinet. When extended, the glass element helps capture the hot air for the venting system. To use it, you simply pull the glass toward you and turn on the vent fan. When finished, you push the glass back under the cabinet, where it disappears.

Another device, marketed by General Electric and others, is a see-through visor that can be shifted into position when needed.

(Above) A glass visor is another option when faced with tight space parameters. This one folds under the microwave when not in use.

(Left) In this small but beautifully designed stainless-steel kitchen, cabinet space was at a premium. The best solution was a high-quality sliding vent hood. This one has a variety of ventilation speeds and its own light.

Typically the visor is mounted inconspicuously beneath a microwave directly above the range. When you're ready to cook, you flip the visor toward you, where it acts like the front surface of a hood.

Still another retractable ventilating device, made by Broan and others, is a hooded vent, styled to resemble a wall cabinet and mounted above the cooktop. When you need it, you extend the bottom of the unit a few inches toward you, which allows the pseudo-cabinet to function as a hood and vent. The fan is concealed in the interior of the "cabinet," which also has some storage space. When you're done cooking, you push the cabinet back toward the wall, where it blends in with the wall cabinets.

Calculating Ventilation Needs

The Home Ventilating Institute, a trade organization in Arlington, Illinois, recommends the following method for calculating the capacity of your fan or blower. To find the necessary CFM for wall and ceiling fans, simply measure the square footage of your kitchen and multiply it by two. (A 10x12-foot kitchen, for example, contains 120 square feet, which, when doubled, results in a CFM requirement of 240.) If your cooktop is island or peninsula mounted with a hood above it, multiply the lineal footage of the cooking surface by 50. For a hood mounted along a wall, multiply the lineal footage of the cooking surface by 40. Whatever the result of your calculations, keep in mind that the U.S. Department of Housing and Urban Development recommends that the minimum power for any kitchen ventilation device should be 150 CFM. Downdraft vents, because they must fight the natural tendency of hot air to rise, need more power than a range hood.

Noise, Air Infiltration, Lighting, and Other Considerations

Any ventilation system will make some noise. Sound level is measured in sones, one of which is roughly equal to the noise level created by a modern refrigerator. The noise levels of different manufacturers' fans and blowers vary, even units with the same CFM ratings, so it's a good idea to ask about the noise when choosing a ventilation system. Powerful fans tend to be noisy, so many of the fans with the highest CFM ratings are mounted on the house's exterior, which makes for a quiet interior when the fan is running. Exterior-mounted fans, which must be weatherproof, are considerably more expensive than interior-mounted fans.

Most ventilation devices have more than one fan speed, letting you control the noise level as well as the intensity of the air removal. Some hoods are even equipped with sensors, which detect

This is a great hood. Simple and straightforward of line, it contains excellent lighting, which also illuminates the counters on either side. Fixtures inside the hood should be encased in a cleanable glass covering to protect them from grease. Make sure the lighting and the ventilator are on separate circuits; you will certainly want to light the stove area without turning on the fan.

excess heat in the cooking area and automatically turn the fan on. When the temperature has fallen, the fan automatically turns off.

Most hoods are equipped with some sort of lamp to illuminate the cooking surface. Cooking is a task that requires excellent illumination, so give this feature close scrutiny.

Since the hood and grease traps must be clean to function properly, check whether they have been designed specifically to make cleaning easier, with no sharp or rough edges or unreachable crevices. If you opt for a downdraft system instead of a hood, keep in mind that the grill above the air intake and the grease traps below it will need frequent cleaning, so make sure they are easy to remove.

●

One final precaution: If your house is exceptionally well sealed against air infiltration and you're planning to install a high-capacity ventilation fan, it would be worthwhile to consult a ventilation specialist to make sure that the kitchen's system will not cause air-quality problems in the rest of the house. In the well-insulated houses built in recent years, air infiltration into the house is so minimal that a powerful extractor fan can actually reverse some of the usual air flows through the house. In the worst case, the kitchen ventilation system may pull flue gases from a gas- or oil-powered furnace and hot water heater down the chimney and fill the house with deadly carbon monoxide, creating a grave threat to your family.

The southwest design theme in this kitchen is carried through to the stucco and tile cooktop enclosure and hood, which is reminiscent of an old-fashioned outdoor oven.

A very tight house may, in fact, need what is called a "make-up air" line run to the furnace and hot water heater. This is a duct that brings fresh air from the outside directly to the furnace to be used for combustion.

A tight house may also need some type of *air-to-air heat exchanger,* a device that expels stale air while bringing in fresh air from the outside. A system of fins in the unit transfers about 85 percent of the heat from the outgoing air to the fresh incoming air. Our Concord barn project was so tight that it required such a device.

Amos Winter, who manufactured the foam core sheathing panels used on the barn project and who manufactures his own line of energy-efficient homes, told me that he learned how to operate sophisticated test equipment so he could personally investigate the complaints of poor air quality (the so-called sick house syndrome) in some of the houses his company had built. He was prepared to find high levels of formaldehyde and other chemicals "out-gased" by modern building materials such as particleboard and plywood, but what he found instead were high levels of carbon dioxide — stale air — which accumulated in the houses simply because they were so tight. Winter's solution was an air-to-air heat exchanger.

As the need for energy efficiency collides with that for interior air quality, we expect to see better and cheaper ventilation devices. Because most ventilation devices are installed before the walls are covered, it is worth thinking carefully about your needs before you begin your project.

●

8 Lighting

The lighting in this kitchen, both natural and artificial, gives the room drama it would not otherwise have. The skylight brings lots of light in by day, but without the halogen up-lights would be a dark and looming space at night. Recessed lights give additional general illumination, and flu-orescents under the cabinets provide good task lighting for the work surfaces.

Once, before I went off on a six-month research trip to the small, remote Micronesian island of Satawal, I took my wife on an extravagant (and therefore brief) visit to the Mauna Kea Hotel on the big island of Hawaii. The rooms opened onto a dramatic three-story atrium, an architectural feature that had not yet become the cliché it is now. What impressed me upon stepping out of the elevator that night was not the expansiveness of the atrium but rather its extraordinary sense of intimacy. Clearly visible on the distant balconies were brightly painted basket and mosquito masks from New Guinea, bronze Buddhas from China, and stone goddesses from Thailand. Each piece shimmered in a light that it seemed to radiate, rather than reflect. As we strolled to our room, I paused at the railing to try to discover what design secrets the atrium possessed. When I turned to our door to seek the keyhole, I noticed it was illuminated with a single, barely perceptible shaft of light from a fixture concealed in the ceiling. In the morning I saw that the atrium was indeed a beautiful space, but it was the lighting design that spun the sense of nighttime magic.

This experience taught me the importance of lighting, and in no room is it as important as in the kitchen. In the past, kitchen lighting consisted of a single fixture in the center of the room, another above the sink, and perhaps a third over the table. The fixtures lit the room, it's true, but they also produced a lot of glare and little atmosphere.

Today the prevailing theory about kitchen lighting (and lighting in general) is to design a system of multiple light sources that illuminates the room without revealing the sources of the light, like the system at Mauna Kea. This reduces glare and makes the kitchen easier to work in. Because today's kitchens often serve multiple functions — workshop, dining, and living area — the lighting system must be quite flexible.

Lighting designers break lighting into three categories: *task lighting*, designed to illuminate working surfaces such as the cooktop, countertops, sink, and island; *general lighting*, which illuminates the room so you can walk through it and see where things are;

and *decorative, mood, or accent lighting,* which enhances the kitchen's attractiveness, highlights architectural features or art objects, and helps to create an intimate, friendly, or romantic atmosphere. A modern kitchen needs all three capabilities in order to be a safe, efficient, and enjoyable space.

Natural Light

The first step in your lighting plan is to consider how to bring the most natural light into your kitchen, for it not only saves money on electricity but greatly adds to the functionality and comfort of the room as a workshop. There are some imaginative ways to do this that do not sacrifice precious cabinet or counter area. One is to install a long, fixed window between the countertop and the bottom of the wall cabinets. In addition to giving the room a very slick look, daylight bathes the counter, and the window opens up an unexpected view of the landscape. If the view is not something you particularly want to look at, install frosted glass, which will give you the light without the view. A similar strategy is to use operable windows in the same space to add cross-ventilation, always useful in a kitchen.

Skylights, as we discussed in chapter 4, are an excellent way to pull natural light into the kitchen without sacrificing wall space. In placing them, one of the most important considerations is where direct sunlight will fall in the room. You don't want it to strike the refrigerator, overheat a seating area, or create excessive glare. But it may be an advantage to have the sunlight fall on a masonry surface in order to "bank" some of the sun's heat for later in the day, when the temperature drops.

If your kitchen has a door to the exterior, you might consider replacing it with an insulated glass door, which will admit a lot of light without undue loss of heat.

Planning Your Lighting Layout

In most rooms you don't need to plan the lighting scheme with tremendous precision. After all, changing the lighting in a bedroom or living room is usually an easy matter of adding, removing, or relocating table or floor lamps. But in a modern kitchen most lighting fixtures are built in, either recessed "cans," track lighting, fluorescent fixtures, or a combination of all three. Such a system is modified only at significant expense, so give your lighting plan the same care and attention as your general kitchen plan.

At this point in the project, we'll assume you know where the cabinets, counters, sink, and appliances are going. A good way to start the lighting layout is by asking yourself which work surfaces

The unusual choice of full-length windows brightens up the eating area and makes the whole room seem much larger. The counter takes full advantage of the structural capabilities of solid surfacing by curving around without supports from the floor.

High, barn-style windows fill the upper reaches of this kitchen with natural light, which diffuses throughout the whole room. The strong line of the upper cabinets, which repeats that of the revealed beams, keeps the eye grounded to the earth while the delicate line of the roof urges the eye up to the light-filled heavens. These features give this kitchen a sense of privacy, order, and serenity.

need illumination. You will, of course, want good task lighting at the sink, as well as the cooktop and any countertops to be used for food preparation. If there's a center island, it, too, should be illuminated. You may also want task lighting at a desk, table, or message center.

You might also give some thought to placing the fixtures, the cardinal rule being to position them so that no shadows will be cast on the work. The fixture illuminating the sink, for instance, should be directly above it so your body doesn't create a shadow when you're working there. For the same reason, lighting for perimeter counters should be installed fairly close to the wall.

In considering general lighting, keep in mind that the level of illumination doesn't have to be tremendously high. Its purpose is to help you find your way through the kitchen, not to provide enough brightness for reading recipes or preparing food. The lighting consultant for "This Old House," Dick Metchear of Watertown Electric Supply, points out that task lighting can often double as general illumination. Not all the light from under-cabinet or recessed ceiling fixtures remains in its target area; some spills out to brighten the room as a whole. Depending on your task lighting scheme, you may need few, if any, general lighting fixtures.

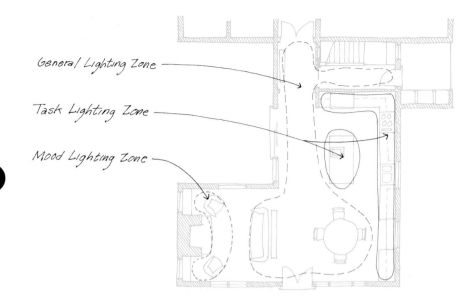

General Lighting Zone

Task Lighting Zone

Mood Lighting Zone

In most other rooms of the house you can re-arrange the lighting to suit the task. Not so in the kitchen. A lighting plot plan like this one will help you evaluate your requirements for the three types of illu-mination: task, gen-eral, and mood.

Finally, consider decorative, mood, or accent lighting. If you want to wash walls or paintings with soft light, provide for mood light-ing at the dinner table, highlight unique objects, or dramatize special architectural features such as a cornice, columns, or fancy molding, you will need to select and place fixtures to do so.

In my own kitchen, the same set of fixtures functions for all three types of lighting. I light my counters, island, and peninsula with recessed fixtures placed in the ceiling. They are all on one circuit and on a dimmer so they can either be turned up all the way for task light-ing or dimmed down for mood lighting. I have another series of re-cessed fixtures in the aisles for general illumination, but they also serve to light the perimeter counters as well as the interiors of the cab-inets. I installed a third circuit of fluorescent fixtures under the counters, for task lighting, and over the cabinets to wash the ceiling. These lights are useful on hot summer nights, when the recessed fix-tures would generate too much heat, and on dark, rainy days when you need a bit more light in the kitchen. Above the table I installed two recessed cans, which can be turned up when paying bills or reading the paper or dimmed for dining. I also installed wall washers on the sidewall and in the niche, which can be turned up bright for general illumination or dimmed for mood lighting.

After you have pondered your lighting requirements in gen-eral, you are ready to draw a *lighting plan.* If you are working with an architect or designer, he or she will probably draw this plan, which specifies fixtures and details their placement. If you're draw-ing your own kitchen plan, or intend to save on your design fees by making preliminary sketches before going to a design professional,

In a kitchen with no windows, lighting and materials need to interact for added brightness. The under-cabinet lights have baffled covers that cast a textural pattern on the stainless-steel backsplash. Reflective surfaces everywhere — floors, cabinets, and counters — increase the bounce of light. Surprisingly, this kitchen doesn't feel claustrophobic, even though it is small and windowless.

you might consult a lighting specialist at a lighting supply house. These people work with lighting every day and can come up with good solutions. In general, they are familiar with the types of fixtures available and how they can best be utilized. Electricians, while expert at installing lighting, may not be skilled at designing it, so you may not want to turn the design aspect of your job over to your electrician. Yet electricians implement lighting designs every day; as in all other aspects of your renovations, be prepared to accept good ideas wherever you may find them.

The Attributes of Lighting

There is no single satisfactory standard for how much illumination to provide in a kitchen. Different people have different physiological needs as well as different tastes. As a general rule, the older the individual, the more light he or she needs. The safest course is to install more lighting capacity than necessary, since it's generally expensive to augment the lighting system later. If the full capacity isn't needed, less powerful lamps can be substituted, some of the lamps can be left turned off, or the whole system can be dimmed. You want your kitchen lighting system to be as flexible as possible.

Output

Light output is not measured in watts, those being a measure of how much electricity the lamp consumes. Rather the gross output of a lamp is measured in *lumens,* and the illumination it casts per square foot of surface area is measured in *footcandles.* A high-wattage lamp does not necessarily deliver high output. An incandescent lamp converts much of the electricity it consumes to heat, rather than light. Incandescent lighting, the main source of artificial illumination in the home, is, in fact, the least efficient type of lighting currently available. But incandescent lamps remain popular because they bring out the warmer colors in objects, flatter people's complexions, and make foods look appetizing.

Kitchen lighting tends to be used for longer periods than the lights in other areas of the house, so incandescent lamps can be both

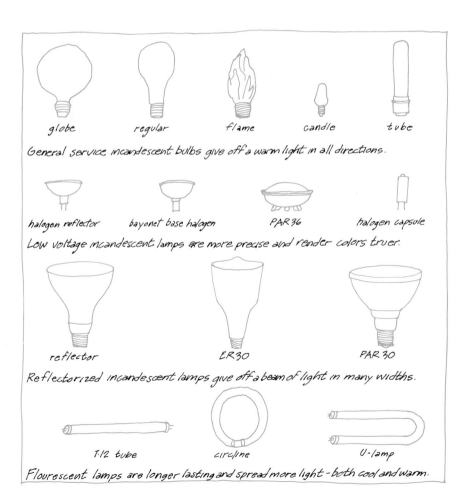

| globe | regular | flame | candle | tube |

General service incandescent bulbs give off a warm light in all directions.

| halogen reflector | bayonet base halogen | PAR 36 | halogen capsule |

Low voltage incandescent lamps are more precise and render colors truer.

| reflector | ER 30 | PAR 30 |

Reflectorized incandescent lamps give off a beam of light in many widths.

| T-12 tube | circline | U-lamp |

Flourescent lamps are longer lasting and spread more light – both cool and warm.

Four types of lighting fixtures add life and vitality to an urban galley kitchen: recessed fixtures for both general and task, under-cabinet fluorescents for task, and a pendant in the foreground to light the table. The neon strip adds movement and a sense of play. It can be left on as a night light for the kitchen and dining area. Neon has an extremely long life span and consumes very little power. Notice the formidable bank of switches and dimmers on the kitchen end wall.

expensive to operate and require frequent replacement. This is why fluorescent lighting is so common in kitchens. For the same electrical consumption, a fluorescent lamp can generate four times the light of a standard incandescent bulb. The most common fluorescent lamps are labeled "cool white," which means that they accentuate the cool, blue colors of the spectrum and deemphasize the warm, red colors. Cool fluorescents are inexpensive, and if you ask for a fluorescent lamp without specifying its color, you'll probably be given a cool fluorescent. Since cool lamps make people look ghostly and food unappetizing, we specify "warm white" lamps, which bring out the reds and pinks instead of the blues and grays. The extra cost of warm white lamps is well justified; they still last much longer and operate much more efficiently than incandescents.

Glare reducing baffles.

If you want the advantages of a fluorescent lamp in a standard incandescent fixture, consider using a compact fluorescent lamp. These U-shaped lamps have a screw-in base just like a standard incandescent bulb yet contain a small solid-state ballast, a device that increases the voltage to a level sufficient to cause excitation of the mercury vapor inside the tube to emit ultraviolet light. The ultraviolet light in turn strikes the phosphor coating on the inside of the tube, which emits white light.

Pinhole downlighting.

Compact fluorescents currently cost up to $20 per bulb, but because they last many times longer and consume a quarter of the electricity of a standard bulb, they are more economical in the long run. The newest generation of lamps manufactured by Phillips and Siemens have excellent color rendering — in fact, nearly identical to standard incandescents — which makes them a viable option anywhere in the house.

Wide angle wallwasher.

Encouraged by lighting manufacturers such as Lightolier, a growing number of "lighting labs" have been installed in lighting showrooms around the country. These provide the opportunity to learn about the color rendering and other characteristics of various lamps and fixtures before you make your final selection. If you have samples of paint colors, curtains, upholstery, or wall coverings that you want to use in the kitchen, you can take them to a lighting lab to see for yourself which lamps complement them. It is a simple way to avoid disappointment later.

Eyeball accent lighting.

Task Lighting

One of our favorite places to install task lighting is on the bottom of the wall cabinets. Fluorescent or incandescent tubes installed here can throw plenty of light onto the countertops, where most of the kitchen work is done. The cabinets must have a lip at the bottom which ex-

Vertical grooves baffle.

Reflector downlighting.

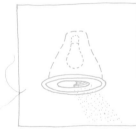

Low intensity wallwasher.

Recessed accent lighting.

tends low enough to hide the tube from view when standing *and* sitting. Seeing the light source not only detracts from the room's appearance, it also interferes with normal eyesight. The glare causes your pupils to contract, making it harder to see dark areas of the room. It is often possible to add a lip to cabinets that lack one.

Typically, under-cabinet lighting is placed at the front edge of the cabinet because it will illuminate the front of the counter where most work takes place and because it is easier to hide there. Mechear prefers thin fluorescent tubes enclosed by a plastic cover for under-cabinet lighting. They are only an inch in diameter and thus easier to conceal. The disadvantage with these thin fluorescents is that they require a standard ballast rather than a rapid-start ballast, which results in a slight flickering before the light reaches full strength and a gentle hum while the lamps are in operation. (Mechear told us he once lit a kitchen for a college professor who liked to read there but was irritated by the noise. Metchear took all the ballasts out of the fixtures and installed them in a closet, an effective, if expensive, solution.) Thin fluorescent fixtures typically measure five inches from front to back, come in several lengths, and may come enclosed by a plastic cover.

A number of companies make linear incandescent lamps. These offer better color rendering than fluorescents with no ballast hum. Linear incandescents can be dimmed, whereas the typical fluorescent cannot. Alko, of Franklin Park, Illinois, and Aamsco, of Jersey City, New Jersey, manufacture fixtures that allow linear incandescent tubes to be butted together in long rows. Fixture and tube together measure as little as $1\frac{1}{8}$ inches high.

Recessed Lighting

Another way to provide task lighting for counters, sinks, and cooktops is with *recessed fixtures* set into the ceiling over the area to be illuminated. Recessed fixtures, often called "cans" because of their shape, or "downlights" because they direct their light downward rather than out in all directions, come as a frame or base into which a number of different types of inserts can be mounted. To minimize glare, choose an insert that allows the lamp to be deeply recessed. The glare is also reduced by black baffles, which are part of the insert. In general, the quality of the insert is consistent with its price, and glare is more of a problem with the cheaper inserts.

The area a single recessed fixture will illuminate depends on the kind of lamp used. A spotlight will produce a narrow beam spread, whereas a floodlight will distribute the light more widely. A larger variety of beam spreads can be achieved with low-voltage lighting systems, some of which allow you to focus the beam. These

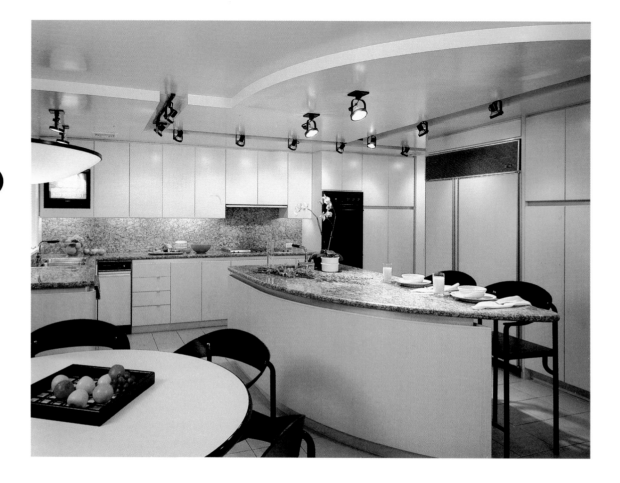

require, among other things, a transformer to convert ordinary 110-volt household current to 12 volts. We tend to avoid low-voltage lighting because the fixtures and bulbs are expensive. However, because of the bulb's long life and the ability to select a fixture with a specific or even variable beam spread, these systems may have applications in high-end kitchens.

●

In general, recessed fixtures are an excellent solution to lighting requirements in the kitchen. They are relatively unobtrusive and make but a modest design statement, and thus may complement many styles of decoration. Installed (as they typically are) in a series, downlights cast even, shadow-free illumination on counters and work surfaces. Yet, in most applications there is sufficient light "spillage" that no additional general lighting fixtures are necessary. When dimmed to a low level, recessed fixtures provide good mood lighting, too.

On the negative side, a high-quality recessed fixture with bulb and reflector will cost $90 or more. You might need anywhere from four to ten (there are thirteen in my kitchen). Add to that the cost

Track lighting illuminates the cabinets and perimeter of this kitchen. Minispots give a slightly brighter light on the island and kitchen sink. Undercabinet lights show off the richly patterned granite, helping to emphasize the contrast in textures between the stone and wood-paneled kitchen. The black "industrial" look of the track lighting ties in with the chairs, stools, oven, and television, unifying the room.

of switches, dimmers, and an electrician to install and wire them (unless you live in a jurisdiction that allows homeowners to do their own wiring), and you end up with a hefty investment in lighting. They also throw off a great deal of heat, which may add to air-conditioning costs in a hot climate. But because they do their job so well, and often satisfy all the lighting requirements in the kitchen, we consider recessed lighting worth the investment.

Surface-Mount Cans

If you want the lighting effects of recessed lighting but cannot, for structural or architectural reasons, actually recess the fixtures, you can achieve nearly the same result with surface-mount cans, cylindrical metal fixtures that contain the same type of reflector and bulb as recessed fixtures but mount on the surface of the ceiling.

Track Lighting

Another solution is track lighting, which offers the same characteristics as recessed and surface-mount cans, but with the added capability to move the lighting heads anywhere along the track, which contains the electrical bus. We've used track lighting in "This Old House" projects and our homeowners have been pleased, but we still have mixed feelings about the system. For one thing, track lighting is very conspicuous — the light heads will become part of the room's decor whether you want them to or not — and if not used sparingly, they may give the kitchen a cluttered look. The system is promoted on the basis of its flexibility, yet, while the ability to move the light heads around might be an essential feature in an art gallery, we question whether it will ever be used in a kitchen. Most people, including the "This Old House" homeowners who installed the system, report that they never readjusted their track lights after the first few weeks of living with them. In addition, the light head's complex and exposed component parts present many surfaces on which dust and grease settle — surfaces that are difficult to clean. Since the working surfaces that need good lighting are predictable, we prefer to light them with a well-designed system of recessed cans. The cost of high-quality track lighting is roughly equal to recessed fixtures.

Yet there are applications where track is an excellent choice. I used it in one of my own kitchens, the 1846 Greek Revival. Installing recessed lighting would have meant trying to saw circular holes in an old horsehair plaster ceiling, the prime characteristic of which is that if you leave it alone it is fine, but once you cut into it the whole thing crumbles. I fed electricity to the track from an existing ceiling box, and thus incurred no additional expense in wiring the system. And, finally, the modern look of the heads was a pleasing contrast to the old-fashioned cabinets and plumbing fixtures.

Old-fashioned pendant lights combine with fluorescent ceiling fixtures to provide excellent overall lighting in this country kitchen.

Pendant Lighting

Pendant lighting refers to that class of fixtures which are suspended from the ceiling either by their electrical cords, or by a small chain or metal conduit. They come in a variety of shapes: luminous plastic spheres and hemispheres, domes, cones, beveled-glass pentagons, and so on. There are literally dozens of styles. Pendant lights can be hung from individual electrical boxes in the ceiling or from a track. They offer excellent task lighting, good general illumination, and can be dimmed for mood lighting as well. We have seen kitchens lit solely by two or three of the luminous globe type of fixtures suspended in the center of the room.

Hang pendant fixtures high enough that they do not obstruct your view across the peninsula or island (approximately 36 inches above the countertop). Over a table, the fixture may be lower, but not so low as to block your view (30 inches is considered standard in a room with 8-foot ceilings). Also consider whether the table will be permanently in one location. If it will occasionally be moved or folded against the wall, a suspended fixture will become an obstruction.

Fluorescent fixtures do not have to mean inelegant design. This suspended fluorescent fixture casts 40 percent of its light toward the ceiling for reflected light and 60 percent down for direct illumination. Continuous under-cabinet fluorescents light the work surfaces. Do not fail to consider fluorescents in your kitchen. They pump out a lot of light and are very economical to operate.

General Illumination

Some people (including my own designer, Marilyn Ruben) reject the concept of fancy and expensive multipurpose incandescent lighting in favor of good, high-output fluorescent fixtures that fill the room with enough light for both general and task lighting. Fluorescent fixtures are available in both recessed and surface-mount models. They come in standard sizes, 2, 4, and 6 feet long, and in standard widths. In her own kitchen, Marilyn used two 2x4-foot fluorescent fixtures that flooded the room with light. Of course, she was from the old school and did *not* believe in entertaining guests in the kitchen, preferring to use her wonderfully appointed living, dining, and studio rooms. Marilyn was the only hostess I have seen who succeeded in getting her guests out of the kitchen.

In some of her other designs Marilyn used what is called a luminous ceiling, an array of fluorescent lamps fitted in either a recessed or surface-mounted box in the ceiling and covered with translucent white plastic.

Any carpenter can make a luminous ceiling by building a

simple wooden box to insert in the ceiling. The interior is then painted white to reflect the light down into the room. The electrician may then mount the fluorescent fixtures and the carpenter can cover the box with ¼- to ⅜-inch-thick translucent plastic — thick enough so the tubes cannot be seen through it, yet thin enough to let most of the light pass through. The goal is to make the entire panel uniformly bright, with no dark areas. Proper placement of the fluorescent tubes is critical. When two or more tubes are installed in a row, they should be butted together. When installed parallel, the distance from the center of one tube to the next should be half the distance from the tubes to the plastic panel.

One of the objectives of a luminous ceiling is to eliminate glare, which can obstruct vision and cause discomfort. Glare can be aggravated by glass and metallic surfaces, such as polished aluminum, and by high-gloss finishes on cabinets. Strong contrasts of light

(Left) Some people, my own designer among them, eschewed the use of fancy fixtures, preferring instead the bright, even illumination afforded by well-designed overhead fluorescent fixtures. This one lights the whole kitchen. Task lights under the cabinets illuminate the counters.

(Right) Uplighting in the soffits makes for dramatic lighting in this city kitchen, and shows off the rich collection of ceramics.

and dark can also cause discomfort. Since people become more sensitive to both glare and extreme contrast as they grow older, this is a consideration that may deserve attention.

General illumination with little glare can be had by *washing* the ceiling with reflected light. This is typically done by installing fluorescent (and sometimes incandescent) fixtures on the cabinet tops. You need 6 to 12 inches of clearance between cabinet top and ceiling. Paint the cabinet top white to bounce more light onto the ceiling, and either build a lip on the outer edge of the cabinet to conceal the light source or place the fixtures sufficiently back from the edge that they are not visible.

Decorative, Mood, and Accent Lighting

Decorative or mood lighting can be provided by a number of the fixtures we've discussed, including track lights, suspended fixtures, or recessed downlighting. Some recessed inserts are available with a small aperture that emits a narrow beam of light, which can be used to dramatic effect in spotlighting a table top or art object.

Another type of decorative lighting consists of tiny half- or one-watt bulbs used to outline the interior of frosted-glass cabinets or to draw attention to other kitchen features. Although these *subminiature lamps* are not powerful enough to serve as task or general illumination, they can be used as accent lighting. Subminiature lamps, which operate almost indefinitely without burning out, are often joined as a string of lights inside a transparent tube, which can easily be attached to cabinetry. These are *low-wattage* devices, which are not to be confused with the low-voltage systems mentioned earlier which require a transformer to reduce the voltage. The subminiature systems do not require expensive electrical work.

Finally, there are a host of decorative lights intended to be a focal point of the room. This category of decorative fixtures is a large one, ranging from wall sconces to chandeliers. Some kitchens successfully employ decorative fixtures while others get along just fine without them.

Dimmers and Other Controls

For the incandescent systems described above to be flexible enough for kitchen duty, they must be fitted with a dimmer. There are a great many dimmers on the market today. Some are operated by turning a knob, others with a slide control, still others with a push pad that when stroked one way turns the lights up, and when stroked the other dims them. Now there's even a dimmer you can actuate by an infrared remote-control unit — yet another "clicker" to keep track of, along with those controlling your TV, VCR, air conditioner, garage door, CD player, and stereo.

It's worth noting that the incandescent dimmers manufactured today reduce electrical consumption as the volume of light decreases, so dimmers can pay for themselves by saving electricity. They can also extend the life of light bulbs. Bulbs burn out partly because the intense heat they generate causes the filament to evaporate. Dimming a bulb allows it to operate cooler. GTE-Sylvania says that dimming an incandescent bulb 25 percent can triple its life span.

Fluorescent lamps require a special ballast and dimmer and are therefore more difficult and expensive to dim than incandescents. Dimmed fluorescent tubes have a shorter life span than those that operate at full power.

In general, we believe in simple dimmer controls. When selecting controls, ask yourself if it is easy to tell what level of lighting the control is set to provide. (A sliding control passes this test.) Can the level of dimming be changed without having to follow complicated procedures? Since children and visitors also operate switches, an easy-to-understand system is best.

With the proliferation of lighting and electrical devices in the house, it's sometimes hard for people to remember which switch operates which light. We know one couple who live in a house that has four switches ganged together at the kitchen door — one switch for recessed lighting, one for under-cabinet lights, one for a hanging fixture over the kitchen table, and one for a mystery device they have yet to find. After seven years in the house, they confess that they still push the wrong switch half the time. To eliminate confusion of this sort, it may be desirable (but not always possible) to put no more than two controls together in any one place. We would consider distributing the controls throughout the room, close to the points where the light is needed. The control for a fixture above the sink should be near the sink; the control for fixtures above a center island should be installed nearby.

If, on the other hand, you're a gadget lover, a handful of computer lighting controllers have come on the market in the past few years that enable you to program your house room by room. By pushing a single button, recessed lights over, say, your counters come on at half-power, your under-cabinet lights come on at full intensity, and a light above the kitchen table comes on dimmed way down. Automated systems can program electrical consumption in every room of the house and even allow the instructions to be changed via a telephone call. Sensors can turn lights on whenever someone enters the room and turn them off after everyone has departed. These may be

Standard Dimmer

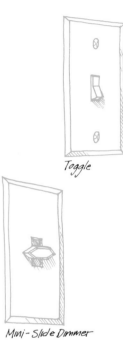

Toggle

Mini-Slide Dimmer

Rocker

Toggle Dimmer

Dimming the recessed fixtures allows the kitchen to disappear when it's time to dine.

Touch Sensitive Dimmer

Wheel Dimmer

Slide Dimmer

very useful devices for children and the handicapped. *Electronic House* magazine in Mishawaka, Indiana, is a source of information about these electronic systems.

Three- and Four-Way Switches

Because one of the main considerations in selecting lighting controls is convenience, we like to install three- and four-way switches and dimmers, which allow you to control a lighting circuit from two or three locations. In a three-way circuit, you can have two switches or one dimmer and one switch. In a four-way circuit, you can have three switches or one dimmer and two switches.

In my own kitchen, I put all the lights on four-way switches. I located a bank of six dimmers in a central location and spotted on-off switches at the two doors coming into the room. This arrangement is admittedly a bit complicated, but once you get used to it is extremely flexible and convenient.

●

There are many other types of lighting — much more than can be discussed in this chapter. Manufacturers such as Sylvania, General Electric, and Lightolier publish catalogues that illustrate their whole product lines and give detailed specifications. You can also learn a lot from consumer-oriented books on lighting.

When you dream of your new kitchen, you don't typically spend a lot of time thinking about recessed downlights or luminous ceilings. Yet the difference between a good and a great kitchen may depend on it.

●

9 Floors

Pattern in flooring should balance the scale of the room. Here, the rhythm of beautifully grained cherry can be fully appreciated, while adding a classic, homey element.

In all but the most privileged households, no other floor gets as much wear and abuse as the kitchen floor. From spilled milk to overturned pizzas, children's experiments in food chemistry (those infamous mixtures of "Bola Cola" and other delights), to dog hairs, bunny droppings, and scuffs from impromptu games of floor hockey, the kitchen floor gets it all. From a kid's point of view, antics unthinkable anywhere else in the house are permissible, or at least not squelched so quickly, in the kitchen.

And yet, of all the design elements in your kitchen — style of cabinets and counters, choice of wall coverings and paint colors — perhaps none influences the room's overall look as much as the floor. Ceramic tile will give the room a crisp, functional look, while wood parquet provides a formal look, terra-cotta tile a French country flair, and vinyl a . . . well, a standard American kitchen look.

When you choose flooring, take into consideration the room's relationship to its surrounding spaces. In renovating the kitchen of a small urban condominium with hardwood floors throughout, you would probably want to continue the same flooring into the kitchen to give the space a sense of unity. If, on the other hand, you are rehabbing the kitchen of a suburban household with young children, you may opt for the functionality, comfort, and low cost of vinyl.

There is a very wide range of flooring materials available today, everything from marble to cork. To decide among them, you will consider a number of factors, but probably the key issues are appearance, cost, maintenance, comfort, and durability.

Vinyl Flooring

Sheet vinyl is by far the most common choice in kitchen flooring. Manufacturers call it "resilient flooring" because it provides a slight cushioning that is easy on feet and legs. Vinyl is warmer than most other floor materials, is impervious to water, resists stains, has good traction, and is cost effective.

Most varieties of sheet vinyl come in 6- or 12-foot widths. The ideal is to cover the whole floor with a seamless sheet, for a visible seam will not only detract from the floor's appearance but is the most vulnerable part of a vinyl floor. If the installation is poorly done, the seam may eventually pull apart. Since many kitchens are too large to be covered in a single sheet, a seam will be required. Fortunately, today's seam sealers, when properly used, can hold two sheets of vinyl firmly together in a strong and inconspicuous juncture.

Most vinyl flooring is composed of three layers: the *backing*, usually made of vinyl or felt, the middle *design layer*, containing the floor's color and visual pattern, and the top *wear layer*, which protects the color and pattern from being rubbed away by traffic. Manufacturers now apply a vinyl wear layer, which eliminates the need to wax the floor. This type of sheet vinyl is promoted as "no-wax."

"No-Wax" Vinyl

Although waxing might be eliminated, no-wax vinyl floors do require care. A spokesperson for Armstrong World Industries, one of the major vinyl manufacturers, said that all vinyl floors lose their shine soon after they're installed. If you don't mind a dull-looking floor — and many people don't — you needn't do anything except clean as necessary. Sweep or vacuum and wet-mop the floor to remove dirt particles that would otherwise grind in and dull the surface. Some manufacturers advise customers to reserve one bucket and mop for cleaning and a second bucket and mop for rinsing, because the film left from inadequate rinsing can make the surface look dull.

Once a vinyl floor starts to look dull and scuffed, and damp-mopping no longer restores its luster, some additional treatment will be required. Armstrong suggests periodic applications of a polish to restore the shine to a dull no-wax floor. Cleaning and polishing should be repeated whenever the floor looks dingy.

"Never-Wax" Vinyl

In addition to no-wax floors, one manufacturer, Mannington Mills, makes an extensive line of what it calls "never-wax" vinyl flooring. According to Mannington, its wear layer is much thicker and therefore longer-lasting than that of a standard no-wax vinyl floor. If a never-wax floor becomes dull and scratched and cannot be restored by damp-mopping, the manufacturer recommends lightly buffing the floor with a buffing machine with natural felt or lamb's wool pads, which are soft and won't scratch the floor.

Armstrong counters that the difference in the thickness of the wear layer has no practical consequences, and that while its wear layer is thinner, it will never be "walked off" in household use. If you want a tougher finish, Armstrong recommends you buy its line with a vinyl surface coated with a urethane layer, which keeps its shine

Dark blue vinyl tiles with a white border was a good choice for this remodeled family kitchen. The dark blue hides dirt, while the white gives it a crisp, classic look that goes well with the white beadboard paneling.

longer (but still needs periodic polishing). Congoleum and Tarkett, other major manufacturers, also offer similar products.

Since all vinyl flooring needs maintenance, one of the factors you might consider when selecting a brand is what type of maintenance you're willing to do. Mannington estimates that a never-wax floor in a kitchen that gets a lot of foot traffic (such as a home with active children) may need buffing four times a year, so you'd have to rent a buffing machine. A no-wax floor doesn't need buffing, but you would have to apply polish.

When choosing vinyl, pay attention to the thickness of the overall flooring, not just the wear layer. Generally, the thicker the vinyl, the more durable (and expensive) the floor will be. Also, different kinds of flooring resist certain stains better than others. You would be well advised to go to a retailer or installer who handles several manufacturers' products and get him to explain the advantages and disadvantages of each, as well as to recommend cleaning agents or polishes. Some manufacturers sell cleaning products formulated especially for their brands.

Some vinyl flooring is embossed with indentations that enhance the design or create a pattern of light and shadow that makes

blemishes less noticeable. Any flooring with a texture, though, will be harder to clean. Note that light colors tend to hide scratches and blemishes, while dark colors make them stand out. Also keep in mind that vinyl can fade after prolonged exposure to intense sun, just as draperies and upholstery do. This might not be a danger in most kitchens, but it's worth taking into account if the flooring is to be installed in a sunny space or next to a glass door.

Inlaid Flooring

Another vinyl product, called inlaid flooring, gets its pattern and color from a different process. Instead of a printed design layer, thousands of colored vinyl granules are fused onto the flooring by heat and pressure. Armstrong claims this process gives the flooring greater depth and richness of color (and, not surprisingly, greater cost).

"Interflex" Flooring

Vinyl flooring is usually installed over a plywood underlayment, which is first nailed to the existing floor to even out any irregularities. There is, however, one vinyl product that can be laid directly on any existing floor. Called interflex flooring, it contains a vinyl backing that can span minor irregularities. Interflex is generally chosen to save on installation costs. But some people select it because they want a vinyl floor now, but don't want to rule out the possibility of eventually exposing the wooden floor underneath. Since interflex doesn't require nailing down underlayment, its use avoids scarring the wood floor with hundreds of nails. Interflex also lends itself to do-it-yourself projects. After adhesive has been applied along the edges of interflex flooring, it shrinks and pulls taut, increasing its ability to span irregularities.

Linoleum

Years ago, linoleum was a favorite flooring material. It was made of linseed oil, wood dust, cork, and resins. Its drawback was that it required waxing, and after no-wax vinyl flooring appeared on the market, demand for linoleum plummeted. Armstrong, the last major American maker of linoleum, stopped production in 1974. But fashions go through cycles, and now there is a small but growing demand for the look of linoleum — especially for a patterned field with a contrasting border. Linoleum can still be obtained through a few companies that import it to the United States. Recently, vinyl imitations of linoleum patterns have been introduced, and it's possible to order flooring with one pattern for the field and another for the border. If you're willing to pay premium prices, you will find other kinds of vinyl flooring, most of them tough, durable materials used in commercial buildings.

Installing Vinyl Flooring

The critical step in installing vinyl flooring is to prepare the subsurface. What's needed is a solid, uniform base, free from irregularities. Sheet vinyl can be laid over an existing floor (vinyl or another material) as long as it is smooth and stable. Any ridges must be sanded down and filled or they will cause visible high spots and be felt underfoot. A leveling compound similar to spackle can even out some depressions, and sanding and scraping can bring down some high spots. However, the installer may be unwilling to guarantee the floor will remain smooth, since it could still be pushed out of shape by pressure from the old flooring underneath. The safest course is to rip out old vinyl or linoleum and start anew by putting down plywood underlayment. Removal is a more critical issue if the old flooring contains asbestos, as many old floor tiles did. They are considered hazardous waste and should be disposed of properly. There appears to be no health hazard in leaving the tiles on the floor and covering them. The hazard, to the extent one exists, is in breaking the tiles and scattering asbestos fibers into the air. Do not sand them — no one should breathe asbestos dust. In making plans for floor removal, make certain the installer will discard the material in accordance with state or local laws and codes governing hazardous materials.

Underlayment is important even in a new house, for the wooden subfloor constructed by the homebuilder is not structurally sufficient and usually too rough and uneven a base for vinyl or other flooring materials. While lauan plywood (a species of mahogany) is the most common underlayment, "This Old House" 's vinyl flooring specialist, Paul Vogan of Belmont Flooring in Belmont, Massachusetts, prefers Structurwood Underlayment, made by the Weyerhauser Company.

The importance of underlayment is emphasized by the fact that vinyl manufacturers will not warrant their products if installed without it. Some installers *will* guarantee their installation for at least a year, although few, it seems, are willing to put this in writing. The haziness of some guarantees points up the importance of discussing warranty coverage before agreeing to use a particular installer or product.

Installing vinyl flooring is slightly more complicated if the kitchen is built on a concrete slab over an unventilated crawl space. Moisture can penetrate the floor from below and, trapped by the vinyl, form bubbles. If the builder has installed a vapor barrier over the soil before pouring the concrete, there should be no moisture problem. If the kitchen sits above a crawl space, moisture problems can be alleviated by installing a vapor barrier over the ground in the crawl space.

Vogan recommends a simple do-it-yourself test to determine whether moisture will be a problem in a slab floor. Tape several pieces of plastic to different parts of the floor. Check the plastic every day to see if it has trapped any moisture. If, by the end of the week, no moisture buildup is noticeable, the floor has probably been sealed against vapor transmission. Also check for depressions or unevenness before installing the vinyl. A fine cement can be applied to level the concrete.

Once your floor is installed, remember not to damage it when you reinstall the appliances. Use a dolly or even a rug to keep from gouging the floor. Even the small casters on a refrigerator may leave marks, and stoves and dishwashers, which are equipped with ad-

These vinyl tiles introduce movement and vitality to this simple kitchen layout. The pattern on the tiles hides dirt and contrasts crisply with the ash cabinets and white laminate counters.

justable legs instead of casters, need to be moved very carefully. Vogan recommends placing appliances on protectors that will distribute weight widely rather than on a small point. Also check that your chair and table legs will not damage your new floor. A variety of protectors are available at hardware stores. It's worth noting that vinyl (and almost every other kind of flooring) can be damaged by high-heeled shoes.

Vinyl Tiles

For low cost and ease of installation, it's hard to beat vinyl tiles. They come in 9- or 12-inch squares, and have long been favorites of do-it-yourselfers. Vinyl tiles are particularly suitable if the kitchen is built on a concrete slab. They're less suitable for use over a wooden floor, since wood may shift and cause tiles to come loose. Vinyl composition tiles have now replaced the older squares made of vinyl and asbestos. Some tiles are $1/8$ inch thick, but many people find it easier to work with tiles $3/32$ inch thick. Generally, tiles cost less than sheet vinyl.

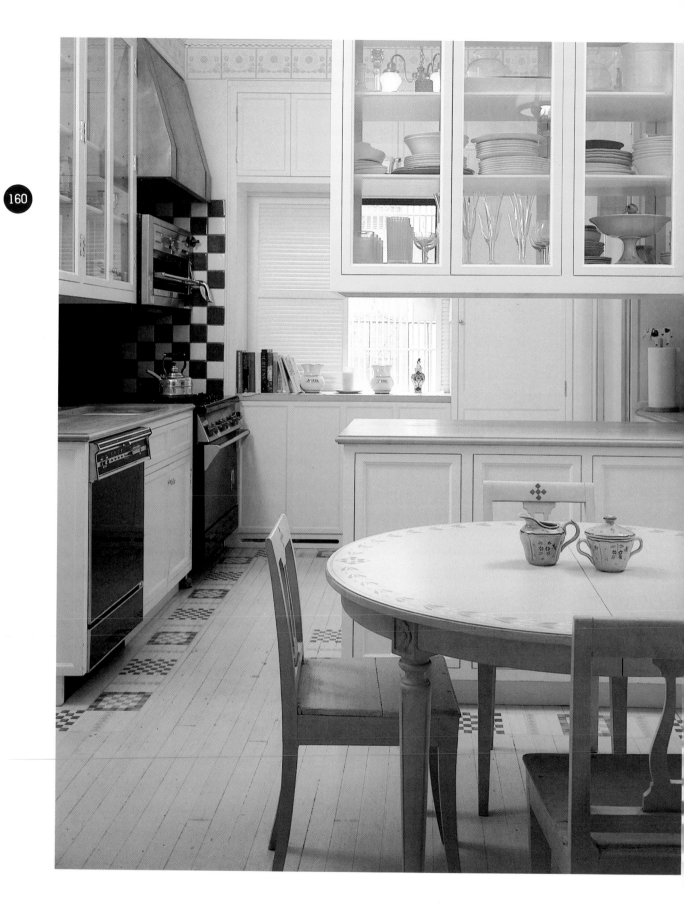

Preparation for vinyl tile installation is the same as for sheet vinyl. Easiest to install are the tiles with an adhesive backing exposed by peeling off a layer of paper; but we have more faith in tiles that are secured with a separate application of trowel-applied adhesive.

Some floor tiles have a no-wax finish and are constructed like sheet vinyl; others are solid vinyl and are more expensive. Some solid vinyl tiles imitate the appearance of wood, ceramic tile, or slate. Tiles are available in commercial grade also.

Yet another product is cork tiles, which are covered by a wear layer of clear vinyl. These combine the look and springiness of cork with the superior wear characteristics of vinyl.

Vinyl and cork tiles are perhaps the ideal do-it-yourself item because few tools and little experience are required. If you make a faulty cut, you've only ruined one tile, not the entire floor.

Rubber Flooring

Rubber flooring is used predominantly in commercial buildings. It has a high-tech look and comes in a variety of surface patterns: raised circles, raised dots, grids, bars, and leatherlike textures. It is resilient, slip resistant, and withstands cigarette burns. Some rubber flooring requires no waxing. It wears like iron and is easy to care for. It comes in the form of tiles and is therefore a candidate for do-it-yourselfers. The only real drawback is its high cost, close to the most expensive sheet vinyl.

Wood Flooring

Wood has excellent qualities as flooring: it is softer and quieter to walk on than ceramic tile; it shares vinyl's advantage of being relatively warm to the touch; and it's good-looking. It requires more upkeep than other materials, making it a questionable choice for a household with small children. For many households, however, it is quite practical, especially with the tough polyurethane coatings available today.

The favorite wood flooring is oak, and for good reason: it's hard enough to be quite durable and it's reasonably priced. Maple is also very popular, as is ash, a beautiful wood. A number of exotic woods, such as Brazilian cherry, purpleheart, and bubinga, are also durable. Woods such as pine, cherry, and walnut are too vulnerable to be recommended for a high-traffic area like the kitchen, although yellow pine is harder than other pines. These softer woods do, however, make distinctive borders around the edges of the room.

While color and pattern vary among species, they also vary within species. Not all red oak, which is often used for kitchen cabi-

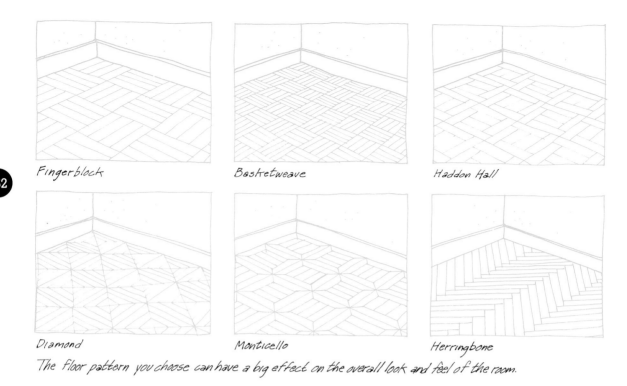

Fingerblock

Basketweave

Haddon Hall

Diamond

Monticello

Herringbone

The floor pattern you choose can have a big effect on the overall look and feel of the room.

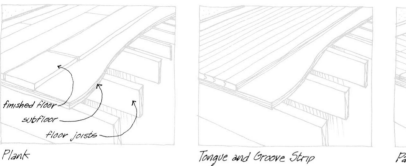

finished floor

subfloor

floor joists

Plank

Tongue and Groove Strip

Parquet

Wood Flooring Patterns and Types

nets, looks the same, and red oak has a different tone and grain from white oak. Also bear in mind that consistency of color varies with the wood's grade. Clear wood, which contains no knots, is highly uniform in color, whereas lower grades contain a mix of colors. While the clear grade (or "v.g.," vertical grain) is the most costly grade in any species, price is also influenced by other factors, such as the length and width of the stock. Two of the lower, more irregular grades of wood, #1 common and #2 common, may not look good in a formal dining room, but be just fine in a kitchen if a rustic look is desired.

Another area of choice is the style of flooring: strip, plank, parquet, and tile. *Strip* flooring, probably the most common type, ordinarily comes $2\frac{1}{4}$ inches wide and $\frac{3}{4}$ inch thick; it can be specified in

other dimensions as well. It is tongue-and-grooved on all four edges, which makes a strong interlocking structure. Typically the stock comes in bundles of random-length boards.

Plank flooring consists of wider boards up to 12 inches or even wider. The planks can be of uniform width or random widths mixed together. The wider the plank, the greater the risk of its cupping.

A third kind of flooring is parquet tiles, which can be up to 12 inches square. Each tile is made of a number of small pieces glued together. Although parquet flooring in some herringbone patterns can be expensive, simple patterns, such as rectangles, can cost less than strip flooring. Parquet flooring is a reasonable choice for do-it-yourselfers, since it is easy to lay.

Here is a tail-wagging-the-dog story. This room with the beautiful parquet floor was once the parlor of this historic 1892 house. In 1940 the kitchen was relocated here. The owners were so smitten with the beauty of the floor they didn't want to hide it under appliances. Therefore, for the next three years, the lady of the house attended woodworking classes at night, learned the craft of cabinetmaking, and built these legged cabinets that show off the floor. The cabinets are first class, too: all mortise-and-tenon, with dovetailed drawers — no nails were used. Check the sliding library ladder, too. Look out, Norm!

Installing and Caring For Wood Flooring

The proper sequence of kitchen work calls for laying down the wood flooring before installing base cabinets. This makes it easier for the floor specialist to cover the entire kitchen without having the flooring interrupted by cabinets. A continuous wood floor will also make it easier to remove and repair or replace built-in dishwashers, trash compactors, and other appliances. If the cabinets must be installed before the flooring, they will have to be blocked up so that they're even with the top of the finish floor.

There are a number of methods of installing wood flooring. One of them is *face-nailing*, which is frequently used with wide, square-edged oak or pine flooring. The nails — often wrought-iron "cut nails" — are driven through the tops of the boards, creating an old-fashioned look, with the nail heads visible. *Blind-nailing* involves driving nails or staples into the tongue-and-groove flooring so that when the job is completed, the nail heads are hidden.

Some floors, especially tile and wide planks, must also be glued to the subfloor. Planks are often blind-nailed as well. For a still greater margin of safety, they may also be screwed to the subfloor, after which the screwheads are covered by wooden "bungs," which, when sanded smooth, greatly enhance the floor's appearance.

"Floating" Wooden Floors

Prefinished laminated flooring, or floating floors, is one of the newer varieties of wood flooring to appear on the market. It is a flooring system consisting of plywoodlike laminated wooden planks with a veneer of the finish wood species bonded to the top surface. The planks have a tongue on one edge and end and a groove on the other, similar to strip oak, and they fit together with very close tolerances.

The rubric "floating floor" comes from the fact that the planks are glued to each other at the edges but not fastened to the subfloor. Instead they rest or "float" on a thin carpet of polyethylene foam. This makes them quieter and warmer than conventional strip or plank floors. They are available in a variety of finish species, some rare and difficult to obtain in strip or plank form.

The flooring stock comes from the factory in sections 6 to 8 inches wide and 8 feet long. Since each plank is quite large, the floor is much quicker to install than strip flooring, and since it is manufactured to such close tolerances it goes down faster than plank. However, floating floors require a very level substrate, whereas plank and strip flooring can be shimmed to bridge small depressions in the subfloor.

Since the planks of a floating floor are glued to each other but not to the subfloor, the whole floor expands and contracts as a single unit with changes in temperature and humidity. To give it "breathing room," a $1/_2$-inch gap should be left between the floor and the wall. This gap is concealed by the baseboard molding, which is held just off the floor so as not to inhibit its movement.

Conventional wooden floors also respond to environmental changes by expanding and contracting, as all wood does, but they do so as individual planks or strips, and not as a single unit.

In addition to installing quickly, floating floors come from the factory prefinished. Once the floor is laid, the job is done. Manufacturers claim that their coating, applied in controlled conditions in the factory, is tougher than coatings applied at the job site. This claim might be true, but the coating is broken at each seam, and it appears to be much thinner than the three coats of polyurethane we like to apply to plank or strip floors. Our concern is that in the course of the hazardous duty the floor will see in the kitchen, spills and wash water will penetrate the joints between planks, causing discoloration or delamination.

Some manufacturers of prefinished laminated flooring mill a chamfer into the edges of their planks, which form a series of V grooves when assembled. Because laminated flooring is not sanded to a uniform height after installation, the grooves distract the eye from any differences between planks, and draw the eye to individual boards rather than the floor as a whole. Some people like this look, others don't. Our objection for kitchen duty is that the grooves give dirt and moisture a place to penetrate into the flooring.

Perhaps the greatest disadvantage of a floating floor in a kitchen is its service life. Whereas a conventional hardwood floor is a solid $3/4$ inch thick, a floating floor is only $5/8$ inch thick, of which only the top third — about $1/8$ inch — is the finish veneer. The bottom two-thirds is laminated wood backing. Jeff Hosking, a floor refinishing expert in Walpole, Massachusetts, says that a floating floor can be sanded and refinished only two or three times before the veneer is worn away. Strip flooring, if sanded properly, can last through as many as seven refinishings.

In a "This Old House" project in Boston some years ago, we installed a beech floating floor. We returned after a couple of years to find out how it held up. The owners pointed out indentations around the kitchen island (where party guests tended to gather) made by high-heeled shoes. In another Boston-area house, we installed a pine floating floor throughout the ground floor. The manufacturer had claimed the pine had been compressed, making it more resistant to gouges and dents than ordinary pine. But when we went back to visit after only one year, the pockmarks were so bad that the owners hid much of the floor under rugs and walked around in socks. If you sanded these floors enough to remove the gouges, you'd sand right through the pine veneer. Floating floors are certainly not the only flooring susceptible to damage, but in our experience they are fragile, and we would not recommend their use in the kitchen.

Finishes

Traditionally, wood floors were finished with coats of stain, sealer, and wax. But wax tends to show water spots, and needs annual re-waxing and buffing to look good. A heavily used floor may need re-waxing twice a year.

Most floor installers and refinishers now prefer a polyurethane finish. Hosking cautions against using a cheap product: "If

(Above) In renovating this kitchen, the designers wanted to keep the existing parquet floor and simply refinish it. They laid a granite "rug" in front of the commercial range rather than leave the parquet exposed to the heat and spills.

(Above right) This pre-painted wood floor system is comprised of short strips, here laid on the diagonal in parquet fashion.

you're going to all the trouble of sanding a floor down, you want the best polyurethane money can buy." Three coats are better than two, especially in the kitchen, where there's plenty of traffic.

Most refinishers prefer a glossy finish, which is a harder coating than a satin finish, but satin hides scuffs and scratches better than glossy. If you desire satin, use gloss for the first two coats and satin for the final coat. Some polyurethanes tend to darken wood unless a sealer is applied first. Many refinishers use shellac because it dries quickly.

Over the years, we've had good experience with *European* or *Swedish finishes*. These alkyd-resin compounds are extremely tough, resist moisture and nearly all household chemicals, and will not yellow over time. They make an extremely handsome finish, bringing out the grain of the wood.

In some states, Swedish finishes are being phased out because they contain volatile solvents that fail to satisfy the increasingly stringent clean air standards. Swedish finishes are applied only to bare wood, or to an existing base of Swedish finish, but not to an existing coat of shellac or urethane. Swedish finishes "off-gas" amounts of formaldehyde and other organic solvents in excess of U.S. government limits, so use of a respirator with activated carbon filter cartridges is *mandatory* — reason enough, we think, to leave application of Swedish finishes to the experts.

Recently a new breed of water-based polyurethane has come onto the market. We used it on the pine floors of our Concord barn project and our Jamaica Plain triple decker, and are suitably impressed. Manufacturers claim that water-based polyurethane is twice as hard as the solvent-based formulations. It is applied with inexpensive foam brushes and rollers, dries in minutes, and is nontoxic and odorless. Jeff Hosking has been using this product commercially with favorable results.

Carpeting

People either love or hate the idea of a carpeted kitchen; there seems to be no middle ground. One couple we interviewed raised their children in a carpeted kitchen and had nothing but praise for it. They covered the existing asphalt tile floor in commercial carpeting with a thick rubber backing and a very short, tight weave — so tight that spills floated on top of the nap. The pattern was a combination of red and green leaves in an unobtrusive but very busy design that hid the dirt and stains. The carpet was such a success that several neighbors did the same thing.

Paul Vogan thinks that this *short-pile commercial carpeting* is the best for kitchen use. It has a tight, gathered weave that repels dirt and spills. It is one of the more expensive kinds of carpeting, but is available in a wide variety of patterns and colors. He says to avoid carpet backed with natural jute, which can absorb moisture, providing a perfect habitat for bacteria. Instead, look for foam-rubber-like *action-back carpeting*. He also advises not to install a pad beneath the carpeting since it may soak up spills.

Nylon carpeting resists stains better than Olefin, another commonly used synthetic fiber. There are various spray stain repellents on the market, but those incorporated into the carpet's fibers during manufacture are most effective.

Two less-expensive types of carpeting are also suitable for kitchens. One is commercial "level-loop" carpeting, which should be sprayed with a stain repellent once a year. You can also use indoor-outdoor carpeting, which is flat and smooth with no pile at all. Spills can usually be easily removed if not allowed to stand, according to Vogan. This comes in just a few solid colors and is the least expensive alternative.

Nonetheless, Vogan believes that carpeting is usually not the best choice for kitchen flooring. His experience is that carpets often do suffer stains and also harbor bacteria and odors. At "This Old House," we prefer floor materials that can be cleaned more thoroughly.

(Left) Since this small urban kitchen is located just off the foyer and main hallway, the formal look of the gray and black ceramic tiles is just right. The pebbling on the gray tiles hides dirt and makes a nice counterpoint to the sleek blackness of the rest of the room.

(Right) Ceramic tile can make a small kitchen seem bigger. The 12x12-inch diagonally laid taupe tiles, bordered with fawn gray trim tiles, make a "rug" under the center island. The repeating small tile patterns around the counters, backsplash, and windows give the illusion of greater space.

Tile, Stone, and Other Possibilities

Tile and stone have many drawbacks. They are hard, cold surfaces that are tough to stand on for long periods of time. Glassware and china dropped on the floor will shatter immediately. The kitchen will be noisier, and in most climates, underfloor heating will be necessary. Yet these floors can be extremely handsome, and when installed properly, long-lasting and low in maintenance. In Europe, one sees tile floors everywhere.

Ceramic Tile

Ceramic tile comes in various sizes and shapes. The most popular in kitchens are 8-inch and 6-inch squares, but 12-inch squares and hexagonal shapes are also available, as are 1-inch squares in sheets measuring 12 inches square or 12x24 inches, making them as easy to install as the larger sizes. The two types of ceramic tile most commonly used on kitchen floors are *red-body* and *porcelain* tiles. Red-body tile is made from red clay, which is refined and fired at high temperature to achieve hardness. They come both glazed and unglazed, in a variety of colors. Scott Broney of American Olean, tile manufacturers, cautions that a glaze with a high gloss could show scratches. The high-gloss tiles are best as accents, not for an entire floor.

Unglazed terra cotta is a more uniform leather color but must be sealed; even then, some staining is unavoidable. Over time the stains just add to the character. The look of terra cotta is particularly suited to an in-door-outdoor space, where rooms lead onto a garden or patio. Because I have lived in Provence, terra cotta has a special place in my heart.

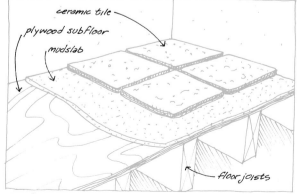

ceramic tile

plywood subfloor

mudslab

floor joists

Mortar Bed Method

Porcelain tiles are made from a refined and very dense clay. They are smooth and shiny with a consistent color all the way through from face to back. They get their shiny surface from a polishing process rather than from a glaze, which makes them fairly easy to care for. Porcelain tiles are also available with a matte surface.

A third kind of ceramic tile, *white-body*, is vulnerable to scratches and tends to be slippery, so it's rarely installed on the kitchen floor except as accent. In general, unglazed, low-glazed, and irregularly surfaced tiles show the effects of wear less than shiny, smooth tile. (Further discussion of ceramic tile appears in chapter 12.)

Installing Tile

Tile must be set on a very stable subsurface because any movement in the floor will cause cracks in the grout. While a concrete slab will have no deflection, a typical wood frame floor is bound to have a bit. One way to reduce the chances of the grout cracking is to put a layer of $5/8$-inch plywood on top of the subfloor. For greater stability, this layer should be laid at right angles to the subfloor and secured with construction adhesive and closely spaced screws or ring-shank nails. One-eighth-inch gaps should be left between the plywood, creating expansion joints to accommodate some movement.

There are several methods for actually setting the tile. Perhaps the most common is the *thin-set method*, which calls for spreading a thin coat of mortar on the plywood or concrete substrate, into which the tiles are set. A stronger but more difficult technique is the *mortar-bed method*, which calls for laying a $1^{1}/_{4}$-inch to 2-inch-thick bed of mortar over the substrate and forcing the tiles into it. A third method entails the application of mastic over the substrate, to which the backs of the tiles adhere. Our experience has been that tiles installed this way sometimes come loose; we prefer the mortar-bed or thin-set method. Often in a rehab, your only choice is the thin-set method, as the thickness of the mortar-bed may be too great for the heights of door openings and adjacent floors. (For more on tile setting methods see chapter 12.)

The most troublesome element in a tile job is the grout. A tiled kitchen floor will be regularly exposed to dirt and water, so a first-quality stain- and water-resistant grout, such as epoxy grout, should be used. But although it resists staining, epoxy grout darkens over time. Cement grout is less expensive, will not darken, but *will* stain unless protected by periodic applications of sealer. The grout color is also critical, especially white, which is the hardest to keep clean.

But consider that it's not the nature of a tile floor to look pristine. If you don't like the thought of the tile or the grout turning dark as time goes by, you should probably rule out tile as a flooring material.

As for routine maintenance, a tile floor needs frequent sweeping and damp-mopping to avoid excessive scratching of the tile faces. To wash the floor, ordinary household cleaners are recommended.

Red clay, quarry tile is another possibility for the kitchen. It is available glazed, but is most often left unglazed for a soft, rustic look. The unglazed tile will absorb oils and gradually darken, taking on the character of old leather.

Another choice is Mexican Saltillo terra-cotta tile. These are big tiles, 12 or 16 inches across, available in both squares and hexagons. Saltillo tiles are sun-baked rather than fired in a kiln, which gives them a wonderfully funky look. We used Saltillo tiles on the first floor of the Concord barn project to stunning effect. Some of the tiles even bore the paw prints of peripatetic dogs, which just added to their (the tiles', not the dogs') character.

These tiles are available unglazed, glazed, and sealed with an epoxy sealer. Like other types of terra cotta, Saltillo will stain if left unsealed. In Santa Fe, where we did our adobe rehab, Saltillo is extremely popular. John Wolf, our contractor for that project, used them in his own and many of his customers' homes. John recommends Saltillo be sealed with a 50-50 mixture of raw linseed oil and mineral spirits. It should be applied in several thin coats until it begins to pool on top of the tiles. Any excess should be wiped off immediately. John has tried a variety of sealers on Saltillo, including products by Minwax, Johnson Wax, Stone Glamor, Mex Seal, and Floor and Gym. Still, he prefers the rich look of the linseed oil–mineral spirits mix.

Being unfired, Saltillo tile is soft and will mar and chip. Even if sealed, it will most likely stain and darken with age. But if there is one floor surface that actually improves with age and blemishes, it is Saltillo. If it gets intolerably marred, Saltillo is soft enough that it can be sanded down with a floor sander and resealed.

Other Possibilities

A number of other masonry and stone products can also be used for a distinctive kitchen floor.

Recently Italian tilemakers have begun producing glazed ceramic tiles that have the look and warmth of terra cotta but are stain resistant and easily washed with a sponge mop.

Slate is cold, hard, durable, and elegant. It has the same positive and negative qualities as tile, but because of its dark color shows dirt, dust, and scratches. Unlike marble, slate is reasonably stain resistant, although still up there in the price range.

Marble is beautiful, rich, and warm in appearance. It is the hallmark of elegance. Marble is expensive, stains easily, and in some areas of the country just finding a tile setter willing to work with it

Slate is cool, elegant, and sophisticated. Tiles are available either honed smooth or with their natural texture, or cleft. Not all sealers leave the stone this glossy.

(Above) Glazed terra-cotta tiles come in variations of color, from light to dark rust. They are highly stain resistant. Note the hand-painted tiles on the walls and ventilation hood. Counters are laminate, the wood trim oak.

(Right) The bluestone floor of this country kitchen is rough cut and casually laid.

(Top) This beautifully patterned floor is made of terrazzo. Molds are laid on the subfloor into which the terrazzo, a mixture of dyed concrete and marble aggregate, is poured, one mold for each color. After the floor has set up, it is ground smooth, polished, and sealed.

(Bottom) When "This Old House" remodeled an adobe house in the historic quarter of Santa Fe, New Mexico, we traveled to Ashfork, Arizona, to learn how flagstone is quarried. This stunning rose-hued stone was laid by artisan John T. Morris. Nowhere have we seen craftsmanship better than his. In any cold climate a tile, slate, or stone floor would be uncomfortably cool. But when laid over radiant floor heat, these surfaces are extremely comfortable to live with — so much so that in my next renovation I will go this route.

may be a problem. Recently, Mexico has begun exporting quite acceptable grades of inexpensive marble tiles, so check twice before you reject this material on the basis of price alone.

Several other possibilities are flat slabs of granite, bluestone, flagstone, brick, and even fieldstones. In Santa Fe, where masonry floors heated by underfloor hydronic heat are the norm rather than the exception, we saw some stunning flagstone and brick kitchen floors. We've never seen a bluestone, granite, or fieldstone kitchen floor, but we don't see any reason it wouldn't work. Certainly the rough surfaces of these materials might pose a mopping-up problem, but by experimenting with the array of sealers available today, you should be able to strike a balance between practicality and beauty.

Sealers

As we have mentioned, unglazed tile and stone should be sealed to prevent water penetration and to increase stain resistance. A mixture of equal parts of linseed oil and mineral spirits does a good job, but requires several thin coats. If applied too heavily and allowed to stand on the surface of the tile, it will form a gummy residue. Floors treated with this concoction should be resealed whenever it appears the coating is breaking down.

Epoxy sealers avoid the drawbacks of the linseed oil–mineral spirits mix. They are typically applied once, penetrate into the tile or stone, and dry to a tough, durable finish. However, epoxy sealers may darken the color of the floor unevenly or give it an "artificial" look.

Silicone sealants, similar to the compounds used to waterproof shoes and gloves, may also deepen the color of tile and stone, but in our experience they tend to do so evenly. These sealers more closely mimic the rich tones imparted to the floor by the linseed oil–mineral spirits mixture.

Oil-based sealers such as Val-Oil do a good job sealing the floor; they also deepen the color of the masonry, but do so evenly.

Before you select a sealer for your tile or stone — or allow your mason or tile setter to apply one — we recommend you test a variety of products on samples of your floor. Each product imparts a different color quality to the floor, and if you've gone to all the expense and trouble to lay tile or stone, you want it to look just right.

●

Equipping the Kitchen

Here is a simply designed, well-thought-out kitchen that is superbly — but not excessively — equipped. On the far wall is a dishwasher, wash-up sink with hot-water maker, microwave, trash compactor, and coffeemaker. The ash cabinets below and metal cabinets above hold everyday dishes. To the right is a bank of cold storage: the refrigerator farthest from camera holds everyday items, the freezers are in the middle. Refrigerators to the right hold long-term cold storage. The cooking area was isolated to discourage intrusions and given a vinyl floor for comfort and ease of cleaning. Note the use of a commercial gas cooktop with double residential electric ovens, the gas grill to the right of the cooktop, the ample, stainless-steel backsplash and hood, which also contains lighting. Both sinks have high curving spouts, making it easy to fill pots, single-action levers, and sprayers. Next to the sink in the foreground is another trash compactor. All counters are solid surfacing with integral sink bowls.

When I was a kid, I remember vividly the day my family got our first dishwasher. Even though it was a cumbersome affair that rolled about the kitchen on casters, drew its water from the kitchen faucet, and expelled its waste water into the sink, it seemed a truly exotic and futuristic machine. My mother loved the fact it relieved her of the drudgery of washing by hand; my brothers and I liked to try to open the door of the running machine fast enough to see the water swirling around inside.

These days, of course, a built-in dishwasher is standard equipment in all but the most budget-minded kitchens. A well-equipped kitchen will likely boast a trash compactor, microwave oven, garbage disposal, boiling water dispenser, built-in refrigerator, and a restaurant-type range. Because of the tremendous variety of kitchen appliances, and because the appliances have such a big impact on both the design and the ultimate functionality of the room, we at "This Old House" urge you to evaluate your choices carefully. Once installed, you tend to keep stoves, sinks, refrigerators, and garbage disposals a very long time — typically until the next renovation — so you want to buy appliances now that will still please and serve you ten years down the line. Select your appliances first on the basis of quality, functionality, and beauty and then on the basis of price. Even if you plan to sell your house in several years, you want to install high-quality, brand-name appliances that will reflect the quality of your home. It's often hard to adhere to this principle when the top-quality products sell at a premium, but in our experience, we've regretted being stuck with an inferior or inappropriate product.

The Proverbial Kitchen Sink

One of the first pieces of equipment you'll probably choose is the sink. Sinks are made in a number of materials, of which the most popular is porcelain-enameled cast iron. This material gives you a heavy, sturdy sink that can take a lot of hard use yet remain impressively glossy. Porcelain-enameled cast iron is available in traditional white as well as black, red, blue, almond, and other colors.

Porcelain has several drawbacks, one being that it can chip if struck by a heavy object, like a frying pan. The iron beneath will then rust. Another drawback is that the rim or lip surrounding the sink has a high profile, making it difficult to sweep crumbs or water on the counter directly into the sink.

Enameled steel closely resembles cast iron but is much thinner and may flex under pressure. When it does, pieces of enamel may pop off. Enameled steel is used mainly by speculative homebuilders because of its low price.

Stainless steel, like porcelain-enameled cast iron, is very durable. Because the lip on a stainless sink is low, water or debris on the counter can easily be swept into the sink. (Most sinks these days are *self-rimming*, which means that the lip sits on the edge of the surrounding countertop. Some sinks still require installation of a separate rim, covering the juncture of sink and countertop.)

Some people dislike stainless steel's cold appearance, but it is important to note that there are big differences between one alloy of stainless and another. The better sinks are constructed of an alloy containing more nickel, which gives the sink richer luster, a warmer color, better cleanability and resistance to spotting, and an ability to conceal scratches. Also, these sinks are made of a thicker gauge steel, making them quieter and sturdier than the cheaper sinks.

European companies such as Francke, Blanco, and Belinox and some American manufacturers, including Moen, offer a new kind of sink, referred to variously as quartz, silicate quartz, acrylic dispersion, or resin-impregnated ceramic. Whatever name is used, it refers to a composite material which contains quartz and plastic, giving the material both flexibility and chip resistance. These sinks usually have a smooth or textured finish on the bottom of the bowl and on a patterned nonslip drainboard. The texturing prevents dishes from sliding, diffuses the impact from knives and other objects dropped into the sink, and helps to hide any cuts or dents.

Other sink materials include china (handsome, fragile, and expensive), fired ceramic, and solid surfacing such as Corian or Fabulon. These sinks can be bought as an *integral bowl,* molded seamlessly into a counter of the same material; as an *undermount,* attached to the counter from below; or as a *drop-in* sink, with the lip resting on the surrounding counter. Integral bowls tend to be shallow, so make sure the depth will be comfortable to work with and deep enough so that water doesn't splash outside the bowl. Solid surfacing is for folks with a fairly generous budget. (For discussion of solid surfacing as a counter material, see chapter 12.)

●

(Left top) **An old-fashioned butler's sink, of enameled cast iron, is nestled in a drainboard of well-oiled teak. The right side has been lifted to facilitate draining.**

(Right) **A solid surfacing counter with integrated sink. With no rim seal to collect water and grunge, cleanup is very easy. Around "This Old House," opinion about the "best" sink/countertop configuration is currently divided between solid surfacing with integrated bowl and stainless-steel with integrated bowl.**

(Left bottom) **Several serious cooks I've talked to rave about these three-bowl sinks fitted with cutting board and wire basket. The garbage disposal mounts to the center bowl. The hot water dispenser, soap pump, and sprayer speak of serious culinary intentions, but the television mounted just six inches above the sink? Come on, must be a manufacturer's photograph.**

Sinks come in a myriad of shapes and sizes. Some have one bowl, some two, and still others, three. Which is best depends largely on your work habits and the availability of counter space. Two bowls often work well, as long as at least one is large and deep. Even better, if budget and space allow, is two separate sinks, one in a preparation area and one in a wash-up area.

There are two other appliances to consider while discussing sinks. One is a dish-soap dispenser, which stores liquid soap in a well under the sink and squirts it out of a small pump-action spigot installed next to the faucet. I have used these handy devices in my last two kitchens and like the fact that they eliminate the unsightly soap bottle from the sink area.

The second appliance is a hot-water dispenser, which instantly supplies boiling water for tea, coffee, soup, and parboiling. The heated water is kept in a small tank beneath the sink. These units typically hold about a half gallon and can deliver about 60 cups of boiling water per hour.

The reason to consider your sink-side appliances now is that both the hot-water dispenser and the soap dispenser may install in one of the four predrilled, or precast holes in the sink rim. If you want one or both of these appliances as well as a spray nozzle, then you

Four-holed exposed fau-
cet with spray.

Ledge mounted com-
pression faucet.

Hi-arc three-hole.

Hi-arc swivel spout with
retractable hose.

might be limited in your choice of faucet. In our kitchen, my wife and I
wanted a soap dispenser, a spray nozzle, a high, curving spigot to
accommodate large pots and pans, and a single-lever faucet. We
also wanted everything finished in white epoxy. We satisfied these
requirements by using one of the integrated faucet and spray units
discussed below. With the increasing number of sink-installed appliances available, think through the best use of your sink-side real estate before you buy.

Faucets and Fittings

A tremendous number and variety of kitchen faucets have come on
the market in recent years, something for every taste and budget. The
easiest place to shop for faucets is a retail establishment where
knowledgeable salespeople can explain the pros and cons of each.
Usually this means a large kitchen and bath showroom or a plumbing supply house, although for standard types of faucets the local
home center may offer lower prices.

In choosing a faucet, quality and durability are the rules. The
quality of a faucet is determined to some extent by its materials. The
elements that carry the stream of water are commonly made of brass,
which resists corrosion. Typically, the brass core of the faucet is
plated with chrome, which is easy to clean and will stay shiny for
years. Many faucets are now available in an epoxy coating, which
is tough and smooth and comes in colors. Some brands are vulnerable to chipping when struck by a heavy object, such as a pot, while
other brands are more chip resistant, so it's worth inquiring about
durabililty.

Faucets use several different kinds of mechanisms to regulate
the water's flow. The oldest and most common type is known as a
compression faucet. A threaded metal stem rises as you turn the handle counterclockwise to allow the water to flow. When you turn the
handle clockwise, the stem descends and compresses a rubber

packing nut
packing ring

stem

seat washer
screw

Compression Faucet

Single lever, elongated spout.

Four-holed concealed faucet with spray.

Single lever with instant hot water and purification.

Swing spout one-hole.

washer against a seat, stopping the flow. This is a very simple mechanism, and compression faucets are low priced. The problem with them is that the washers wear out from being repeatedly squeezed, and the faucet then drips until the washer is replaced.

To avoid this maintenance headache, a number of varieties of "washerless" faucets have been developed. Many combine control of both hot and cold water in a single lever. One of Delta's washerless faucets has a single lever that swivels on a round base, inside of which are grommets and a plastic ball with holes in it, which regulate both the flow and the mix of hot and cold water.

Another kind of single-lever faucet, produced since the mid-1960s by Moen, has a cartridge that regulates the water flow. The mechanism is durable, and if the cartridge does go bad, it can easily be replaced. For homes with wells, the design is available in Bakelite plastic, which stands up better to acidic and alkaline water. Other manufacturers, including Kohler and Price-Pfister, make faucets with similar controls.

The top of the line in cartridge faucets (both for single-lever and two-handed faucets) uses *ceramic disk valves* to regulate the flow and temperature. Harden, American Standard, and the Swiss firm KWC offer faucets of this kind in their product lines. Ceramic disks are tough and can be expected to perform for many years without maintenance or failure. Some of these faucets feature built-in temperature and flow resistors, which limit the maximum temperature and volume of water. Considering these features, it is no surprise that ceramic-disk faucets are the most expensive on the market.

A kitchen faucet gets frequent, hard use, and a breakdown of this vital device can cause kitchen operations to grind to a halt. Fortunately, most of the brand-name faucets are very reliable, but it is worth inquiring about this before you buy. Plumbers are generally a good source for this information because they are the ones who end up fixing all brand names and have no particular ax to grind, as

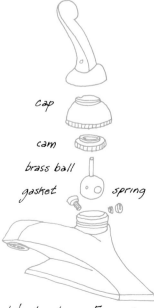

cap

cam

brass ball

gasket   spring

Washerless Faucet

Two bowls, disposer bowl and side drain.

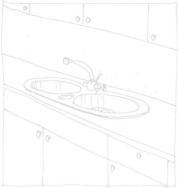

Two equal-shaped bowls.

Double corner sink.

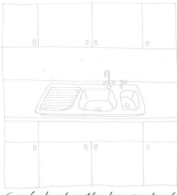

Single bowl with disposer bowl and side drain.

Single bowl with disposer compartment.

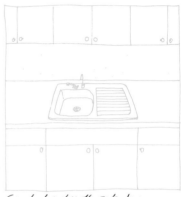

Single bowl with side drain.

Single bowl.

Two bowls with disposer bowl and dishrack accessory.

Two bowls with cutting board accessory.

Three bowl corner type.

Two bowls with side drain and dishrack accessory.

Single bowl with disposer bowl.

A garbage chute installed next to the chopping board lets peelings drop into their own waste receptacle, where they can be added to the compost pile or tossed into the garbage. Wonderful idea, beautiful execution — but you have to ask yourself how easy will it be to clean?

might be in the case in a showroom, in which the salesperson is pushing a particular brand or brands. Also worth asking your plumber is whether parts for your prospective faucet will likely be available several years hence, because parts from different manufacturers or even different models by the same manufacturer are not interchangeable.

Although most faucets require no maintenance, many are equipped with a wire mesh aerator, which traps particles in the water supply. The aerator is merely threaded into the end of the spigot and should be removed from time to time and cleaned.

Configuration of the Faucet

The configuration of your kitchen faucet — tall or short spigot, single lever or two knobs, integrated or separate spray — is entirely a matter of your personal preference.

For straightforward practicality, we prefer a tall, curved spigot, which makes for easier filling and cleaning of tall pots, and a single-lever valve for one-handed operation. We also like a separate pull-out plastic hose for washing bulky roasting pans and other objects that won't fit under the spigot. Recently, European manufacturers have introduced faucets in which the pull-out hose and spray are integrated into the faucet head. These are particularly handy if you want a clean, minimalist look to your sink area, or, as in my own case, you want more sink-mounted devices than there are holes in the sink rim.

Garbage Disposers

It is extremely convenient to have a garbage disposer installed in the sink, which explains why it is a nearly ubiquitous kitchen appliance. There are two general types. One is a *batch-feed* disposer, which is switched on and off by a cover plate inserted into the opening. If you have concerns about small children getting hurt by a garbage disposer, or if placing a switch is problematic, this is the type to install. Certainly it solves the problem of silverware falling into a running disposer.

If you have neither of these concerns, we recommend a *continuous feed* disposer activated by a wall switch. You can run it as long as you want, processing a continuous stream of garbage without the bother of stopping to cover or uncover it.

Garbage disposers are powerful little machines. They can shake a sink made of a thin-gauge stainless steel. The reverberations are especially annoying when a cheap, uninsulated metal sink is teamed up with a bottom-of-the-line garbage disposer. The better disposers are sound insulated, have stainless-steel interior parts, and are designed to avoid jamming. If you do a lot of cooking, or if you plan to live in your house for many years, do not try to save a few dollars by buying a cheap garbage disposer; a high-quality unit will serve you for many years.

Those who cannot install a disposer may be interested in a sink (such as that made by Blanco of Germany) with a built-in waste-disposal chute. You remove a cover and drop scraps and cuttings into a garbage bin below. This feature may be especially handy if you prefer to compost your food scraps instead of adding them to the waste that must be processed by the already burdened municipal sewerage plants.

Refrigerators

It goes without saying that a good refrigerator is an essential part of an efficient and satisfying kitchen. These factors can help you identify the refrigerator best suited to your needs and budget.

Storage Capacity

The first thing you have to look at is the size of the refrigerator. Don't be fooled by gross interior volume. The organization of the space is just as important as the amount. Shelves should be easily adjustable in the interior and on the door, and there should be provision for eggs, butter, cold cuts, and fresh fruits and vegetables. Also keep in mind that the more the space is cut up with individual compartments, the less room you have for groceries.

The unit should be matched to your particular needs. If you do a lot of freezing, for instance, you will want a big, conveniently located freezer. If you cook with a lot of fresh vegetables, you'll want ample storage for them, perhaps at the expense of freezer space.

You will also want to consider the configuration of the unit: side-by-side; freezer on top, fridge below; or fridge on top, freezer below. The side-by-side looks great in the design magazines, but consider that the long, narrow refrigerator and freezer spaces are the least efficient in terms of practical storage. The freezer on top, refrigerator on bottom solves this problem, but it places the refrigerator down low where you have to stoop to reach in. For most families' needs, we feel the best configuration is the refrigerator on top accessed by a single door (which provides maximum storage on the shelves) and a pull out, drawer-type freezer compartment below. A split door reduces the room required in front of the refrigerator for the door swing, but also reduces the practical storage on the shelves.

Energy Efficiency

Refrigerators carry easy-to-understand stickers grading them for energy efficiency and comparing their electricity consumption to that of

Designed for entertaining large groups with the assistance of a caterer, this professional kitchen has it all: stainless steel throughout (note the countertop); a full bank of restaurant cooking equipment — griddle, range, grill, and ovens; marble top on the island for baking; glass rack above the sink for crystal; and glass doors on the refrigerator so the contents are easy to see and get at. This kitchen reminds me of the engine room of a German luxury yacht — exquisitely designed and flawlessly engineered.

(Above) My great-aunt, "Auntie Daint," had a '54 Cadillac DeVille and one of these refrigerators. Now, I wish I had both. A fresh coat of taxicab yellow paint gave this old reliable a facelift, while the chrome refrigerator was designated for pantry use. You'll notice this is the back side of the kitchen in the illustration on page 144.

(Left) Although she is a professional cook and food writer, Nina Simonds did not feel a commercial refrigerator was necessary. She painted a mid-price, double-door fridge shiny black, and slid it into a pantry cabinet. The electric range is for testing recipes. On the other side of the kitchen is a commercial gas range.

the most and least efficient refrigerators in their class. Despite the extra electrical consumption, you may want automatic defrosting, an automatic ice cube maker, cold-water dispenser (both of which require a small water line to the refrigerator), or other features such as a through-the-door ice cube dispenser. This feature may even save electricity if it eliminates frequent opening of the freezer door.

Ease of Use

In most instances, the refrigerator door should open away from a counter, so that you can easily transfer things in and out. Some refrigerators have reversible doors. If the freezer compartment is on the bottom, a roll-out bin rather than a conventional door makes it easier to find things and helps limit the volume of warm air entering the freezer.

Temperature Control

Wanda Olson of the Department of Design, Housing, and Apparel at the University of Minnesota says a freezer compartment at 15° (the temperature some freezers maintain) will not keep frozen food at its best quality for the maximum recommended storage time. A freezer section that can achieve zero to 8° is better. Temperatures of 33° to 38° are needed in the refrigerator's fresh-food section. Some refrigerators offer separate temperature and humidity control for compartments holding fruits, vegetables, and meats.

Appearance

Because the refrigerator is one of the most prominent appliances in the kitchen, you will want to consider its appearance. The standard refrigerator is about 30 inches deep, making it project into the room half a foot past the cabinets and counters. One scheme to make the refrigerator less intrusive, which we tried at our Concord, Massachusetts, barn rehab, is to simply provide for an additional recess behind the refrigerator (or alternately build the cabinets extra deep) so that the front of the refrigerator is flush with the cabinets.

More expensive refrigerators, manufactured by Sub Zero and General Electric, are 24 inches deep and designed to be permanently installed in a bank of cabinets. These units come with unfinished doors into which the cabinetmaker can insert a panel to match the cabinets. These units feature two compressors, one for the refrigerator and another for the freezer, which are top-mounted both for appearance and energy efficiency (the hot air from the compressors rises up and away from the cooled storage compartments). The internal space of these units is very well organized and easy to reach, and they are quiet running. As you would expect, there is a price for all these features; these refrigerators can cost twice as much as a standard one.

When Nina Simonds, a well-known Chinese chef, food

Professional ranges are now almost *de rigueur* for the serious kitchen renovation. The newest models are "zero clearance," meaning they can be installed next to combustible materials (the old ones could not), and have insulated oven handles — the old ones did not, and when the oven was on, the door could only be opened with a hot pad. The size, BTU output of the burners, overall functionality, and great looks of a professional range have to be balanced against the use you will put it to, the real estate it will command in your kitchen, and the hefty price tag — the high-end models cost what Volkswagens used to.

writer, and a friend of the show, recently renovated her kitchen, she could not see spending all that extra money on a fancy refrigerator. She bought a standard unit, had the doors painted jet black, and installed it in a special recess in a wall that also contains a large pantry cabinet, a broom closet, and a dispenser for bottled water. The refrigerator is flush with the surrounding cabinet fronts, the black door hides smudges and dirt, as well as contrasting handsomely with the cherry, maple, and oak that compose her casework, counters, and floors.

Ranges

The most cost-efficient answer to cooking needs is a freestanding range containing four burners on the top and one or two ovens below. At a sacrifice of some capacity, the oven can be equipped with a *self-cleaning* mechanism, which uses intense heat to burn deposits off the oven walls. Much less popular is *continuous cleaning*, which uses a lye-treated, textured coating, activated by the oven's heat, to combat grease and deposits. But a continuous-

Old stoves bear testimony to the sentiment "They don't make them like they used to." A circa 1920 estate range was the starting point for the design of this Art Deco kitchen. The curved hood plays up the lines of the stove, while the glass-front, tile-topped cabinets on either side maintain a traditional feel. The pendant light is a halogen.

cleaning oven never really looks clean, and the surface is easily damaged by a scouring pad or other abrasive.

Restaurant ranges, very much in vogue these days, offer a larger number of burners with more power, large ovens, and built-in griddles. Most professional cooks prefer these ranges because they accommodate more pots and pans and put out much greater heat. Designers and many homeowners love their industrial look. In the past, restaurant ranges had many disadvantages: standing pilot lights that consumed fuel and kept the kitchen hot in the summer, uninsulated oven handles which could burn an unwary child, and uninsulated sides so the units could not be placed directly against either wall or cabinets. Now, however, manufacturers like Viking and Wolf offer residential versions of their commercial models, which feature electric burner ignition, insulated oven handles, and insulated side walls Some manufacturers even offer cooktop versions.

If you are a serious cook, especially of cuisines that require high temperatures, such as Chinese, Indonesian, and Cajun, you might seriously consider a restaurant range. They can get expen-

If you want six burners and a grill but do not have room for a commercial range, take a look at this cooktop, which sits inconspicuously on a solid-surfacing countertop.

sive — from $2,000 all the way up to $6,000 for the top-of-the-line, zero-clearance Viking! Also, being wider and deeper than conventional ranges, restaurant units command a great deal of kitchen real estate. Nina Simonds recommends a four-burner instead of a six-burner model, which both costs less and commands less space. This decision, like the one about which type of refrigerator to purchase, demands a cool, rational evaluation of your family's needs and budget.

Separate Cooktops and Ovens

The all-purpose range containing burners on top and a broiler and an oven or two below enjoyed a long reign in the kitchen. But increasingly these functions are being separated into independent appliances: a cooktop installed in the counter, and an oven or ovens located elsewhere. This division increases the cost, but provides a number of advantages. One is visual: A cooktop and a separate oven tend to look nicer than a range, and since the two units are each less bulky, you have more flexibility of design. Better ergonomics can also be achieved, since the oven can be placed at whatever height you find most comfortable. A shelf-mounted cooktop, open beneath, could easily be used by a person in a wheelchair.

With the cooktop independent of the oven, it becomes a straightforward matter to use different fuels for each. For the oven,

Solid disk elements are made from cast iron and are sealed into their mounts so drips won't run inside. Sensors in the center of the front disks monitor the actual temperature of the utensil and automatically adjust the heat to stay at the selected setting. The rear disks are equipped with temperature limiters that reduce the heat if a pot or pan boils dry.

most cooks prefer electricity because the temperature is more even and the self-cleaning feature more effective. For the cooktop, natural gas is the fuel of choice because the burner heat can be instantly adjusted and one can gauge the intensity simply by watching the flame. Also, gas cooktop burners last indefinitely whereas electric burners will wear out.

Gas Burners

Burners on a conventional gas range generate about 9,000 BTUs. A restaurant-style burner may generate 15,000 BTUs, bringing water to a boil faster and improving the performance of a wok, which requires high heat to sear meats and vegetables quickly. Many cooktops feature burners of different BTU ratings to accommodate a cook's varied needs.

Electric Coils

These have been around for many years and still rank among the best burners powered by electricity. They transfer their heat to the pots and pans fairly well and, when turned on, their cherry red glow warns of danger, which is useful especially in a home with young children. Electric coils are attractively priced.

Solid Disks

These cast-iron electric elements look nicer than coils, and because they merge neatly into the cooktop surface they simplify cleaning. But disks are slow to heat up and cool down, which is a major drawback, and their failure to turn red when hot could result in some burnt fingers. Some cooks are disappointed to discover that their old pans, which worked fine on conventional electric coils, are not sufficiently flat-bottomed for good heat transfer from disks. Some disks have thermostatic controls that sense the temperature of the pan bottom. Disks also discolor over time, and, according to some users, do not produce sufficiently intense heat for sautéing.

Glass Ceramic Elements

Electric resistance coils beneath the smooth glass ceramic top provide the heat in these elements. Pots and pans must be very flat bottomed or they will not perform adequately. The yellowing once characteristic of glass ceramic tops has reportedly been eliminated in new models, which also provide more heat per watt of electricity than did the originals. They are still slow to heat up, and some glass tops become marred by spills on the burner areas.

Halogen Elements

These, too, use electricity to generate heat from beneath a smooth glass ceramic cooktop. As the electrical current passes through the element, the halogen radiates warmth much the same as an incandescent light bulb. Turn on the burner and it immediately glows red,

A glass ceramic element is another cooktop that lends itself to sleek design. The drawback is relatively slow heat-up time. Here the owner has installed a two-burner halogen cooktop (under the teapot) to compensate.

like neon, and starts to heat up. Halogen is slower heating than the best conventional electric coils, but much faster than the glass ceramic elements.

Ovens

Conventional ovens do their cooking mainly with *radiant heat.* As the bottom, top, and sides of the oven become hot, they radiate warmth into the food. *Convection* ovens circulate the hot air with a fan, so the heat penetrates the food faster, which in most instances reduces cooking time and keeps the food more moist.

At the top of the price scale are ovens that let the cook choose among two or more cooking methods: radiant baking, convection baking, and even microwave cooking. In the fanciest of kitchens, where a great deal of baking is done, some homeowners go so far as to buy appliances like the British-made AGA stove, a versatile, enameled behemoth that has a couple of griddles on top and two to four ovens below, heated all the time, each at a different temperature. The bigger AGA models weigh more than *half a ton.*

●

When choosing an oven, consider whether you need double ovens or can do with one. Some models are available as double ovens, often with one of the ovens a combination microwave, convection, and conventional. Double units are also available with small bread ovens

These homeowners installed working 1927 appliances into their 1887 house. They tore up three layers of linoleum to reveal the original flooring, and repainted with an old-timey color scheme. The soapstone sink is original to the house, as are the walk-in food and butler's pantries.

instead of a second, full-sized oven. When evaluating your options, don't forget to check the interior dimensions of the ovens. Some units are too small to accept a standard roasting pan or cookie sheet.

●

Microwave ovens are now nearly indispensable. Some people just use them for defrosting frozen soups, making popcorn, and reheating Chinese takeout, while others use them for actual meal preparation. We've seen accomplished cooks who precook various dishes for a meal, leaving them just a bit underdone. A brief period in the microwave completes the cooking so that all the meal's courses are ready at once.

Microwave ovens are really not "ovens" at all. Microwaves are extremely high-frequency radio waves that penetrate deep into the food, exciting the water molecules such that they generate heat. It is this heat that cooks the food.

Power and performance of microwave ovens vary considerably from model to model, so comparison shopping is a good idea. In

An induction burner heats utensils by magnetic friction rather than heat conduction, so the burner itself stays relatively cool. Burner response time is very fast and the cooktops can be covered with glass and thus easily cleaned. Cookware must be cast iron or steel, and have flat bottom surfaces.

general, the microwave ovens with the most power are the most useful. Mastering the microwave can be tricky, but there are plenty of guides to cooking with them successfully.

Since microwave ovens are bulky and somewhat ugly, do not neglect to incorporate a place for one into your design — you will need to provide cabinet space along with an electrical outlet, preferably on its own circuit. Placement of the microwave should reflect how you use the appliance. If it is used primarily for heating snacks (I use mine mostly for heating the milk for *café au lait*), then you might place it next to the refrigerator. If the microwave is a main-line cooking tool, then you might want it next to the regular oven or elsewhere in the cooking area.

Dishwashers

It is no longer true, as it was with that first machine my parents bought, that you must prewash every dish before it goes into the dishwasher. Rather, it depends on how good (and usually how expensive) the dishwasher is. Ordinary dishwashers have just one wash arm, so dishes have to be prerinsed. Lacking a soft-food disposer, the dishwasher may redeposit food particles on dishes and glasses. Somewhat better (and more expensive) dishwashers have two wash arms or one multilevel wash arm, and a filtering system to strain food particles out of the wash water, eliminating the need for prerinsing. Still better (and more expensive) models can even clean dirty pots and pans without rinsing. These models may also be quieter. A few models feature a built-in water softener that uses rock salt to eliminate spotting on glasses.

As the price goes up, so does the manufacturer's attention to appearance. The more expensive machines can be fitted with a front panel that matches the cabinetry. The toekick, too, is adjustable to line up neatly with the cabinets.

My wife was complaining about the noise and long cycle time of our dishwasher to Jock Gifford, who designs many of our "This Old House" projects. He suggested we consider a commercial dishwasher, which will blast a load of dishes clean in under *three* minutes. Even though they have no internal dryer, the water temperature is so high that the water evaporates from the dishes in just minutes.

Commercial dishwashers are available in under-the-counter sizes which are the same dimensions as domestic units: 34½ inches high by 24 inches wide by 24 inches deep. Those offered by Hobart are all stainless steel, and some models are equipped with an internal water heater, which boosts the wash-water temperature to 180°, sterilizing everything. (The water heater requires 220 volts, and because of the high-temperature water, Hobart recommends that you install a stainless-steel sheet underneath the counter substrate to prevent condensation from penetrating the plywood or particleboard.) These units are truly industrial strength, having been designed for the rigorous demands of fast-food restaurants. They are extremely reliable, can withstand many years of use, and have a price tag to match: they list from $2,500 to $3,100, almost ten times the cost of a standard domestic dishwasher!

Trash Compactors

Trash compactors are great at reducing the sheer volume of trash, even though they require the purchase of special bags. Odors can

If you are serious about wine storage, a dedicated refrigerator assures careful temperature control for your wine futures. This unit above has individual climate-controlled upper and lower cases, one for aging red (temperature kept at 52°–59°), the other for serving whites. Correct levels of humidity are maintained to prevent corks from drying out. Smoked glass doors increase ultraviolet protection. Extravagant? Perhaps, but the unit is still cheaper than digging a wine cellar.

But then again, maybe not as much fun as the cellar to the left, accessed via the hatch. If you have the room beneath your kitchen, a renovation is a good time to design a special place for wine.

develop if you throw unwashed bottles and cans into them. The better compactors offer an antijamming design, easier bag removal, and a charcoal filter system for odor control.

I have found that ordinary heavy-duty plastic bags can be used in the trash compactor if you do not compact glass. This not only saves money on bags, but provides some incentive to recycle bottles and jars. This practice also controls odors without need for filtration systems.

Small Built-in Appliances

There is available a motorized apparatus that can be built into a countertop to run a mixer and other appliances. The device has been on the market for a long time, but most serious cooks reject it because it reduces usable counter space and limits them to using appliances from a single manufacturer. It is better, we think, to choose each hand appliance on its own merits.

How to Choose

In the last few years a tremendous variety of new appliances have come on the market. Your choices now range from high-styled German diswashers and ovens, to minimalist Scandinavian faucets, to Japanese compact refrigerators, in addition to all the well-known American brands. The design magazines incorporate these fancy appliances into their beautiful and alluring photographs, but do not be seduced by looks alone. To really know you are buying the best appliance for your particular application, read the magazines, look at advertisements, talk to salespeople in the showrooms, and then try to find people who own and use the particular ones you're interested in and listen carefully to their observations. Your kitchen is still basically a workshop, and the appliances are your tools. It is better to have good, sturdy, workmanlike, and serviceable tools than fancy ones that break, are difficult to use, or are expensive to service.

A classic butler's pantry in a country farmhouse holds the family treasures.

11 Storage: Cabinets and Pantries

Often the fatal flaw of an old kitchen is insufficient storage for the dry goods, pots and pans, small motorized appliances, and other *batterie de cuisine* we now consider essential to the process of meal preparation. Indeed, the key goal of many renovations is to provide more storage, and when many of these renovations are complete there is *still* not enough. Storage needs to be adequate in volume and functionality. As anyone who has ever cooked on a yacht knows, a small well-thought-through and well-organized kitchen is far easier to work in than a sprawling, poorly designed one. Storage problems that many people think are due to lack of space are in reality caused by lack of good design. In this chapter let's look at the considerations of storage: from design considerations for pantries to the design, construction, and choice of materials for cabinetry.

The Pantry

Before you start filling (in your mind's eye, anyway) your kitchen with expensive casework, consider the pantry. It was a necessity in nineteenth-century kitchens, and even today is far from being an anachronism. A pantry is a highly efficient, inexpensive way to store a great deal of stuff. Unlike casework, the only highly finished surface a pantry needs is a door, which can be an ordinary interior door at that. All you need inside is some sturdy shelving.

In some houses, a butler's pantry is used as a walk-through room connecting the kitchen to the dining room, and it can be elaborate indeed, with fine glass or wood cabinetry, high-quality countertops, even a small sink or refrigerator. A butler's pantry can be wonderful, if you have the space and budget, but the pantry we recommend is a small room that is not on display to guests and makes no contribution to the kitchen's decor.

In chapter 2 we discussed where to put the pantry. If at all possible, we recommend a pantry/mudroom located between the kitchen and an attached garage. Another possibility is a vestibulelike room between the kitchen and the door leading in from the driveway. In either location, the room reduces the distance you must carry heavy items such as soft drinks and canned goods.

A traditional butler's pantry was a place where serving dishes and food were organized to take into the dining room. Here, a hanging cabinet and marble-topped shelf create a serving island for this Victorian home.

The location of the pantry and the purpose it will serve must be closely coordinated. If the pantry is to be outside the kitchen's work triangle, it will probably function best as a place for storing things that aren't in constant demand. On the other hand, if it is meant to hold everyday supplies, it must be close to the food-preparation area. In all cases, the pantry should be *close* to the kitchen.

Some of the things stored in a pantry, such as apples, potatoes, onions, are best kept at relatively cool temperature, so we advise against heating the pantry, either purposely with warmth from a furnace, or inadvertently with waste heat given off by a refrigerator or freezer.

The floor of the pantry should be covered in a material that's easy to mop. The pantry itself should be rodent-proof and well lit. Even if it has a window (which does sacrifice some storage potential), you'll want good artificial lighting. We recommend a large fluorescent fixture in the ceiling.

Special metal bins inserted into the drawers add pantry storage space to under-counter cabinets.

You can build your pantry to any size and layout. Probably the most functional is a walk-in pantry equipped with shelves on every usable wall. In most circumstances, the shelves shouldn't be very deep (12 to 14 inches is sufficient) so that you can see everything at a glance. You shouldn't have to move cans and packages at the front of the shelves to see what is at the back. But some deeper shelves should be available to store large objects such as soup kettles, appliances, and so on. For maximum efficiency, shelves should extend from floor to ceiling. Additional compartments can be hung on the back of the door to hold small items.

Generally, 4 by 4 feet is the minimum workable size for a walk-in pantry. If the depth is greater than 4 feet, it's worth considering expanding the width as well. You need a floor 30 to 36 inches wide for comfort; this, combined with 12-inch shelving on each side, would bring the pantry's interior width to almost 5 feet. If a small space presents design problems, perhaps a long narrow space will solve some others. In a Japanese-style house built by Lee Davidson, a friend of the show, we saw a traditional Japanese storeroom, 6 feet wide by 20 feet long. This room functioned as a pantry as well as a storage area for cameras, luggage, and sports equipment. Located between the master bedroom and the kitchen, it was convenient to both, yet isolated the bedroom from the eating and food-preparation areas.

As years go by, your storage needs will change, so we recommend adjustable shelving for maximum flexibility. I use brackets and standards manufactured in England by Spur. They are rugged, good-looking, and come in many colors. For the shelf itself, I use 1x12-inch pine or laminate-covered plywood (whatever you choose should be easy to clean). The shelving should be supported along its length every 16 to 24 inches; if the span is greater, the shelving will sag.

Steelwork-grid shelving has become popular in recent years, and its price is competitive with other systems. The grid allows you readily to see objects on the shelves, and offers less surface on which dust and dirt can accumulate. But beware of the cheaper coated wire, which may chip, discolor, or get sticky. Although wire-grid systems are not adjustable, they are easy to install, even by those who don't consider themselves handy.

The critical requirement for any shelf system is to secure it to the studs. Builders sometimes attach wire shelving only to the gypsum-board walls, using toggle or molly bolts. Although this is what some of the wire-shelving manufacturers recommend, it's risky, especially in a pantry, where the shelves may be loaded heavily. To avoid their pulling out of the wall, secure the brackets or standards with screws directly to the wall studs.

Pantry Cabinet

A space-saving alternative to a walk-in pantry is a pantry cabinet that extends from floor to ceiling with open shelves inside. This is typically a large, expensive unit, but many consider it worth the cost. I have one in my current kitchen. It measures 6 feet long by 7 feet high, is 12 inches deep, and is covered by six 12-inch-wide, full-height doors. This was custom built with the rest of the casework, but pantry units are available premade, and manufacturers offer a number of choices for outfitting the interior. One system has shelves 18 inches deep, augmented by shallow shelving on the back of the door. The only drawback to this arrangement is that if the shelves are stacked full, it might be difficult to see some of the items at the rear. A better arrangement might have narrow banks of shelves in the cabinet and shallow shelves on the back of the pantry door to pack a great deal of usable storage into the unit.

A sliding minipantry holds a great deal and is accessible from both sides.

The famous American naval architect John Alden is said to have asked his clients for a complete list of all their shipboard tools, spare parts, cooking equipment, and other gear before he designed the casework for their yachts. Before you decide on the final configuration of your pantry closet or room, it might be a good idea to think through your storage needs. This will help you determine the size of the pantry and shelves that will work best for you.

Yet another offshoot of the traditional pantry is a tall, sliding minipantry cabinet, which extends from floor to ceiling. Some cabinets are quite narrow, but by pulling out, like a drawer, present an assortment of canned or other goods within easy reach. While these cabinets are rarely as economical on a cubic-foot basis as the larger pantry units, they might be a good choice for a cook whose needs are limited, or who has to make do with a compact kitchen. Keep in mind that packaging is subject to fashion; your favorite canned goods might suddenly start to be manufactured in short, stout cans that don't fit in your unit's shelves. In any storage device, adjustability is worth looking for.

A variation of the pantry unit is to cover a whole wall with 12- or 16-inch-deep cabinets with adjustable shelves. If you have a short corridor between the kitchen and the dining room, for example, these cabinets could line one side of it, running from floor to ceiling to maximize the storage potential. Or, the lower cabinets could be separated from the uppers by a counter and a space tall enough to accommodate decorative items or serving dishes. Jack Cronin, who has built

This narrow kitchen had to accommodate a lot of storage, but without causing claustrophobia. All appliances were mounted below the counter, including an under-counter refrigerator, and closed storage on the working wall is way up high. This leaves all the eye-level surfaces open, creating an illusion of spaciousness.

many of the cabinets for "This Old House," suggests that 16-inch-deep base cabinets and 12-inch-deep uppers make pleasing proportions, similar to those of a hutch, and the counter is still deep enough to be useful. This configuration also keeps the storage wall from appearing too monolithic. A corridor storage wall works best when the hall is fairly wide. After installation of the cabinets, the aisle should be at least 36 inches wide to avoid crowding when one person walks through while another is opening a cabinet.

While thinking about storage, also consider whether everything needs to be placed out of sight. A large pot rack hanging over a counter can free up a great deal of cabinet space while giving the kitchen a country flair. Don't forget, professional cooks keep all their utensils in plain sight, readily at hand.

In summary, it's best to think in terms of usable, convenient storage that fits your space and your budget.

Cabinet Strategies for a Limited Budget

In general you will get your best value for dollar by buying stock cabinets. But in that category you can still stretch your renovation dollars to their utmost by considering the following tips from Glenn Berger.

- Fill the space with fewer, larger cabinet units. The cost of cabinets is related to the size of the units — an 8-foot run made up of four 2-foot carcasses will cost far more than a run of two 4-foot units. Also, fewer units will keep installation costs down.
- Buy lower-priced cabinetry — do you really need dovetailed drawers or all of the accessories available? Spend a little more for a really good-looking countertop.
- Add accessories as you can afford them. Most of the pull-out trash bins, tray storage, and silverware containers available for cabinets today are modular, that is, they will fit many cabinets. Buy your cabinets without these and add them over time.
- Purchase high-quality cabinetry, but leave out pieces that can be added later, for instance some of the upper cabinets or a pantry unit in a far corner.
- Often the best way to save money is to hire a kitchen designer or architect. These design professionals will help you focus on the real problems in your kitchen, often recovering their fee. A good design conserves both space and dollars.

Choosing Cabinets: Custom Versus Stock

Regardless of whether your kitchen has a pantry, you will undoubtedly need cabinets, but what kind? You'll find that your first choice is between *stock cabinets,* mass-produced in a factory, and *custom cabinets,* which are hand-built for a particular kitchen. The biggest difference between the two is the range of choices available. To make mass production possible, stock manufacturers limit their production to the most popular sizes, finishes, colors, and features. They will probably offer cabinets with doors faced in oak — the most popular wood in American kitchens — and perhaps in a few other species, such as maple or hickory, but to get a less-common species, such as walnut or butternut, you may have to go to a custom cabinetmaker.

Many stock cabinets are available surfaced in high-pressure laminate such as Formica or Wilsonart. This provides a smooth, easy-to-clean surface that resists damage from blows and abrasions. Stock cabinets are available in a few of the popular colors, whereas custom shops offer a broad selection of colors. As a rule, stock cabinets are less expensive than custom, although some of the highest-quality stock cabinets sell for the same as custom. If you're on a tight budget, stock cabinets help you keep it. (I should note that for my laminate cabinets, I use a commercial cabinetmaker who builds for department stores, hospitals, and boutiques. His operation is so efficient that he can offer his product at the same or even slightly lower cost than average-quality stock cabinets. Perhaps there is such a shop in your area.)

Special collections of kitchen equipment are easier to use — and fun to look at — when put on display. This baker designed a special glass-fronted pantry to house her collection of small molds and baking utensils. When my wife, an avid baker, saw it, she said with great seriousness: "I want you to make me one. Perhaps, you know, as an anniversary present."

In addition to being attractively priced, stock cabinets are available quickly. Retailers such as home-improvement centers, lumberyards, and kitchen dealers either have the cabinets on hand or can deliver within a week or two from a warehouse or factory.

Stock cabinets are usually manufactured in these standard dimensions:

- Base cabinets: 24 inches deep by 34½ inches high. A 1½-inch-thick countertop will bring the counter to a height of 36 inches.
- Wall cabinets: 12 inches deep by 30 inches high. A smaller number of wall cabinets are available 12 inches deep by 42 inches high. This height is specified if you want your cabinets to abut an 8-foot ceiling or close the gap to an even higher ceiling. There are shorter wall cabinets for use above refrigerators, ranges, and other appliances.
- Base and wall cabinets are sized in 3-inch increments. For example, you can get a cabinet 36 or 39 inches wide, but not 37 inches. Since stock cabinets may not fit your kitchen exactly, strips of wood, known as fillers, are used to stretch out a group of cabinets.

Shopping for custom cabinets is a little different. Home-improvement centers and lumberyards are seldom a source; kitchen design stores usually are. Typically, the store's in-house designer collects your measurements, designs the cabinets, and orders them from a large factory. There are also a number of small custom cabinet shops and even skilled carpenters who will build cabinets.

A custom cabinetmaker can tailor the casework to the dimensions of your room and your particular needs and tastes. For example, nearly every stock base cabinet is made with one drawer at the top, which may result in too many drawers scattered around the kitchen. Custom casework can be configured any way you prefer.

If you want counters lower than normal, the custom shop can oblige. The lowest possible counter height, if a dishwasher or garbage disposal will be installed beneath the counter, is 34½ inches to the *underside* of the countertop. Customers often want their counters higher than the customary 36-inch height, a standard established years ago when Americans were shorter. At "This Old House," we often build counters 37 inches high, which many people find more comfortable.

Similarly, custom wall cabinets can be built to whatever height is dictated by the proportions of the room. In a tall kitchen, standard 30-inch-high wall cabinets may look too small. A custom shop can build cabinets that extend to a soffit, to the ceiling, or to

some other elevation that seems appropriate. Taller cabinets may create better visual balance in the room, while boosting the kitchen's storage capacity.

Eighteen inches is the standard distance between the top of the kitchen counter and the bottom of the wall cabinets, but this is only a guideline, and a custom cabinetmaker will occasionally build to a different dimension. The Kennebec Company of Bath, Maine, which built the custom cabinetry for the Weatherbee Farm in West-wood, Massachusetts, generally prefers to place the wall cabinets slightly closer to the counter, and make the wall cabinets a little taller than standard. "We think 15 to 16 inches between counter and wall unit is adequate," says Kennebec's David Leonard. "Dropping the wall units slightly allows us to make taller, more aesthetically pleasing doors, minimal space is wasted, and children can reach the wall cabinets a little more easily."

In a small or oddly shaped room, custom cabinetry may be

Building custom cabinets means you can squeeze the maximum possible storage out of your kitchen space, even the dead space above the door to the garage. These lovely cabinet doors are of teak, as is the bullnose edge on the counters.

essential in order to obtain enough storage and to mask the shape of the room. Indeed, one of the great advantages of custom cabinetry is that it can seize every square inch of potential storage, while making an elegant design statement in the process.

Just as the height and width are completely flexible dimensions with custom cabinetry, so is depth. You can, for instance, order the cabinets along the refrigerator extra deep so that their fronts line up with it, giving the room a more unified look. The extra-deep interiors can be made accessible with roll-out shelves. If 12-inch-deep wall cabinets look out of balance above such hefty base units, order them 16 inches deep. The cost of these departures from the norm is minimal.

You can also reduce the depth of custom cabinets to solve particular design problems. In one of his projects, Jack Cronin had difficulty finding enough room for a dishwasher and a trash compactor along one wall. He reduced the depth of the base cabinets on an adjoining wall to 21 inches to find the necessary 3 inches for installing the appliances. These examples illustrate the flexibility of custom cabinetry.

From an aesthetic standpoint, there are at least two consistent differences between stock and custom cabinets. First, as we've discussed, custom cabinets are more precisely fitted to the room, giving the kitchen a more refined look. There is a visible line (actually a tiny gap) where each stock cabinet is joined to its neighbor. Custom cabinets can be built without such lines. How important these differences are, or whether they matter at all, depends on your personal preferences, the demands of your job, and the constraints of your budget.

As one would expect, working with a custom cabinetmaker involves more advanced planning. Glenn Berger, who provided casework for our Concord barn and our Jamaica Plain triple decker, can typically build cabinets in five to seven weeks, but there are always prior orders to be built first. "If you find a cabinetmaker who can do your kitchen immediately, that may be a red flag," Glenn warns. "Good cabinetmakers are in demand. At our shop, people usually wait six to eight weeks."

Though all custom cabinetmakers pride themselves on meeting each homeowner's individual needs, there are sizable differences between one shop and another. Big factories often offer a wide variety of materials and colors, while small shops might specialize in laminate-faced cabinets, or wood. Some shops, like Jack Cronin's, build wood cabinets in a number of traditional styles; others, like the Kennebec Company, concentrate on eighteenth- and nineteenth-

century Shaker styles. Still others, like Glenn Berger's, which is incorporating more computer design and manufacturing technology, will build anything in wood from Shaker to contemporary.

Each custom cabinetmaker has his own perspective on which materials to use. Cronin, for example, prefers hardwoods — oak, hickory, maple, cherry, mahogany, and others — but is willing to build in pine, which many cabinetmakers shy away from because it's easily gouged or dented. According to him: "Pine has a busy grain that makes the blemishes less noticeable. Imperfections aren't necessarily bad. In antique furniture, they're called 'distress marks' and are quite acceptable." A good cabinetmaker has a great deal of knowledge that you can call upon in making your decisions. If you haven't decided whether to go stock or custom, most cabinetmakers will take some time to explain the differences in construction and quality.

Custom cabinetmakers earn their pay, in large part, from their attention to aesthetics. Part of their job is to blend the cabinetry

(Right) These cherry cabinets have perforated stainless-steel fronts reminiscent of the old pie safes. Cabinet composition provides an opportunity to mix materials and establish the look of the kitchen.

(Left) Curly maple cabinets with granite counters produce a very elegant kitchen in this formal home.

into the kitchen as a whole. Where the cabinet stops at a window, for instance, he can provide transitional elements such as shelves for flowers or special objects. He can design moldings for bottom and top edges of wall cabinets, and even make curved wood transitions between counter and refrigerator.

●

There is a middle range of cabinetmakers who offer more individualization than stock cabinet manufacturers but less than a true custom shop. These producers, which the industry refers to as "semi-custom" cabinetmakers, usually take orders through kitchen dealers.

Yet another source for your cabinets is a skilled carpenter, but it's difficult to predict how satisfactory working with him will be. One couple we know hired a local carpenter to build pine cabinets for their kitchen and had a very enjoyable time of it. They wanted to save money, so he gave them the job of staining the cabinets. They enjoyed making a satisfying and money-saving contribution to their project, and the carpenter avoided the part of the task he disliked. Everyone contributed ideas as the project went along. When a boxed-in pipe chase for the second-floor bathroom seemed to render a vital corner useless for storage, the carpenter and couple together designed a small medicine cabinet to disguise the chase.

Responding quickly and imaginatively to such unusual situations is one of the advantages of working with a skilled carpenter, but there may be drawbacks too. A carpenter may have less experience building cabinets than a cabinet shop and may lack the specialized tools required to build high-quality casework. Know your man (or woman), his work, and his reputation before you sign him on.

Construction Methods: Face Frame Versus Frameless

There are two basic methods of cabinet construction: face frame and frameless, also called European style. Both methods begin with the fabrication of the storage compartments, or carcasses, usually out of particleboard or plywood. The difference between the methods lies in the way the front face of the carcass is trimmed out. In face frame construction, which has long prevailed in the United States, a rectangular frame is attached to the carcass, which helps to strengthen it and provides a mounting point for the cabinet doors. After the cabinet doors and drawers are installed, you can still see a portion of the frame, which gives these cabinets a rustic, early American look. In frameless construction, the cabinet doors cover the entire carcass, giving European cabinets a sleek, seamless appearance.

European manufacturers now export their casework to the United States and as the style gains popularity, many American shops are building it. Since frameless is faster and simpler to build, some American manufacturers have ceased to build the face-frame style altogether.

Hinges

Face-frame cabinetry can employ either visible or concealed hinges. Frameless cabinetry requires concealed hinges to hold the doors straight and square, within a fraction of an inch of each other. Because the doors are continuous, any misalignment will catch the eye, so the hinges must be of the adjustable type. European-style doors must be realigned every couple of years, so a high-quality adjustable hinge will make it easier to do both the initial installation and to realign the doors later. Some concealed hinges come with detachable mounting plates, which allow easy removal of the doors prior to mounting the carcasses. Afterward, the doors can be quickly reinstalled. Another handy piece of hardware used by European cabinet

The oak doors of these visually demanding cabinets were finished with cobalt blue–tinted varnish and the carcasses lined with yellow laminate. Handpainted tiles in the same blue tie the casework to the solid surfacing countertop.

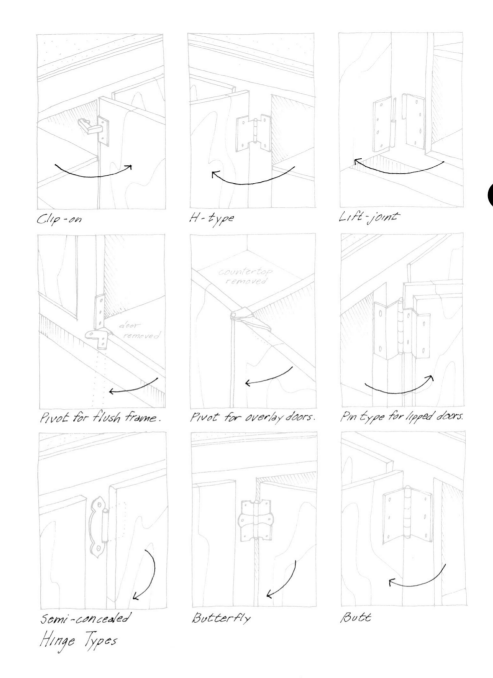

Clip-on   H-type   Lift-joint

Pivot for flush frame.   Pivot for overlay doors.   Pin type for lipped doors.

Semi-concealed   Butterfly   Butt
Hinge Types

manufacturers is an adjustable leg mounted on the bottom of the carcass, which eliminates the need for shims, or small, tapered strips of wood to level the base cabinets. Once leveled, a toekick molding is installed and the legs disappear from view.

The least expensive hinge allows the door to open only 90 degrees — perpendicular to the cabinet itself. Some people find this bothersome or even hazardous, as there's a possibility that a child might run into an open door. More expensive hinges open to 120 and 180 degrees.

Today many cabinetmakers value an uncluttered look so

highly that they conceal hardware even on face-frame cabinetry. This is accomplished with a wraparound hinge, which secures to the back of the door with a metal plate, and to the face and edge of the frame with an angle bracket. The wraparound hinge holds well and can be repositioned, if necessary, without detracting from the cabinet's appearance, for it remains out of sight behind the closed door.

Many older cabinets use magnetic catches to hold doors shut, but after a while, the catches get out of alignment and must be re-adjusted. We prefer hinges with a self-closing feature, a built-in tensioner that pulls the door shut once it gets within range of its closed position.

Materials and Quality

Wood Doors

In wooden cabinetry, the majority of the work lies in building the doors and face frame. Wood is a tricky material, since it expands and contracts with changes in temperature and humidity. Cabinet-makers employ a number of techniques to compensate for wood's liveliness. One is to construct the doors from narrow strips of wood glued together. Another is to make a door frame with four pieces of wood, forming the top, bottom, and sides, and let a center panel "float" within the frame. The inside eges of the frame are grooved or *rabbeted*, to accept the panel, which "floats" in the groove, freely expanding and contracting with the seasons and weather.

If you're buying stock cabinets with stained wooden raised-panel doors, make sure that the center panels were stained before the door was assembled. If they weren't, you may have an unwelcome surprise when the center panel contracts — an outline of unstained wood at the perimeter.

Veneer Doors

Another approach is to use wood veneer doors, which have a thin skin of the finish wood species over a core of plywood or particleboard. Veneer plywood is available in a variety of species, including oak, ash, birch, beech, and teak. Since the veneer is made by peeling thin layers of wood from a single log, the doors are very uniform in appearance, and since the structural core is plywood or particleboard, they resist warping and cupping with changes in temperature and humidity. Some people regard veneer as inferior to "real" wood.

What's unquestionably a poor value is a door of particleboard or fiberboard covered with paper or vinyl to simulate wood. Leaving aside the question of aesthetics, paper and vinyl are easily cut, scratched, and dented. Once damaged, it is impossible to restore the surface to its original appearance.

This handpainted case-work creates the sense of a collection of individual pieces of furniture assembled over time.

213

Most flat-panel all-wood doors are composed of laminated strips for stability. You can assess the quality of their construction by whether the color, tone, and grain of the wood are well-matched, both from lamination to lamination and from door to door. In high-quality work, the grain, tone, and color are consistent, whereas in low-quality work, there tends to be a lot of variation. Poorly matched wood can sometimes be given a dark stain to downplay the variations, but this assumes you don't mind a darker appearance. When shopping for stock cabinetry, check if the display models are matched well enough to please you. If so, ask if the retailer or manufacturer guarantees the cabinets you order will be equally well matched.

Some people contend that differences in grain and tone are part of the natural character of wood and should be accepted as such, but the eye is naturally drawn to contrasts, and sharp ones usually take away from the cabinetry's attractiveness. The best cabinetmakers match their wood so meticulously that the seams between one piece and another are hardly noticeable. Consistency is one of the standards by which cabinetry is judged.

High-Pressure Laminates

In Europe, where the supply of wood is more limited than in North America, plastic laminate has long been a well-accepted surface for cabinets. In recent years, it has caught on here as well. Laminate cleans easily but also requires more cleaning since it shows smudges more readily than wood. It can be given a wood or metal accent along the edges.

Doors surfaced in laminate usually have a core of particleboard or medium-density fiberboard (MDF). This makes the doors heavy, but since laminate cabinets are typically of European frameless design, they are hinged with recessed adjustable hinges which provide excellent support for the door. My own laminate cabinets have stood up to four years of constant use without a problem. Particleboard core is now the industry standard for laminate doors.

Medium-density fiberboard, made of finer sawdust particles and more binder, is smoother than particleboard, reducing the likelihood of the texture "telegraphing" through to the surface of the laminate. For this reason, it is often used beneath high-gloss laminate surfaces, which are most likely to show irregularities. Plywood has been used in many doors over the years, but Formica Corporation cautions against it, as it poses too great a risk of warping and telegraphing its grain through the laminate surface. Both fronts and backs of doors should be covered with laminate, for strength and to eliminate any tendency of the doors to twist or warp.

Sometimes a color-through laminate such as Colorcore is used for door panels. Since the surface color of this laminate is consistent through the depth of the material, its use avoids the dark brown lines where the interior of the laminate is exposed. It's expensive, though, and most people, myself included, don't consider it worth the extra cost. It is a great alternative for countertops, though, where the brown line really distracts the eye.

Lacquered Doors, Glass Doors, and "CAD" Doors
For elegant casework, a rich, deep, lacquered appearance can be achieved by applying a high-gloss polyester coating to the door's core material. The lacquered effect, once reserved only for very-high-end budgets, is becoming more affordable as more and more cabinet factories install automated fabrication equipment. Also in this category are multipaned glass doors and doors that have been given a raised-panel effect. These doors are made from a single piece of medium-density fiberboard rather than from many pieces of solid wood.

Both the cutouts for the glass and the raised-panel effect are created by a computer-driven router. As computer-aided design, computer-aided manufacturing, and computer-integrated manufacturing (CAD, CAM, and CIM) technologies are adapted by the cabinet industry, expect to see prices drop and variety and quality increase.

(Above) Butcher block deepens in color as it ages. It works well here with the white laminate cabinets and the brick floor.

(Right) Frosted glass allows you to see into the cabinets, but you don't have to be quite as meticulous about arranging the contents as with clear glass. In comparison to a solid door, frosted glass can lend a sense of depth to the room.

These steel cabinets give a crisp, airy feeling to a small city kitchen. Although the room is windowless, light bouncing off the shiny surfaces of metal and glass helps to liven up the space. Shelves inside the cabinets are adjustable.

Steel Cabinets

On the other end of the technology spectrum is yet another cabinet material — metal. Forty years ago, steel doors and cabinets were common, but no longer. One of the best-known manufacturers of metal cabinets is St. Charles Kitchens in Chesapeake, Virginia. They make rustproof cabinets insulated with wood slats for sound deadening, available with lacquered or stainless-steel finishes. The wall cabinets come with built-in fluorescent fixtures to illuminate counter surfaces. The units with glass doors are especially handsome.

Construction Quality

Inside the Cabinets

In most cabinetry today, the carcass is made of particleboard, which used to contain glues that gave off formaldehyde gas. It is our under-

An appliance garage is best made with a sliding, tamboured door. Electricity can be supplied by outlets in the back wall or by a wiremold raceway as shown here.

standing that most particleboard manufacturers have eliminated formaldehyde from their glues. But even a small volume of formaldehyde can bother some people, so you may want to take this into account. The National Kitchen Cabinet Association, an organization of manufacturers, has responded to this issue by requiring that its members give all the exposed interior surfaces of their cabinets at least one coat of a finish designed to eliminate or substantially reduce "outgassing." The blue seal of the association is displayed on cabinets that meet this standard.

In any case, all exposed particleboard inside your cabinetry should be sealed or surfaced. Some manufacturers line their boxes with self-adhesive vinyl, but this is easily damaged. Laminate makes a very durable liner, but to use it on all interior surfaces will run costs way up. Some cabinetmakers spray the interiors with lacquer or polyurethane paint that seals the wood, is durable, and is easy to clean.

Particleboard carcasses are assembled with glue and staples driven with a pneumatic staple gun. For greater strength, the bottoms of the carcasses should be fitted into *dadoes* or grooves cut in the sides. We've seen flimsy-looking clips in the corners of some inexpensive cabinets, which don't inspire much confidence. The strength of a particleboard carcass depends chiefly on the strength of its glue joints, so don't think you can buy a cheap cabinet and beef it up with additional screws and nails.

A superior, though more costly, material for building carcasses is plywood, preferably with a hardwood veneer such as maple or birch. Plywood is durable, holds fastenings well, resists damage from being banged by pots or pans, and the carcass interiors can be sealed with several coats of clear urethane or lacquer. Birch-veneer plywood is favored by cabinetmakers because of its subtle graining and neutral color. In custom cabinetry, specifying birch plywood instead of particleboard for carcasses and drawers will increase costs 15 to 20 percent.

Drawers and Accessories

Drawers are subject to rough treatment, so it's important that they be well built. Good drawers start with a solidly built compartment, which is then joined to a decorative drawer front. Cheap drawers eliminate the front wall of the compartment, joining the sides directly to the decorative front. Look also at the joints of the drawer boxes. Dovetail joints are a sign of premium construction; a glue-and-staple joint, lower quality.

Avoid drawers that operate on a single runner or glide because it will break or jam when the drawer gets pushed and pulled from different directions. A good drawer has two runners, and the

This is what I need, a spice drawer that holds up to fifty spices — all easy to identify and keep organized.

better ones have ball-bearing nylon rollers for smooth, quiet performance. Some runners are painted or epoxy-coated and a few expensive cabinetmakers even enclose the runner mechanisms in sleeves to protect them from dirt and make them less conspicuous when the drawer is open. The cheapest runners extend only a third of the way back the drawer, whereas high-quality runners extend along the entire length to provide more stability. A good runner is also equipped with a stop, which prevents the drawer from rolling all the way out of the cabinet.

Shelves

Adjustable shelves enhance the cabinet's flexibility. Typically, in stock frameless cabinetry shelves in both base and wall units are adjustable. In stock face-frame cabinetry, some cabinets have adjustable shelves and some don't. Wall cabinets with one door, for instance, are usually adjustable. If there are two doors, the shelves may be in fixed positions because they're providing structural support for the cabinet. Stock face-frame base cabinets tend to have fixed shelves. A custom cabinetmaker, of course, can equip any cabinet with adjustable shelves.

Pull-out Bins

Shelves or bins that roll out of base cabinets provide easier access to

(Above) Inside the cabinets, a hinged spice cabinet and door shelves increase the usable storage space.

(Below) Roll-out bins make everything more accessible — from pots and pans to trash and cleaning supplies.

things stored at the back, minimizing bending and searching. Using these may eliminate the need for a pantry cabinet.

Inside Corners

One of the hardest problems to solve is how to make best use of an inside corner. There are various approaches, the least successful being a "blind" cabinet with no door directly into the corner. A second contrivance is a lazy Susan with attached corner doors. The entire assembly — doors and shelves — revolves to expose shelves, or close the doors. The doors are slightly smaller than their opening so they don't collide with the surrounding cabinet frame. These units have several disadvantages, though. The weight of the goods on the lazy Susan can throw the doors out of alignment so that they rub against the cabinet frame. And there is always the danger of small children's fingers getting pinched in the revolving doors.

Yet another approach has two doors in the corner, hinged to each other at a 90-degree angle. When you pull on one door, both of them swing out of the way. Often this kind of cabinet is equipped with stationary shelves, but it can be equipped with lazy Susans. Two independent lazy Susans operate more stably than a pair on the same mechanism.

The best solution we've seen to the corner cabinet dilemma is a device called a "half-Susan." Semicircular shelves are attached to a single door at the junction of the two banks of cabinets. By opening

(Above left) A half Susan lets you get the most out of the dead space where lower cabinets meet at a 90-degree angle.

(Above right) For bird lovers, a special place to collect those crusty crumbs!

the door you extend shelves into the room. Even though its arrangement may offer slightly less storage, it is more easily accessed.

Additional Features

There are a vast number of features that can be incorporated into the cabinetry. Generally, the more expensive the stock cabinets, the greater variety of optional accessories. Custom shops, of course, can provide virtually anything your budget will bear. Among those features are:

- An elevator shelf, which rises out of a base cabinet to counter height. It might hold a food processor or mixer, plugged in and ready for use.
- A spice drawer to hold jars on their sides for quick identification.
- A knife drawer containing a slotted holder.
- A pull-out cutting board.
- Cabinets subdivided to hold cookie sheets and trays.
- A small tilt-out compartment in front of the sink for sponges and soap pads.
- A folding ironing board cabinet.
- A toekick panel that pulls out to provide a small step-ladder.
- A cabinet containing a swiveling shelf for a television set.
- An "appliance garage" — a countertop enclosure with a tambour door, which houses appliances not in use, such as a blender. Probably the best location for this is in a dead inside corner of the countertop.
- A built-in desk.

Cabinetry presents a dizzying array of options, so try not to let yourself be rushed into a decision. But also keep in mind that cabinetry isn't the most important aspect of your renovation. In the best kitchens, the casework is an integral part of a well-conceived overall design, which includes comfortable places for working and eating, a pleasing blend of natural and artificial light, agreeable circulation patterns, and good heating and ventilation.

Thus far in my own kitchen renovations, I have opted for laminate casework (sometimes even using stock units), because they are cheaper than all-wood cabinets. I spend the extra money on better lighting, higher-quality countertops, and a better flooring. It is the total look and function of the kitchen that will make it successful, not just top-of-the-line cabinetry.

●

A one-piece, 300-pound stainless-steel countertop with integral sink and backsplash is the focal point of this sleekly remodeled ktichen in a 1940s house. The induction stove pictured in chapter 10 is barely visible at the far end. Stainless counters are hard to beat for looks and serviceability.

12 Counters

Counters have a big visual impact in the kitchen. Situated at waist height and close to the eye, they make an immediate statement. Counters are also the most tactile surface in the room. As the workshop's primary working surface, we do everything on them from re-potting the geraniums to making peanut-butter sandwiches for school lunches. In any kitchen other than that of genteel city dwellers who dine out every meal, the counters get a lot of abuse, so the problem before us is to select a material that looks good, doesn't break the budget, and can still stand up to hot pots, drip-drying dishes, coffee grounds, plant fertilizer, tamarind paste from your latest experiment in Thai cookery, spilled red wine, and dirt from the vegetables you just brought in from the garden. In this chapter we'll take a look at our options.

This counter looks like stained wood, but is actually laminate with a simulated wood pattern. The trim is oak painted black to match the counter, with a red solid-color laminate decorative strip.

High-Pressure Laminates

Of all the counter materials on the market, the most widely used is plastic laminate. Many people know it only by the brand name "Formica" rather than its generic moniker. There are several U.S. manufacturers of this smooth, easy-to-clean surfacing material — Formica Corporation, Wilsonart, and Micarta — but the product is basically the same: a series of thin layers bonded together under heat and pressure.

The topmost layer is melamine, a clear plastic coating that protects the lower layers from abrasion and water penetration. Next is a layer of pigmented or decorative paper for color and pattern, and beneath that are several more layers of craft paper impregnated with phenolic resin, to give the laminate body and impact resistance. Printed patterns, like wood grain, have an additional protective layer of *alpha cellulose*, a white, parchmentlike paper, applied over them to keep the pattern from being rubbed away by repeated cleaning. The finished laminate is about $1/_{16}$ inch thick.

Countertop Construction

To make a sturdy countertop, the laminate must be bonded (with contact cement) to a *substrate,* or deck, of particleboard. One might think plywood better, but particleboard is the preferred material (with the added bonus of being slightly less expensive). It is harder than plywood, offering better impact resistance, smoother, which allows a better glue bond with the laminate, and it has no grain structure that could be telegraphed through to the finished countertop. Also, particleboard has a coefficient of expansion similar to laminate, which means that the two materials expand and contract at the same rate with changes in the temperature and humidity. Plywood's coefficient of expansion is higher than laminate, which can weaken the glue bond and cause seams to open up.

The standard countertop thickness is 1½ inches, comprised of a sandwich of two layers of ¾-inch particleboard. The top layer expresses the full shape of the countertop; beneath it, smaller strips, or *fillets,* are glued and pneumatically stapled to the edge and all points where the countertop will contact the base cabinets. The finished countertop is then screwed to the base cabinets from underneath.

Edge Detail

The most common edge treatment is "self-edge," meaning that a strip of the same laminate used on the surface is glued to the front edge of the countertop. A small dark line will show wherever the laminate's core is exposed. Self-edging is usually the least expensive option, and visually the least intrusive, in that the edge will not draw a great deal of attention to itself.

If you like the simplicity of a self-edge but object to the dark line, consider using *color-through laminate,* in which the color is consistent throughout. It is beautiful (and expensive) and can be used to produce the illusion of a solid countertop. Laminate manufacturers produce color-through laminates in the same colors as regular laminate, so you can mix the two types without worry of color differences.

●

Another approach is a *decorative edge detail,* the most common being to fasten a hardwood strip around the perimeter of the counter. Oak, birch, and maple are the most commonly used, either left natural or stained. The laminate abuts the hardwood at the top edge of the counter, so you don't see the brown interior of the laminate as with self-edge. Also, hardwood will absorb the nicks and blows the edge is sure to receive, whereas a self-edge might chip.

The edges of the wood itself can be profiled in several ways. They can be left square, or "eased" slightly for a contemporary look; they can be quarter-rounded, half-rounded, or profiled with a more elaborate ogee.

At "This Old House," a favorite edge profile is a simple 45-degree *bevel* or *chamfer* to ease the transition between horizontal counter and vertical edge. We run the laminate over the hardwood

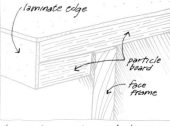

Laminate counter and edge.

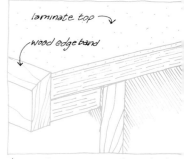

Laminate counter with wood edge.

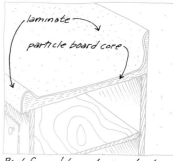

Post-formed laminate countertop.

Laminate Counter Conditions

Because laminate must always have a seam at intersections, corners can be softened by using a bullnose insert. Here, a post-formed laminate counter with a double radius uses a wooden insert to round the corners.

edging, then chamfer both the wood and the laminate with a chamfering bit in a router. You can accent the chamfer by laminating a strip of plastic, a contrasting color of wood, or even aluminum or brass behind the outermost layer of wood. You can also build up a decorative edge without any wood by using layers of plastic or metal.

There are also prefabricated edge treatments in a variety of colors and wood-grain finishes. They install by snapping into a groove cut into in the front edge of the counter.

Since edge treatments can be installed in different ways, ask your fabricator if there will be a noticeable seam between the edge treatment and the laminate and if the seam will be impervious to water, which will destroy a counter if it penetrates to the substrate.

It is also possible to put decorative *inlays* of wood, metal, or a contrasting color of laminate into the surface of the countertop itself. But because this entails exposed joints in the laminate, it increases the chance of water penetration and eventual failure. If you want embellishments in the horizontal surface, it is best to use a solid surfacing material, discussed later in the chapter.

●

The Backsplash

Some sort of backsplash is necessary to finish off the wall edge of the countertop. Standard backsplash dimensions are 4 inches high by ¾ inch thick, and the fabricator of your laminate countertops will probably supply them in the same color laminate as your counters unless you specify otherwise.

The backsplash is bonded directly to the wall with construction adhesive and the top edge caulked with silicone caulk. There are two methods for making the transition between counter and back-splash. One is to install an aluminum cove molding at this juncture, the other is to caulk it with a thin bead of silicone caulk.

Another approach is to bond, directly to the wall, a sheet of laminate that covers the entire wall space between the top of the counter and the bottom of the wall cabinets, eliminating the need for a backsplash altogether. This is typically done prior to installation of both wall units and counter. The wall units overlap the laminate from the top down, and the counters must be scribed to the back wall. It is a slightly more tricky procedure, but offers a cleaner appearance when finished.

Postformed Countertops

One way to integrate the backsplash, the countertop, and the edge detail in a single unit is to install a *postformed* countertop. Postforming refers to the process whereby laminate is heated to make it pliable and bonded to a formed substrate. Since the laminate cannot be bent to extreme radii, the backsplash melds into the countertop in a sweeping curve rather than a sharp edge, and the front edge is given a semicircular wrap or a blunt bullnose. Some postformed counters feature a slight rise at the edge of the horizontal surface, which keeps spilled liquids from dribbling into the lower cabinets or onto the floor.

Postformed counters are available in a limited range of colors and patterns, but special colors may be special ordered. The laminate used on these counters must be slightly thinner than usual (the industry standard is .042 inch, as opposed to .050 inch for conventionally formed counters and .030 inch for cabinets and doors). The chief disadvantage of these counters, aside from their rather old-fashioned look, is that in an L- or U-shaped kitchen the joints between runs of counter will have to be made like picture frames, in 45-degree miters. To make these close-tolerance cuts in the field is difficult to do. Another problem is the difficulty finishing the end of the countertop. In a self-edge detail the top laminate covers the vertical laminate of the counter edge. Since this is impossible to do with postformed counters, a wood or laminate endcap must be fabricated and fitted to the counter end.

Seams

The Achilles heel of a laminate countertop is the seams. Water penetration to the substrate will cause the glue bond between laminate and substrate to fail, the plywood substrate itself to rot, and particleboard substrate to expand — as much as 75 percent. In a word, the counter will self-destruct. Laminate comes in 5x12-foot sheets, so in most kitchen configurations a seam somewhere on a countertop is almost inevitable. A spokesman for the Formica Corporation admits it

Counters both divide the kitchen vertically and unite it horizontally. A seemingly trivial detail like the edge profile can make a big difference in the way a kitchen feels.

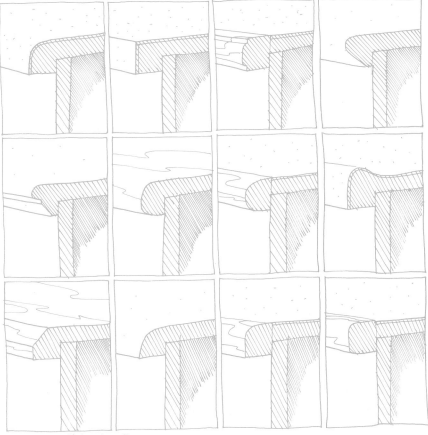

Counter Edge Profiles

comes down to a choice between performance and aesthetics. You can locate the joints away from the sink and danger of water penetration — but they will be the full width of the counter and very prominent. Or, you can locate them at the sink, where they will be much less noticeable — but vulnerable to water. For what it's worth, I have always opted for aesthetics, keeping the water around the sink area mopped up.

Considerations When Choosing Laminates

In a kitchen that gets hard, intensive use, such as a restaurant kitchen, plastic laminate may last only a few years. The surface is vulnerable to nicking, chipping, denting, cutting, scratching, and blistering from hot pots placed directly on it. Yet a laminate counter treated with care is extremely durable. In the very first "This Old House" project in the Boston neighborhood of Dorchester, laminate was used; even after more than a decade of constant use it still looks nearly as pristine (in its eye-opening orange) as when new.

In order to get this kind of longevity out of your laminate counters, consider these points:

High-gloss laminates scratch very easily and show scratches prominently. Since laminates cannot be sanded or otherwise treated to remove scratches, we advise you to avoid glossy laminates for counter duty. A matte finish is best for scratch resistance.

Dark, solid colors show both blemishes and dirt and we generally advise our "This Old House" homeowners against using them. Laminates are also available in a variety of textures — leather, slate, stone, and an embossed grid — which we also advise against, as the high part of the topography is the first to wear through.

Another thing to consider with laminates, as with all finishes and surfaces in your new kitchen, is how enduring will the color and style be from a decorating standpoint. A bright purple floral pattern might be the rage this year, but will you still love it three years down the road? We generally advise our homeowners to choose a neutral white or gray, which will blend with many paint and wallpaper schemes.

High-pressure laminate is an excellent choice for this cost-effective, well-designed kitchen renovation. Laminate is relatively inexpensive, good-looking, serviceable, and, if treated with care, very long lived. Wood edging gives the counter some accent, and here it ties in with the oak floor.

Solid surfacing comes in a wide variety of patterns. In addition to its other properties, it can be machined and formed in a variety of ways. Here are two variations of faux granite. The bullnose was created by a router and the column by a process called thermoforming.

Solid Surfacing

If you like the look of high-pressure laminate but don't like the brown lines at the joints, the vulnerability of the seams, and the fragility of the top clear layer, consider using what is generically referred to as *solid surfacing*, an acrylic-based material invented by the DuPont Corporation and still widely known by its trade name Corian. It was originally available only in white and off-white. Now there are similar products by other manufacturers — Avonite (Avonite Corp.), Fountainhead (Nevamar), Surell (Formica), and Gibraltar (Wilsonart) — and over fifty patterns and colors, including some beautiful granitelike patterns.

Many cooks, contractors, and kitchen fabricators consider solid surfacing the best choice for kitchen counters. It is a structural material that can be used to make cantilevered overhangs along edges of islands or peninsulas, and it is dimensionally stable so it will not warp or shrink as a wooden counter will. The color and pattern is homogeneous throughout, so the material stands up to many years of use. It is resistant to heat, scratching, denting, and staining. If cut or damaged, solid surfacing can be sanded smooth again with an ordinary orbital sander or by hand-sanding. In the worst case, portions of the counter can be filled with a filler that matches the color of the material or the bad spots can even be cut out and patched. Perhaps best of all for the homeowner, solid surfacing is easily cleaned with standard household cleansers.

All these wonderful attributes are not without cost, however. Solid-surfacing countertops are three to five times as expensive as high-pressure laminate, but less than granite or marble.

Fabrication

Although solid surfacing can be worked with ordinary woodworking tools, it is not a project for the average homeowner. In fact, most contractors and carpenters subcontract solid-surfacing work out to a specialist. Specialists, in turn, tend to use one brand exclusively, since each brand has different material properties, working characteristics, factory-recommended fabrication techniques, and proprietary seam adhesives. Beware the fabricator who claims he can work with equal facility in any of the brands. The fact that each manufacturer conducts special training seminars and publishes fabrication handbooks and regular product bulletins, and the fact that some fabricators give their personnel six months' training before turning them loose unsupervised is a strong argument for going to a shop that specializes in just one brand.

The detailing of your solid-surfacing countertop is limited only by your imagination — and, of course, your budget. A variety of edge details can be applied, from a simple quarter- or half-round to chamfers and more complex ogees and laminated feature strips. It is a relatively easy matter to build up the edge to two or three inches to give the countertop the look of a massive piece of granite or stone. Inlaid patterns in the counter surface or edge detailing can be made without fear of damage from water penetration. In general, the more complicated the detailing, the more costly.

The backsplash can be a simple ½- or ¾-inch-thick piece of solid surfacing that sits on the countertop, or it can be let into the countertop with a graceful and easily cleaned integral cove.

Material Properties

Solid surfacing comes in ¼-inch, ½-inch, and ¾-inch thicknesses, and in various size sheets. It can be cantilevered to form overhangs at the edges of peninsulas and islands. The usual rule is that ½-inch-thick material will tolerate a 6-inch cantilever while ¾-inch-thick stock will tolerate up to 12 inches, although some fabricators will only canti-

Solid surfacing again shows off its structural versatility in this "handkerchief" corner.

This sophisticated design takes full advantage of the structural and sculptural qualities of solid surfacing. The double horizontal line of the bar is repeated in the counter beyond, the shelf above it, and again as an edging above the cabinets, giving the kitchen an understated rhythm and cohesiveness. Counter lighting runs under the shelf and under the cabinet, emphasizing the openness of the wall space. The cabinets, a very tightly patterned curly maple, offer a textural complement to the counters, but both have a similar matte finish, to reflect the light in the same manner. The cabinet doors above the stove pull out to become the hood vent.

lever to 9 inches. Some brands, like Corian, do not require a particleboard or plywood substrate — in fact, the use of one will void the manufacturer's warranty, as the substrate inhibits the dissipation of heat from hot pots placed on the surface. Other brands, like Class 3 Avonite, require a full substrate. (Some fabricators claim that Class 3 Avonite will not tolerate overhangs without being supported.)

Part of the differences between brands is accounted for by the fact that they are formulated differently. Corian is an acrylic, whereas Fountainhead and Avonite are a mixture of polyester and acrylic. Surell, formerly called Formica 200X, was recently reformulated and renamed.

Corian, Fountainhead, and Surell all have a Class I fire rating, indicating that they retard the spread of flames. Although this rating is not currently required by code for most residential construction, it does provide an extra margin of safety. Avonite is available in two formulations, a Class I rating and Class III rating.

Many fabricators, designers, and architects consider Corian to be the standard by which all others are judged. It has been in production for over two decades and has a track record of dimensional and structural stability and resistance to environmental factors like strong sunlight. But all of the Class III materials behave similarly.

There are several factors to consider when choosing among brands. First, of course, is the color and pattern of the material — Avonite, for instance, is still favored by designers for its colors. Gibraltar's colors match those of Wilsonart's line of high-pressure laminates, offering the possibility of using a solid surfacing edge detail on a laminate counter. Another factor is the dimensions of the stock. If you are planning an island 36 inches wide, it would make sense to buy the material in that width to eliminate a seam. This consideration would knock Corian out of the running, as it is available only in 30-inch-wide sheets.

A third factor is the accessories, or "shaped products," offered by the manufacturer. DuPont, for instance, manufactures thirteen sizes of sinks and lavatory bowls that your fabricator can bond right into your countertop, an option that, in and of itself (in our opinion), is almost worth the price of solid surfacing as it eliminates one of the most vulnerable areas of the kitchen counter, the rim seal.

You can also undermount either a standard sink or one specially designed for undermounting. This technique offers many of the advantages of an integral sink — a clean look, no rim to collect dirt and water, ease of cleaning the counter area around the sink — while giving you a broader range of sink choices. However, the total installed costs for an integrated sink may be only slightly higher than for a separate undermounted sink when you consider the extra labor required to build a structure to support a standard sink. You can, of course, install the sink in the traditional manner.

A fourth, and critical, factor in your decision among brands should be the availability of a top-flight fabricator certified to work the material of your choice. Even though DuPont, for instance, guarantees Corian against manufacturing defects for ten years, failure to fabricate it using certified techniques and materials will void the warranty. DuPont certifies fabricators through a network of local training seminars. (This policy puts the home craftsman in a bit of a bind, since if you do your own fabrication, you may hinder your ability to prosecute later warranty claims.) Because solid surfacing counters may represent a substantial percentage of your kitchen renovation budget, evaluate your prospective fabricator carefully. Ask him for a straightforward explanation of his and the manufacturer's warranty policy and for the names of several of his customers.

Granite comes in a wide variety of colors and patterns. Here a tight pattern of black, white, and gray stone sets the keynote for this serious-looking kitchen. The cabinets are bleached ash and the floor black granite tiles.

Stone

Many people consider stone to be the ultimate counter material. Stone is beautiful, and so durable as to be "permanent" — just look at the marble counters that have survived for decades in diners and soda fountains. Stone, of course, has disadvantages. It is hard, so plates, cups, or wineglasses dropped on the counter will probably chip or shatter. It is also among the most expensive counter materials, depending on the type of stone and the area of the country you live in. But stone's advantages may make it worth the extra cost, particularly if you are considering another high-end material like solid surfacing.

Slate

From the cost standpoint slate is the most attractive of the types of stone commonly used for countertops. On most of the East Coast it is readily available in sheets of various thicknesses. Slate is soft and therefore easily workable, which may lend itself to advanced do-

it-yourselfers. It cuts with a diamond-tipped circular saw blade and can be smoothed with a belt sander. Like all stone, it can be glued to steel, wood, or just about any other material with epoxy. Slate is available in two surface textures: polished, which has a silky, soapstonelike feel, or with a natural *cleft*. Slate's chief disadvantage is its color, black, which makes any dirt, smudges, water, or crumbs stick out like a sore thumb. Unless you are very meticulous, your slate counter will almost always look dirty.

Marble

For bakers, marble is the countertop of choice. It has a cool, smooth texture, which is perfect for rolling out dough. It is beautiful and available in a variety of colors and textures.

Marble is porous, which makes it easily stained. Sealers are not recommended because they may be toxic. To increase stain resistance, marble can be polished to a high gloss, but acids like lemon juice and vinegar may blemish the surface. Even a wet glass may leave a mark on polished marble.

A *honed* finish will stand up better to kitchen duty. The satiny texture can be scoured with steel wool to remove some stains. Those that remain will be hidden somewhat by the stone's nonreflective finish. You may have to be persistent to obtain honed marble. Most of the imported slabs come prepolished, and domestically produced stone is polished before it leaves the yard. Most people prefer a

(Above left) The marble counter in this baking center is lowered for rolling and kneading dough. Other counters are solid surfacing.

(Above right) Marble makes a major design statement in this kitchen. It comprises all the counters and the backsplash as well. The intensity of color and pattern should be carefully considered when choosing your stone. Like wallpaper, what looks good in a small sample might take on different qualities in a large mass. It's clear that the tones and textures in this Southwest kitchen were carefully blended together.

These ¾-inch-thick black granite counters were given a ⅛-inch radius on the front edge and the top of the backsplash to soften the corners and make them less susceptible to chipping. The glossy finish reflects light into the window-less space. As in the May-Lin kitchen on page 231, texture, color, and light-reflective qualities were carefully bal-anced to get a room that is spare yet not sterile. Cabinets are beech.

polished finish, so dealers and fabricators stock what they can sell most of.

Another way of minimizing the stain problem is to select heavily veined marble so the stains will become lost in the pattern, or a dark color, which tends to hide stains. Inevitably, though, your counters will get stained. There is some consolation in knowing that marble bears the vicissitudes of kitchen duty gracefully — some of those beautiful gray soda fountain counters started out as pristine white marble and gradually changed color with use.

Granite

Granite is a very elegant stone that serves the same function as mar-ble, providing a cool, smooth surface for pastry making, while offer-ing much more resistance to discoloration. It is about 30 percent more expensive than marble, although this comparison is only approxi-mate because there are many grades of granite and marble to choose from. Rare grades of both stones will be more costly than plentiful grades.

Granite has a tighter grain structure than marble, so it looks very uniform or monolithic. Slabs for countertop are usually polished to a smooth, high-gloss surface, which can be washed with soap and water and touched up with window cleaner. Polished granite is im-pervious to stains — boiling oil is about the only thing that can stain it. Like slate, black granite shows every smudge mark and crumb,

Who says you can't have it all? This owner/designer put polished granite on all his counters, then installed six pullout cutting boards around the kitchen at key points. All are mounted at a good chopping height and lock securely in place when in use. The device next to the range is a professional wok.

whereas a more variegated pattern does not. Honed surfaces in granite tend to be dull and lifeless as well as being more vulnerable to stains.

One way to enjoy the benefits of stone for baking without taking out a second (or third) mortgage on your house is to inset a marble or granite slab in a portion of your island or countertop. This is a common feature in many professional kitchens where the expense of full stone counters is deemed unnecessary and extravagant.

Purchasing Stone

Buying stone involves a much different procedure than buying laminate or solid surfacing. Stone dealers, kitchen stores, and designers usually have small sample pieces to show what is available, but placing your order solely on the basis of the sample is risky, especially with marble, which has a prominent vein structure or figure, the full extent of which will not be revealed in a small sample. Stone is a product of nature, and the color and figure will vary even though the stone comes from the same quarry.

If you are ordering your stone from a local stoneyard or distributor, go there with your mason, fabricator, or installer and select the stone for your job in person. If the distributor is too far away, ask

(Above left) Flamed French limestone, heavily sealed, gives a rustic, beautifully textured look to these counters and backsplash.

(Above right) The warm pink-orange domestic granite was chosen to complement the tones of the "red-mouth rift" oak cabinetry. Because the pattern of the granite here is subdued, the effect of wood and stone together is harmonious.

for a sample from the lot from which they will fill your order. For our adobe rehab in Santa Fe, New Mexico, our homeowners selected a pink Mexican marble for their kitchen countertops. While they made their initial color selection from architectural samples, they traveled to the fabricator's yard in Juárez, Mexico, to make their final selection.

In the course of your visit to the stoneyard, you may find that the dealer is willing to offer more attractive prices on stone he's already got in stock. A way to get stone at an even better price is to call a large stone fabricator and inquire about remnant slabs. A yard that turns out big jobs for the facing of office buildings and other large projects inevitably ends up with leftover pieces, some of which may be big enough for your kitchen. If you are willing to do a little legwork rather than simply ordering through a dealer or stonemason, you may find a real bargain.

Fabrication and Installation

To cut the stone to the dimensions of your counters, a full-size pattern or *template* is created. The template is made of a waterproof material such as thin plastic, which will stand up to the large quantities of water used by the diamond-tipped wet saws used in stone cutting. Most slabs used for kitchen counters are ¾ inch thick, although thicker slabs are available. The length and width of slabs varies from piece to piece, but because of the weight and brittleness of stone, 8 or 9 feet long and 4 or 5 feet wide is about the maximum-size slabs quarries like to handle. Obviously these dimensions will dictate the maximum length of a counter without seams.

A granite counter ¾ inch thick by 9 feet long is readily carried and positioned by two workers. Larger or thicker pieces start to present installation problems. Sometimes the slab simply sits on top of the base cabinets and is secured by silicone or epoxy. In other installations it rests on a plywood substrate.

A combination of ceramic tile and maple counters gives this kitchen a maximum of utilitarian surfaces. The blue-glazed terracotta tile is used between the stove and the sink so hot pans and woks can be set down without second thought. The hard maple on the other side of the stove provides a gentler surface for the dishes on their way to the table. Stainless-steel bands edge both counters on either side of the stove.

A fabricator's biggest fear is that the stone will not reach the job site intact. Some yards are willing to precut holes for sinks or cooktops, while others will only make these cuts on site, or will avoid them altogether, instead shipping small sections of stone to be placed at the front and back of the sink or stove and grouted in place. In some cases, these small pieces are reinforced with steel underneath.

The exposed edges of the stone should be slightly rounded or "eased," since a sharp edge is likely to get chipped or cut some unfortunate child's forehead. The edge can also receive a more decorative profile. The backsplash can be made of long pieces of stone, or stone tiles, which are usually less expensive than slabs. In old houses where the walls are extremely uneven, we have seen wooden backsplashes, which are scribed to the walls. Wood is not as durable as stone but may make an attractive contrast.

If you want the look of stone without the high cost, consider using stone tiles, which are sometimes quite attractively priced. Because of the grout lines, a stone tile countertop may not be suitable for rolling dough, but it would preserve the look and feel of a monolithic slab. This is especially the case with precision-cut granite and marble tiles, which can be installed such that the grout lines will be 1/16 inch wide. Stone tiles have the qualities and drawbacks of slabs, but are installed like ceramic tile.

Ceramic Tile

In California and the Southwest, tile is the favorite material for counters. Like stone, tile is hard, durable, and heatproof. Tile costs more than plastic laminate, but may be less than stone and solid surfacing.

The two types of ceramic tile predominantly used for countertops are *white-body ceramic* and *porcelain ceramic tile.* White-body tile is made from white clay, and the face glazed in any of dozens of colors. But beware, brilliant colors tend to show scratches, whereas more subdued colors don't. Similarly, high-gloss glazes tend to scratch easily, and those scratches will stand out on a shiny surface. Matte glazes are harder and less likely to scratch. Even then, the matte finish will hide scratches quite well. Yet a third glaze, called "crystalline" and various other trade names, looks like glass coated with sugar crystals. It is very hard and will stand up to plenty of rough use. Still another possibility is "suede" glaze, a matte finish with some shading. It is also tough and durable.

Porcelain tile has a consistent color all the way through. It is fine textured, nonporous, and usually unglazed, with a smooth, silky surface that hides scratches well. Porcelain tile is not available in the many colors and textures of white-body tile.

In addition to manufactured tiles, we see an increasing variety of handmade tiles. Usually distinguished by its irregularities, the glaze on a handmade tile may be uneven, forming thick pools in some spots while thinning out in others. The edges of the tiles may look lumpy or there may be other imperfections, which can give your counters a distinctive, handmade look. Remember, though, the more irregular the surface, the harder it will be to clean.

Also in this category are one-of-a-kind handpainted tiles. Some tile dealers can arrange to have a craftsman paint tiles to complement the colors in your room or to repeat a pattern or motif which you specify. Handpainted tiles command a premium price, but by buying just a few and placing them in prominent locations, you can liven up a countertop made of relatively inexpensive single-color tiles. At less cost, dozens of standard patterns are available from large tile companies.

Some artisans will construct large-scale designs or paintings on ceramic tile. Behind the meat counter of our neighborhood market, the owner installed, at great expense and trouble, a wonderful panoramic scene from his native Greece, replete with dry hills covered with olive orchards above sparkling bays dotted with the caïques of fishermen.

Handmade and handpainted tiles range in price from several dollars per square foot to twenty dollars per tile.

Size of Tiles

Manufactured tiles are available in many sizes, the smallest being one-inch squares. These are linked into sheets with paper or strands of silicone. A 1-by-2-foot sheet makes it possible to install 288 1-inch tiles in a single operation, saving a tremendous amount of time. For countertops, however, most people prefer individual or loose tiles in larger sizes, 4¼ by 4¼ inches, or, more commonly these days, 6 by 6 inches. Selecting the size that is right for your kitchen is partly a matter of scale and partly a maintenance issue. Little tiles can make a small room seem larger, but the bigger the tiles, the fewer the grout lines to clean.

Installation of Ceramic Tile

There are several methods of installing tile counters. The traditional *mortar-bed method,* or "mud job," is still frequently used in the western United States. The installer lays a bed of portland cement ¾ to 1½ inches thick on a base of exterior-grade plywood covered with building paper and chicken wire. When properly executed, a mud job can last for decades. Most failures of a tiled kitchen counter, such as breakage of individual tiles or cracks in the grout, stem from instability of the substrate rather than from flaws in the materials. The mortar-bed method is extremely stable — the tile setter has, in essence, built a rigid masonry slab — so there is no cracking of the grout or tile. Usually a mud job is more expensive than alternative methods.

●

In most of the United States tile is installed with the *thin-set method,* so called because the mortar can be as thin as $^3/_{32}$ inch. Starting with a deck of exterior-grade plywood, the installer secures to it a layer of *cementitious backer board,* a cement and vermiculite tile substrate available at the lumberyard. He then spreads mortar on the backer board with a notched trowel and presses the tile into the mortar. Several different kinds of mortar can be used, including a high-strength epoxy.

A variation on the thin-set method involves the application of an organic mastic adhesive over exterior-grade plywood. This is quick and inexpensive, and while it is fine for walls and ceilings we

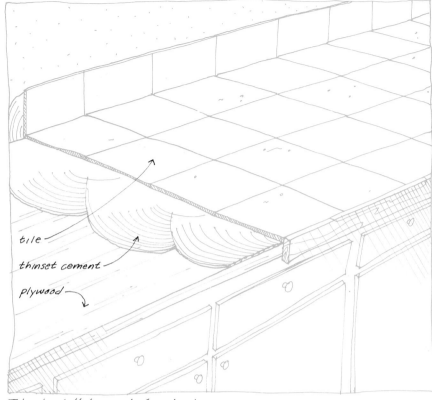

tile

thinset cement

plywood

Tile Installation at Countertop

do not recommend it for countertops. If water penetrates to the plywood substrate, it can delaminate the plywood or loosen tiles. Since plywood expands and contracts at a different rate than tile, it is nearly impossible to maintain tight grout joints between the backsplash and the counter and at the sink's rim seal.

●

There's just no getting around the fact that the quality of installation is critical. If tiles in a countertop break, it is usually because they were not adequately bedded into the mortar base. If cracks appear in the grout, it is most likely caused by shifting of the tile bed, as a result of the house settling or the expansion and contraction of materials in response to changing temperatures and humidity. We see no problem with shopping around for the most economical tiles available, but choosing an installer and an installation method solely on the basis of price is often a false economy. The quality of the installation can be the difference between a counter that begins to deteriorate immediately and one that endures for many years.

Grout

There are a number of grouts on the market, the best being *epoxy*

The chief goal of the rehab of this small 1950s ranch house was to create as much inside-outside space as possible. The tiled kitchen was designed to look like an outdoor barbeque. Absence of small details, such as trim and edgings, helps to reinforce the outdoor look. The sand-colored stone pavers from Mexico continue onto the patio.

grout. It is strong yet flexible enough not to crack with the expansion and contraction of substrate materials. It is extremely stain resistant and its colors (even white) will not darken over time. Unlike traditional grouts, epoxy contains no cement at all. Instead, it is composed of epoxy resins, plasticizers for flexibility, and colored filler powder. It demands special application techniques. Each batch has a working time of about 45 minutes in which it must be applied, or *packed,* and then cleaned. Once the chemical reaction that hardens the grout occurs, the grout will be permanently stuck wherever it is. Epoxy grouts are about three times the price of other types, but according to John Pascoe, of the Tile Council of America, they are the product of choice for kitchen countertops.

In the many years before the advent of epoxy grouts, tile setters used *commercial portland cement grout,* which is simply a mixture of 40 percent commercial portland cement and 60 percent sand. There is nothing wrong with this type of grout; it is dependable and economical, and its properties and application techniques are well known and understood. Commercial portland cement grout has a long working life but must be "wet-cured" in order to harden. After the grout has been applied and cleaned from the joints, the tile sur-

Green rope-braid ceramic tile edging to these tile counters softens the overall look of the room. Note the green-stained oak floors.

face is sprayed with water and covered with a sheet of polyethylene. It takes 24 to 48 hours to cure.

Commercial portland cement grout is inexpensive, and if properly installed performs excellently, although it will stain and darken over time. It can be used with any kind of tile but is ideal for applications where the grout joints are wide, such as with quarry tile in a commercial kitchen.

There are two additives, or *admixtures,* commonly combined with commercial portland cement grout to alter its properties. Addition of .5 percent methyl cellulose (wood pulp) to the standard brew will produce *dry-set grout,* a formulation especially used with terra cotta and other porous tiles. The wood pulp helps the grout to retain water, which would otherwise be sucked out by the tile. If used on less porous tiles, dry-set eliminates the need to keep the tile hydrated with the plastic sheet.

The other admixture is latex, which can be added both to dry-set and to the standard portland mix. It improves the grout's bonding both to the tile and the substrate, its compressive and tensile strength, and its stain resistance. But latex can leach into some types of tile, ruining its appearance. Latex comes as a liquid or a powder. To prevent leaching, it is imperative that latex be mixed in strict accordance to the manufacturer's instructions.

There are two other types of grout. One is a silicone-based mastic grout, which is something like silicone caulk and is still available in hardware stores and home centers. This type of grout is not widely used commercially. The second is a new commercial grout manufactured by the Tec Corporation that has just come on the market, called cementitious mastic grout. It is extremely flexible, and is applied right out of the container.

Edge Detail

There are two common edge details for a ceramic tile counter. Probably the easiest is to use an edge tile manufactured expressly for this purpose. You can also build up an edge with a bullnose tile. These tiles could be the same or could contrast with those of the counter itself.

The other approach is to edge the counter with hardwood, in whatever profile you find pleasing to the eye. This detail can look very good, accenting the tile with a contrasting color and material. The problem with it is that wood and tile expand and contract at different rates and this joint always seems to open up, collecting a bit of everything that is wiped off the counter.

Aluminum, brass, and stainless steel are other possibilities. Metal expands and contracts less than wood and therefore will remain in closer contact with the tile.

Butcher Block and Other Wooden Counters

Serious cooks often insist on butcher block in their kitchens. Some build whole counters or islands of it, others insert a cutting-board-size section into a counter of another material. Butcher block is a highly functional material — you can cut and chop and prepare foods right on it without fear of ruining the counter or dulling your knives. It is also a handsome material that lends warmth to the room, and many people select it for their counters even if they never intend to use it for chopping or cutting.

Hard maple is the species most commonly used for butcher block counters and is the only material approved by the National Sanitation Foundation for commercial kitchens.

To make butcher block, strips of wood two inches wide are laminated with the wood's edge grain up, which will make it more warp resistant and water repellent than with the face grain exposed.

Unglazed handmade ceramic tiles in a range of similar hues make a warm complement to the hickory-covered cabinets in this handcrafted kitchen. The range hood, oven front, and knob plate are sheathed in pounded copper, and the knobs themselves are forged iron. The floor is unglazed Saltillo tile.

Traditional meat-cutting blocks are made with the end grain up, but in many areas their commercial use is illegal because liquids may be absorbed into the wood, creating a health hazard.

Butcher block is commercially available up to 12 feet long, but can be made in any length. It is sealed by the manufacturer with oil to prevent it from absorbing moisture and cracking. Sealing also makes it more resistant to stains. Exposure to foods and repeated cleaning gradually remove the oil, so you must periodically re-oil the wood with a nontoxic oil. Tung oil is best, because it leaves the surface dry to the touch. Mineral oil and vegetable oil can be used but will remain tacky, making the counter sticky on hot summer days.

Keeping the counters clean is one of the biggest headaches of butcher block, since the porous surface is hard to sponge and liquids and oil that have soaked into the wood can become sticky in hot weather. The long butcher block counters in German beer halls are washed each morning with chlorine bleach, which removes any food residue and gives the wood a nice gray patina. The Bally Block Company in Bally, Pennsylvania, one of the largest makers of butcher block in the United States, recommends cleaning the surface with warm water and soap or detergent and wiping it dry immediately. Stains can be removed by puddling lemon juice or diluted chlorine bleach on the surface for a few minutes. For stubborn stains and cutting marks, you can always resort to scouring powder, steel wool, or sanding.

An alternative is to finish the wood with two or three coats of a high-quality urethane. I went this route in my kitchen when, after having laboriously oiled my counters, I found that they were just too rough and porous to clean easily. You cannot cut directly on a urethaned counter, which defeats one of the purposes of installing butcher block in the first place. But with the recent concern about salmonella contamination, many cooks now use plastic cutting boards, which can be washed in the dishwasher.

We advise against using butcher block around the sink, where water from washing and drip-drying pots and pans on the sideboard can penetrate the sink's vulnerable rim seal and warp and discolor the wood. There's a lesson to be learned from my own experience in this regard, for I disregarded both common sense and wisdom and dropped my sink directly into my maple counter. I used a marine-grade polyurethane sealant to caulk the rim seal. The sealant performs well, but unfortunately I had the counters made from 2-by-6-inch maple (to match the scale of the wide pine flooring) instead of the far more stable 2-by-2-inch strips. In winter when the humidity is low, the counters cup so badly that the cast-iron sink breaks the rim

(Above left) This island combines laminate with butcher block to get the best of both worlds. The joint between the two surfaces must be very tight so water and dirt cannot penetrate.

(Above right) Handmade brass plates set into this teak counter protect the wood from the heat of the stove and serve as a pot rest.

seal, letting water in. Despite diligent mopping up around the sink area, the wood is beginning to crack and discolor.

Purchase your counters from a source that specializes in butcher block. If you want to place the sink in the counter, find out if doing so will void any warranties for the material. There are differences in the degree to which different butcher block fabricators match the wood strips for color. If color matching is important, check a representative sample before you place your order. You might also look for the seal of the National Sanitation Foundation, which indicates that the butcher block meets industry standards for sanitation.

You are not limited, however, to maple butcher block. Oak and cherry are also popular choices for residential countertops. Mahogany has been used for bar tops and on yachts for years. It is stable, works beautifully, glues well, and has a close grain structure that is lovely when oiled, varnished, or urethaned. Teak, the premier wood for boatbuilding, is also a good choice. It is extremely stable and, because of its high oil content, resists water, staining, and wood-eating sea worms (in case you have problems with them in your kitchen). On yachts and English park benches, teak is often left unfinished to weather to a pleasing silver color. When coated with oil, varnish, or urethane, it is dark and rich, with some blond highlights. Teak looks like a million, but costs one, too.

The fact is, you can use just about any wood for kitchen counters — yellow silverbali, bubinga, purpleheart, ebony — if it is properly dried and fabricated by someone who knows the characteristics of the particular species. A wood counter, like a wooden yacht, requires more care and attention than, say, a laminate or solid-sur-

facing counter. But after time, the nicks, scratches, and stains blend right into the grain structure and as the wood gets older it mellows in color. What was once part of a living tree starts to seem like an old friend.

Stainless Steel and Copper

In many ways, stainless steel is the ideal counter material — it is tough enough to withstand constant use, stands up to high temperatures, will not stain or rust, and is easy to clean and sanitize. For all these reasons it is used in virtually every commercial kitchen in the country. Some designers have taken the restaurant look in residential kitchens a step further by installing stainless-steel counters as well. There are commercial sinks available with wide stainless drainboards on either side, which can be very successful in residential applications. However, most stainless-steel counters installed in residences are designed by an architect and custom fabricated. Their cost is high and their "warmth factor" low.

(Above left) This cottage already had the spectacular leaded-glass windows and the plank floor. To tie it all together, the carpenter on the job, also a boat-builder, built these handsome splined cherry counters and sealed them with ten coats of marine sealant. The cabinets look to be wood but are in reality plastic laminate.

Stainless steel looks at home in a classic, Old World setting as well as in a modern one. This turn-of-the-century townhouse kitchen needed practicality as well as period style. The library ladder stows out of the way when not needed. Note the old tile floor and white-tiled back-splash.

In the rarest of instances, we've seen copper kitchen counters. They are expensive, of course, but the effect of their warm glow is gorgeous. Copper is soft, so it will easily dent, and has little resistance to acidic substances found in the kitchen. To keep copper from tarnishing, you must polish it every few weeks. A lacquer finish will reduce this, but the finish itself is soft and difficult to maintain. Perhaps this doesn't matter — copper is for people who have other people clean their houses.

●

The materials we've explored in this chapter represent those most commonly used for countertops, but by no means *all* the possibilities. In some restaurants and residences, we've seen lightweight concrete counters, dyed to various colors such as rose, gray, and black. They are expensive but can be cast in any shape and thickness. Concrete counters are durable and easy to clean. And while we're discussing ceramics, there is no real reason you could not use bluestone, or even brick, or granite paving stones for a countertop, although the rough texture might make them difficult to clean.

In wood you are not limited merely to butcher block. The West System is an epoxy laminating technique, commonly used on boats, whereby several thin layers of wood, typically cedar, are glued together over a form. I've never seen this technique applied to kitchen counters, but see no reason why it wouldn't work. You could build a counter with any plan shape and profile. You could even engineer formed wooden sinks into the counter.

The kitchen counter is one of the most visible surfaces in the room — no reason not to have some fun with it!

●

Finishing Touches: Paint, Paper, and the Punchlist

If you love color, don't stop at the kitchen! Continue on to the rest of the house. Here an avid collector of antiques extends her passion to her cozy breakfast room. She sponge-painted her walls green, and continued the hand-painted border from the foyer.

By now, your kitchen should be coming together quite nicely, and you should be down to the final painting, wallcoverings, and finishing touches. It is the decoration that announces to the world your particular taste, especially in a more cost-effective renovation in which stock cabinets, counters, ventilation hoods, and other items have been used.

Painting and decorating is also something you can do yourself. It will save you some money and give you the satisfaction of performing such a visible part of the job yourself. Since these are usually the last steps in a renovation, performed when there are no tradespeople scheduled to follow, you can take your time and do the job right.

Choice of Paints

It is critical to specify paints that stand up well to moisture and grease. The major brands are all of good quality, but stay away from cut-rate brands. For kitchen walls we recommend two coats of gloss or semigloss enamel (the more shiny the surface, the easier it is to clean). Some of us at "This Old House" like acrylic latex enamel for its ease of use and soapy water clean-up. Others, myself included, prefer an oil-based enamel for its handling characteristics and for the way it "lays down" or evens out as it drys. Oil is undeniably harder to use than latex; however, some latex enamels will show brushstrokes or roller dimples if not applied carefully. Here in New England, tradition demands that ceilings be painted with "ceiling white," a flat oil or latex white paint. Out West, I've never seen "ceiling white" and we used to use flat acrylic.

Wood trim, including the baseboard and cornice moldings, should be protected from moisture and grease with two coats of oil or acrylic enamel. For clear finishes, we have been using water-based polyurethane with good results.

If you still can't decide between latex and oil, you should know that the professional painters typically use latex on walls and ceilings and oils on the trim.

Preparation

Preparation is everything. It is the cake — the painting is merely the frosting. Painting "prep," as it's called, is just plain hard work, but it makes all the difference in the final results. Wash anything that isn't new work: all old walls and woodwork that will be recoated. Use trisodium phosphate, or TSP (available at virtually any paint store), according to the directions on the back of the box. Then fill all small holes with vinyl spackling compound, remove the excess, allow to dry, and sand. If you are recoating glossy enamel, whether on walls or woodwork, "key" the surface after washing by sanding lightly with 120 grit paper to give the new coat of paint a texture to which it can form a mechanical bond. All bare wood should be sanded and primed before painting. Knots should be treated first with two coats of sealer (Kilz or Bin) to prevent the sap in them from bleeding through to the finished surface. Vacuum dust off all surfaces before priming or painting. It's not a bad idea to remove the hardware from doors and windows. If you are fortunate enough to live in an old house with lovely glass or porcelain and brass doorknobs, this is a good chance to shine them up. It's a small detail, but you'd be amazed how the eye picks up small details, and it contributes to the impression of a job well done.

Tools

There is nothing more expensive than a cheap brush. As in all trades, high-quality tools are required for a high-quality result. If you're using oil-based paints, invest in a couple of 1½-inch-wide Chinese bristle sash brushes. For latex, use a high-purity nylon bristle brush. These brushes will cost $15 to $20, but if you care for them by cleaning thoroughly after use and storing them in their cardboard jackets, they will last for years. Once you learn how to paint with them, you will be surprised at how much control they give you over the paint. We also use 9-inch rollers. Some people use 3-inch rollers, but I find them more of a nuisance than a help, and much slower than painting the same area with a good sash brush.

Procedure

With both oil and latex paints, open windows and otherwise improve the ventilation, both while you're working and as the paint dries. Paints dry best at "room" temperature (65° to 70°), so you might have to kick the heat up. We recommend the use of cloth dropcloths rather than plastic; they are not as slippery underfoot, they cling to carpets and floors better, and they soak up most of the spatters so you don't track paint into other rooms. Also, you'll need plenty of light for a

(Above) Anticolor:
Black contains many
reflective qualities,
and colors too.

(Right) Color can be
anecdotal. This all-
white kitchen takes on
the blue hue of the
painted wall.

good job, and perhaps a good ladder or even a plank between two ladders to get at the high areas.

Rather than work directly out of the paint can, professionals work from a paint pail. It's not only lighter to hold but has a single rim rather than a paint can's double rim, making it easier to "dress the brush," that is, dip it, gently press paint into the bristles, and then wipe the excess off. Apply the paint to one section of the wall or woodwork at a time, then go back over it with very long, flowing strokes to smooth it. Some people assume that painting is messy by necessity, but a good painter, using high-quality brushes, working methodically, if not quickly, rarely spills a drop. If more than one coat is needed, follow the manufacturer's directions as to how much time should elapse between coats. Sometimes the first coat must dry completely before the second is applied. In other cases, the second coat will bond better if applied while the first coat is still soft.

Resist the temptation to start painting whatever is the most conspicuous or closest at hand. The old maxim is to start with the surface that's farthest away and work to the closest. Generally this means doing the ceilings first, then the walls, and finally the trim. When painting windows, begin with the muntins or sash, then do jambs, and finally the casings. If you're right-handed you'll probably find it easier to start in the upper left-hand corner and work counterclockwise; just the inverse if you're a southpaw. If cabinets are to be painted, do the interiors first, then the exterior frame, and finally the doors. You might find it easier to remove the doors and paint them on a horizontal surface to minimize drips and runs, but considerable labor is involved in removing and rehanging them. In any case, be sure to paint all edges of the door to minimize swelling and warping in times of high humidity. If you're going to paint the floor, do it last.

Wallpaper

Wallpaper is a relatively inexpensive way to change the whole feeling of a room. It can serve to pull a large kitchen-dining area together, or to expand the apparent size of a small room. Most wallpaper stores will loan out their large sample books for you to take home. Prop the candidates up on the counter of your new kitchen and look at them in various lighting conditions and at different times of the day before you make your final choice.

There are some excellent vinyl wallpapers that are sophisticated-looking and also stand up to washing. You can even order custom wallpaper, more expensive than stock papers, but when you consider the expense on a square-foot basis, you'll probably find you get a lot of decoration for the dollar.

(Above left) A beauti-
fully painted door
hides the electrical
panel and intercom
box.

(Above right) A wall-
papered, upholstered
niche by the phone.

Wallpaper can be applied over drywall or skim-coated plaster. Previous layers of paper should be removed. The most effective
method is with a propane-powered wallpaper steamer, available at
rental centers. Electric steamers are also available for the faint-of-
heart (the propane units do look and sound like a tool from Dante's In-
ferno) but they are not as fast as the propane units. If previous layers
of wallpaper have been painted, these, too, should be removed. I
have found no more effective way than to scrape the paper off with a
razor scraper. Invest in several good scrapers, buy an industrial-size
box of single-edged razor blades, and get to work. Experiment with
the angle at which you hold the scraper for best results. This will not
be much fun, and you will probably nick the walls, which you will
have to patch later, but the alternative is to paper over the existing
paper, which may or may not be well adhered to the wall. When the
paper is all off, wash the walls with a mixture of vinegar and warm
water (two cups per gallon or so) to remove the residual paste.

Old walls or new should be sized before papering. The sizing creates a slightly rough texture to grip the wallpaper better. If you're doing the papering yourself, your wallpaper store should be able to provide the advice and supplies you need for a successful installation. Be sure all the materials are compatible with each other.

•

Since paint and wallpaper so influence the look of the kitchen, and may have an impact on the decor of adjacent rooms, you will want to choose your colors and patterns carefully. Many people have a hard time making their choices in the abstract, while contemplating hundreds of paint chips or scores of wallpaper sample books. A proven approach, and one I use for my own projects, is to paint the whole room a pleasing shade of white and live in it until you can settle on the scheme that most suits you. You have this luxury if you're

The spare lines and smooth textures of this modern apartment contrast with the large wall hangings.

Details make the difference!

doing the decoration yourself, as well as the advantage that whenever you no longer like the scheme, you can change it.

The Punchlist

As your project nears completion, it is time for you to draw up what is called a *punchlist,* the list of all the little details still to be attended to. Often the contractor will compile a list and ask you to add to it any other items you think should be taken care of. The punchlist helps everybody understand what will and will not be done to bring the job to a close.

Kitchen projects are very complex, with many loose ends to tie up in the final stages. If you've had little experience with renovation projects, the problems may seem much bigger than in fact they are. If there's electrical, plumbing, or carpentry work unfinished, then by all means the contractor should make sure it is completed. All serious problems should be ironed out before you hand over the final check. But many times the issues that remain are little things, a couple of lines of grout missing from a tile backsplash, some "holidays" by the painters, or the refrigerator left unleveled. If you are capable of taking care of some of these tasks, you may save yourself a good deal of frustration by recognizing that even a conscientious contractor is going to have difficulty delivering the kind of perfection we've come to expect in our automobiles (although in any case, there is no excuse for shoddy work). Carmakers build a prototype of a new design to iron out all the bugs, but your kitchen project *is* the prototype.

Often a written agreement stipulates that the contractor will not be paid the final 5 to 10 percent of the contract price until everything has been completed, which induces him to take care of all the details on the punchlist. But keep in mind that it's expensive for a contractor to return two or three times to attend to minor items, and while he may have technically failed to deal with everything that was called for, he also may have thrown in some extras for nothing. The point here is not to excuse shoddy or incomplete work, but to try to keep the big picture in mind. As we said at the beginning of this book, kitchen renovations are very stressful for most people, because the very heart of your household is in total chaos for a period of weeks, and it's easy to begin to see the contractor as your tormentor rather than the builder of your dream kitchen. Ask him for some touch-up paint for the holidays, or for some grout for the not-quite-completed backsplash, or handle the five-minute job of leveling the refrigerator yourself.

●

D E S I G N   A S S O C I A T E S

58 Main Street
Nantucket
Massachusetts
02554
508-228-4342
FAX 508-228-3428

432 Columbia Street
Cambridge
Massachusetts
02141
617-661-9082
FAX 617-661-2550

Hartford Site Visit - July 27, 1991

Attending: Chris Dallmus (Architect)   Legend: P = Painter
                 Mike DeSevino (Contractor)   PL= Plumbers
                 Corky Malloy (Painter)   C = Carpentry
                 Pam Hartford (Client)   E = Electrician
                                                                O = Other

PUNCHLIST II

Mudroom/Porch
P   Paint outside of entry door
C/P   Install and paint storm/screen door
E   Label all panel box fuses
E   Install entry downlight fixture
C   Complete door hardware installation
E   Install closet light, coat closet
P   Paint trim at microlam to mudroom
C   Install ball catches on door to recycling closet
C   Coat hooks and shelf

Breakfast Area
C   Rework window liners at southeast windows to easy operation
C   Sash lock at southeast window

Kitchen
P   Paint touch-up on ceiling
P   Sand and paint beam separating kitchen and breakfast
PL   Install toe kick on dishwasher
PL   Change color panel on dishwasher to white
O   Replace end panel south end of island (damaged in transit)
C   Adjust all cabinet doors
C   Key all locks to operate with same key (patio, mudroom, courtyard)
PL   Replace chrome soap dispenser with white (as per spec)
C   Install weather cap on range fan exhaust
C   Sand scratches out of solid surface center right of sink

Family Room
O   Fix ice-maker
P   Paint fireplace mantel and trim
C/P   Install and paint storm/screen doors on French doors to patio

Exterior
E   Install patio lights with photocel switch
O   Apply sealer to redwood trim boards
P   Paint and seal patio railing
C/P   Install storm screen doors on French doors to patio
C   Install deadbolt on same
P   Paint trim and new clapboards on rear elevation

Note: Failure to include items on this list does not alter contractor's
responsibility to complete all work in accordance with Contract Documents.

It was noted all around that work in all trades was in progress.

Christopher L. Dallmus, AIA   Jennifer K. Shakespeare, AIA   John F. Gifford

It helps to recognize that from the very moment the job is done, your kitchen will begin to experience wear and tear. Busy kitchens don't stay immaculate for long. Keep all the guarantees and instruction booklets for kitchen appliances, so you can request repairs and order parts, and recognize that regular maintenance is a necessary part of keeping a kitchen in working order. Grease traps in ventilators need to be cleaned, casement windows should be oiled and painted as they are exposed to the weather, grout may need periodic resealing, the refrigerator compressor should be vacuumed several times a year. Cabinet hinges will go out of adjustment with use, so have your contractor or carpenter show you the very simple adjustment procedure and plan on readjusting them every year or so.

Also allow that from the moment you start to use your kitchen you will begin recognizing your mistakes: a window that should have been five inches lower or higher, a poor choice of an appliance, the floor color not quite right, the wrong counter material. I constantly ponder how I would do my kitchen differently if I had it to do all over again. I kick myself for not engineering a mudroom, for instance, and for using large sliding glass doors instead of smaller doors with side-lights and clerestory windows. But if you and your designer or archi-tect did your design work well, you probably considered the design consequences of each alternative and made what you thought was the best decision — again, you're building the prototype.

For me, of course, my doubts are aggravated by my involvement with "This Old House." Every project we do, or house we tour, gives me ideas, and I come home to my own kitchen and want to incorporate them. I try to lie down until the urge passes, or perhaps make a note of it in my "house ideas" file, in which I keep photos or notes of details I'd like to incorporate in some future project.

That's the thing about building and renovation. It is messy, unpleasant, and expensive when you're in the middle of it, but when you finish, you only remember what a wonderful experience it was to have reshaped your own living space. You may even convince yourself it was fun, and think of trying it again someday. Then, little by little, you get these ideas . . .

●

Some people regard renovation as an art form, in which perfection is attempted but never achieved. This space was drawn and executed with the certain knowledge of "kitchenness." Don't be alarmed if you start rethinking your kitchen from the day you start using it. It may be a sign that, like all of us at "This Old House," you too are afflicted with renovator's disease.

Index

Acknowledg- ments

Many people contributed to this book. In no particular order, and without prejudice as to their contribution, we wish to thank the following:

Jay Warren Bright, AIA; Scott Broney, American Olean Tile; Ellen Cheever, CKD, National Kitchen and Bath Association; Jack Cronin, Cronin Cabinets; Glenn Berger, Acton Woodworks; Michael Fried, Gerrity Co.; B. Leslie Hart, *Kitchen and Bath Business;* Joe Fiedrich, Stadler Co.; Jeff Hosking, Hosking Floor Refinishing; Jack Hussey, Jeff Locke, Dick Metchear, Kenneth J. Pfister, and Karl J. Peterson; Silva Brothers Construction; John Valentine; Paul Vogan; Judy Bernstein; Creative Laminates; Somerville Lumber; Karen Fisher, Designer Previews; Mike Strohl, Design Media Research; Margaret Foley, *Home* magazine; Alex Grant, *1001 Home Ideas;* Rich Bilo; Ron Collins, John Ashworth, and Rene Varrin.

Don Cutler managed the whole project. Pamela Hartford was our illustration editor. Chris Pullman conceived the book's design. Design Associates of Cambridge and Nantucket took a great deal of time from more profitable ventures to work on this book, especially Greg Conyngham, who did the computer renderings of the "finished" concept kitchens; John Murphy, who penned the fine illustrations that enliven the book; and Chris Dallmus, who did the design on the concept kitchens and managed the development of the drawings.

No list of acknowledgments would be complete without thanking the "This Old House" team, especially Russ Morash, Norm Abram, Rich Trethewey, and Jock Gifford. Finally I must thank my wife, Evy Blum, who tolerated the intrusion that work on this manuscript made into a year-and-a-half's worth of family time and several vacations. Marilyn Ruben was mentor, friend, and surrogate mother to my wife for more than twenty years. She taught me most of the little I've managed to learn about design. Marilyn died before I became host of "This Old House," but upon hearing the news would have laughed her wonderful laugh and said: "Oh, I think it's *marvelous!"*

Photograph Credits

iii
Design: Shattuck Blair Associates
Photography: George Ross

vi
Design: Sid DelMar Leach, ASID,
Classic Design Associates
Photography: William Helsel

viii
Photography: Richard Howard
Courtesy "This Old House"/WGBH

xi
Photography: William N. Hopkins
Reprinted from *Country Home*.
Copyright 1990 by Meredith
Corporation.
All rights reserved.

xii top
Photography: William Stites
Reprinted from *Country Home*.
Copyright 1990 by Meredith
Corporation.
All rights reserved.

xii bottom
Photography: Neil Jacobs
Courtesy "This Old House"/WGBH

xiii
Photography: Richard Howard
Courtesy "This Old House"/WGBH

xiv top
Photography: Richard Howard

xiv bottom
Photography: Richard Howard
Courtesy "This Old House"/WGBH

2
Design: Frank Faulkner
Photography: John Hall

5
Photography: Richard Howard

6
Design: R. Scott Bromley,
Bromley Caldari Architects
Photography: Peter Vitale

8
Design: Sandy Slepack
Photography: Karen Radkai
Courtesy *HG*. © 1991 by
The Condé Nast Publications Inc.

12 top & bottom
Courtesy The Whirlpool Corporation

13 top right & left
Courtesy The Whirlpool Corporation

13 bottom right & left
Design: Jacobson Silverstein
Winslow Architects
Photography: John Hauf

15
Design: Betti Franceschi
Photography: Norman McGrath

16
Design: The Vassa Group
Photography: Judy A. Slagle

18
Design: Stein + Associates
Photography: courtesy Robert Stein

20
Design: Sortun Vos, architects
Photography: Michael Jensen

21
Design: Peter Gisolfi Associates
Photography: Norman McGrath

27
Photography: Richard Howard

28
Ship: *Sunrise*
Photography: Matthew Walker

33
Design: Amy Scott
Photography: Norman McGrath

34
Photography: Karen Melvin

36
Design: Karen Williams
Photography: John Schwartz

38
Design: Michael Berman
Photography: Jeremy Samuelson
Courtesy *Home* magazine

39
Photography: Bruce Katz

40
Design: Clodagh
Photography: Daniel Aubry

41
Design: Andrew Cohen
Photography: Richard Howard

42 top
Design: Janine, CKD
Photography: Robert Perron

42 bottom
Design: Jim Miller
Photography: John Schwartz

43
Design: Rothzeid Kaiserman
Thomson & Bee,
Carmi Bee, Partner-in-Charge
Photography: Elliot Kaufman

44
Design: Williams Builder
Photography: Norman McGrath

45
Owner: Julia Child
Photography: Jim Scherer

46 top & bottom
Design: Marilyn Ruben
Photography: Richard Howard

48
Design: Doug Fitch and Ross Miller
Photography: Dean Powell

50
Design: William Cohen
Photography: Norman McGrath

52
Design: Louise Levin
Photography: Norman McGrath

54
Design: Charles Myers
Photography: John Hall

56
Designers/Owners: Lou and Lisa
Ekus
Photography: Walter Wicke

61
Design: Pietz and Michal Architects,
AIA
Photography: George Leisey

62–63
Design: Gregory Stuart Conyngham
Software: ArchiCAD by Graphisoft

64
Design: Louis Mackall
Photography: courtesy Louis
Mackall

66 top & lower right
Design: Laura Rose
Artist: Connie Leslie
Photography: Robert Perron

66 lower left
Design: Stuart Wrede, architect
Artist: Sandy Moore
Photography: Robert Perron

70
Design: Cambridge Seven
Photography: Norman McGrath

72
Photography: Bruce Irving
Courtesy "This Old House"/WGBH

74
Photography: Bill Schwob
Courtesy "This Old House"/WGBH

75
Owner: Steve Thomas
Photography: courtesy Steve
Thomas

76
Photography: © ESTO

77
Design: Motif Designs
Photography: John Hall

80 top
Design: Louis Mackall
Photography: courtesy Louis
Mackall

80 bottom
Design: Mullman Seidman
Architects
Photography: John Hall

81 left & right
Design: Brock Simini, Architects
Photography: courtesy Peter Brock

82
Design: Mulfinger–Susanka
Architects
Photography: Karen Melvin

84
Design: Shope Reno Wharton
Associates
Photography: H. Durston Saylor

86
Photography: Bill Schwob
Courtesy "This Old House"/WGBH

87
Design: Sortun Vos, architects
Photography: Michael Jensen

88
Design: Pietz & Michal Architects,
AIA
Photography: George Leisey

89
Design: Stein + Associates
Photography: courtesy Robert Stein

90
Photography: Lizzie Himmel

91 left
Design: William Lipsey
Photography: Robert Perron

91 right
Design: Bennett Wallace
Photography: John Hall

92
Design: Mullman Seidman
Architects
Photography: John Hall

173 top
Design: William F. Stern &
Associates
Photography: Paul Hester

173 bottom
Design: Jan Johnson
Photography: Laurie Black

174 top
Design: Chris Alexander
Photography: Mark Darley © ESTO

174 bottom
Design: John Midyette III
Photography: Neil Jacobs
Courtesy "This Old House"/WGBH

176
Design: Stein + Associates
Photography: Richard Mandelkorn

178 top
Design: Smallbone Kitchens
Courtesy Smallbone

178 bottom
"Corian" sink
Courtesy DuPont

179
Courtesy Kohler Company

183
Design: Smallbone Kitchens
Courtesy Smallbone

185
Design: Robert Schwartz
Photography: John Schwartz

186 top left
Design: Ricki Fingerhut, Blair
Design
Photography: Billy Cunningham

186 top right
Design: Tom Pritchard
Photography: John Hall

186 bottom
Design: Andrew Cohen
Photography: Richard Howard

188
Design: Alison Spear
Photography: John Hall

189
Design: Hammer and Nail
Photography: Spectrumedia

190
Design: Shattuck Blair Associates
Photography: George Ross

191
Courtesy Monogram/General
Electric

192
Design: Doug Fitch and Ross Miller
Photography: Dean Powell

193
Owners: Jim and Mary Boone
Photography: courtesy the owners

194
Design: Stuart Frederick Sidells
Photography: Andrew McKinney
Courtesy *1001 Home Ideas*

196 left
Design: Charles Sieger
Photography: Robert Perron

196 right
Design: Shattuck Blair Associates
Photography: George Ross

198
Photography: John Hall

200
Design: Shattuck Blair Associates
Photography: George Ross

201
Design: Michelle Thunen
Photography: Laurie Black

202
Design: Michelle Thunen
Photography: Laurie Black

203
Design: Mullman Seidman
Architects
Photography: John Hall

205
Design: Barbara Wheaton
Photography: Jim Scherer

206
Design: Louis Mackall
Photography: courtesy Louis
Mackall

208
Design: Lisa Rose, I.S.I.D.,
of Aubergine Interiors
Photography: M. Rogol

209
Design: Hariri & Hariri
Photography: John Hall

210
Design: Catherine A. Duacki, CKD,
with Tina Piper
Photography: Susan Gilmore
Courtesy *1001 Home Ideas*

213
Design: Smallbone Kitchens
Courtesy Smallbone

214
Design: Peter Gisolfi Associates
Photography: Norman McGrath

215
Design: Joe Carter
Photography: Robert Perron

216
Design: Robert Schwartz
Photography: John Schwartz

217
Design: Roger Williams, architect
Photography: Michael Jensen

218
Photography: Karen Melvin

219 top left
Photography: Robert Perron

219 top right
Design: Clodagh
Photography: Daniel Aubry

219 bottom left
Photography: Karen Melvin

219 bottom right
Photography: Mike Moreland
Courtesy *1001 Home Ideas*

220 left
Design: Smallbone Kitchens
Courtesy Smallbone

220 right
Design: Clodagh
Photography: Daniel Aubry

222
Design: Stuart Frederick Sidells
Photography: Andrew McKinney
Courtesy *1001 Home Ideas*

223
Courtesy Wilsonart

225
Courtesy Wilsonart

228
Design: Frank Carroll
Photography: Michael Jensen
Courtesy *1001 Home Ideas*

229 left
Surrell surfacing by Formica
Corporation
Photography: Robert Perron

229 right
Corian surfacing
Courtesy DuPont Corporation

230
Design: Clodagh
Photography: Daniel Aubry

231
Design: May-Lin Architects
Photography: Bruce Katz

233
Design: R. Scott Bromley,
Bromley Caldari Architects
Photography: Jaime Ardiles Arce

234 left
Design: Weinschenk and Company
Photography: Robert Perron

234 right
Design: Michelle Thunen
Photography: Laurie Black

235
Design: William F. Stern &
Associates
Photography: Paul Hester

236
Design: Lisa and Lou Ekus
Photography: Walter Wicke

237 left
Design: David Gibson
Photography: William Helsel

237 right
Design: Brukoff Design Associates
Photography: Michael Bry

238
Design: Andrew Cohen
Photography: Richard Howard

240
Design: Sid DelMar Leach, ASID,
Classic Design Associates
Photography: William Helsel

243
Design: Ron Goldman
Photography: Douglas Kennedy
Courtesy *Home* magazine

244
Design: Susan Preece
Courtesy *Home* magazine

245
Design: Daryl Rush
Photography: William Helsel

247 left
Design: Tony Zunino
Photography: Robert Perron

247 right
Design: Louis Mackall
Photography: Robert Perron

248 left
Design: John and Iris Sutton
Photography: Michael Jensen
Courtesy *Home* magazine

248 right
Design: Rothzeid Kaiserman
Thomson & Bee,
Carmi Bee, Partner-in-Charge
Photography: Diane Hobe

250
Design: Merrill Stenbeck
Photography: John Hall

253 top
Design: Miles Lourie
Photography: John Schwartz

253 bottom
Design: Ted Long
Photography: Robert Perron

255 left
Design: Samuel Botero Associates
Photography: Phillip H. Ennis

255 right
Design: Crystal Kitchens
Photography: Karen Melvin

256
Design: Claudia Librett

257
Design: Louis Mackall
Photography: courtesy Louis
Mackall

259 left
Design: Walz Design
Photography: Barbra Walz

259 right
Design: Natalye Appel
Photography: Hal Lott
Courtesy *1001 Home Ideas*

261
Design: Shelton Mindel
Photography: John Hall

●